FLORIDA STATE
UNIVERSITY LIBRARIES

MAY 19 1997

TALLAHASSEE, FLORIDA

SLEEPING DOGS AND POPSICLES

The Vatican versus the KGB

> *"J' ai eu le courage de*
> *regarder en arrière*
> *Les cadavres de mes jours*
> *Marquent ma route..."*
> **G.A.**

Eugene H. Van Dee

University Press of America, Inc.
Lanham • New York • London

Copyright © 1996 by
University Press of America,® Inc.
4720 Boston Way
Lanham, Maryland 20706

3 Henrietta Street
London, WC2E 8LU England

All rights reserved
Printed in the United States of America
British Cataloging in Publication Information Available

Library of Congress Cataloging-in-Publication Data

Dee, Eugene H. van.
Sleeping dogs and popsicles : the Vatican versus the KGB : memoirs
of an American / Eugene H. Van Dee.
p.   cm.
Includes index.
1. World War, 1939-1945--Secret service--Soviet Union. 2. Catholic
Church--Foreign relations--Soviet Union. 3. Soviet Union--Foreign
relations--Catholic Church. 4. Dee, Eugene H. van. 5. World War,
1939-1945--Personal narratives, American. I. Title.
D810.S7D38   1996   940.54'8647--dc20   96-19051   CIP

ISBN 0-7618-0381-5 (cloth: alk. ppr.)

∞™ The paper used in this publication meets the minimum
requirements of American National Standard for information
Sciences—Permanence of Paper for Printed Library Materials,
ANSI Z39.48—1984

For Derek Sadowski, the preux chevalier "Sir Derek", as a small appreciation of his sterling friendship and trust.

Contents

Preface   vii

Acknowledgments   ix

Chapter 1   The War Years   1
            Germany Invades Poland
            First Encounter with Russian Colonel Grigori
            Escape to Freedom
            U.S. Lecture Tour - FBI Vagaries
            Return to Europe - Colonel Grigori Sends Katyn
                Murder Evidence

Chapter 2   Warsaw - Paris - Rome   37
            Warsaw :   U.S. Embassy
            Warsaw :   U.S. Film Industry
                       Accident & Arrest
                       Flight to West

Chapter 3	The Golden Years		67
	Paris :	Movie Stars and Philosophers	
	Rome :	Dolce Vita Years, Venice Film Festivals	
	Rome :	Ambassador Clare Booth Luce and Eric Johnston	
	Rome :	Free Lancing Movies Dangerous Games	

Chapter 4   The Vatican and Soviet Intelligence Services   133
             Cardinal Vagnozzi's Top Secret Report
                on Vatican Wealth
             Murder in Turin
             Soviet General Grigori Surfaces as Vatican
                Excellency

Chapter 5   Grigori's Story   153
             The 1917 St. Petersburg Tragedy
             The Soviets Win Intelligence War
             The Vatican's Secret Trichéco/Walrus Files
             The Hermitage Coefficient
             General Grigori of Soviet Army Intelligence
                and the Vatican Shake Soviet Economy
             Karol Wojtyla, Archbishop of Krakow
             General Grigori Comes in From The Cold
             When the Greeks Say "No"
             Insh'allah

Index   201

Preface

First let me make it clear that this book is not an autobiography. It was never intended to be one. It's about people and places and extraordinary events, a few irreverent, all of them true, to which I happened to be witness, calling them simply "memoirs", nothing more.

The sole hero is Grigori, whom I first met when he was my interrogator, a colonel in the Soviet army who, over the next thirty years, three times saved my life, rose to become the commanding General of Soviet Military Intelligence, created a secret Society in Russia, *The Hermitage Coefficient*, which in collaboration with the Holy See, played a key part in the unraveling of the Communist system, and who ended his years as a Monsignor at the Vatican.

I felt no compulsion to write this book until 1989, when Mikhail Gorbachev became the catalyst for the revolution that swept through Eastern Europe, fulfilling General Grigori's prophecy, made only a few years earlier, that *The Hermitage Coefficient* "would soon cause the emergence in Russia of a statesman-reformer whose persuasive rationale to fundamentally revise the Communist Party's orthodoxism would have a profound effect on the entire world". His prediction proved so accurate, so true to reality, it excluded any possible correlation with historical coincidence. The time had come for me to pay humble tribute to this Mastermind.

Some will ask why I never mentioned General Grigori's family name. He willed it that way. I could have given him a plausible pseudonym like Alexinsky, Filonenko or Zenzinov, and only his closest friends would know the difference. But revealing his true name could provide tracking scent for the forever vengeful Ishaika sniffing dogs of the many intelligence services he regularly made fools of and lead them to his surviving secret associates. As a further precaution, I also respected his wish not to write or say anything about him for at least ten years after his death, which occurred on November 19, 1982.

Still others will probably wonder where the bizarre title of this book came from. During one of our many reading sessions of secret documents, General Grigori warned me that if I ever committed the indiscretion of making public all the described events, it could agitate sleeping dogs and turn them rabid. On another occasion, this time in his moralistic errand of a Vatican Excellency, Monsignor Grigori observed that the vivid accounts of my exhilarating experiences in, what he called, "the libertine world of cinema", reminded him of the sugary and quickly melting popsicles he used to buy as a boy, for a few kopeks, at St.Petersburg's market place. That is how my title was born. To make it somewhat less obscure, I added the subtitle: *"The Vatican versus the KGB : The memoirs of an American"*.

Acknowledgments

My first tribute of gratitude goes out to a friend of many years, Michael Sakellaropoulo, who after flogging me into opening my files, accompanied this project throughout, giving it an affection, and the concern, that enabled me to turn my hidden remembrances into the book now in your hands.
I am deeply in debt to Monseñor Erique Campos Mevéndez for his judicious counsel. It must not be assumed, however, that he approves everything herein.
I am truly beholden to Helmut Schwarzer, for contributing much precious time, his versatile erudition, meticulous research, and the sophisticated skills that produced for me a publisher.
I am profoundly grateful to my dear friends in Greece, John and Suzie Kehayas, who laboured through the typescript of this book more than once, and made valuable criticisms and suggestions.
For the candor of his advice, my thanks to the cultured James Hepburn of London, who so unselfishly tried to mold me into an author, ultimately acknowledging that as a writer I was beyond all prayer.
For her remarkable perspicacity and unflagging enthusiasm, I thank Julia ('Julie') Kamarinou of Athens.
Sincere remerciement to William LaRiche for his untiring efforts, across the continents, to place my manuscript.
To my dear friends, Don Satisky and Gertrud Olsen, I say thanks for all their support and encouragement.
Last and certainly not least I express my appreciation to Steve Kanavos and Nick Diamantopoulos for their infinite patience and the meticulous professional formatting of the final typescript.
"First Fig" by Edna St. Vincent Millay. From COLLECTED POEMS, HarperCollins. Copyright 1922, 1950 by Edna St. Vincent Millay. Reprinted, with thanks, by permission of Elizabeth Barnett, literary executor (page 100).

Chapter 1

The War Years

Warsaw

It was Sunday and sunny. The first day of September. We were taking a leisurely stroll, my girlfriend and I, over Warsaw's main bridge on the Vistula river. On the banks bathers seemed small and half naked, sort of silly. Something made me look up into the sky. It was so blue. "The airforce is showing off", I said to my companion, as two silver planes buzzed low. Bombs began falling on the beaches, missing the bridge. People screamed, then began to run in panic. For a brief moment we stood frozen. So this was it, I thought. This is war. What am I doing here?

A few months earlier my English friend Tommy Whitehead, who lived in Portsmouth, wrote me: "Wouldn't it be fun to float down the Elbe and see what the Germans are up to?"

For two weeks we knapsacked, sleeping in hostels, getting on and off river boats. There was a spirit of elation in the air. We enjoyed watching the open-faced, healthy, strong, smiling, talkative friendly young Germans jump to disciplined attention at the sound of a leader's shrill whistle. Tommy, I thought, looked uncomfortable at times. The stare of the Führer followed us everywhere.

On returning to Warsaw, where I had studied for several years, I presented a two-piece article to the multilingual magazine of the Polish radio network. I called it "Mobilization for Chaos", a title I had stolen from the Times of London, along with a few ideas. I had the urge to shout. To take the Poles by the scruff of their necks, to verbally kick their derrières. The historic scourge of the Poles: excessive patriotic zeal, pride, insolent hubris, had again infected them. "We are ready to march on Berlin", they were saying. In my article I wrote that there is a way to reach a proper decision and that it is the product of understanding one's limitations. That for many years Germany had been preparing for war with an intensity no other nation could even begin to match. Hitler had already annexed Austria and the Sudetenland, I said, and Poland would soon be invaded by the German military machine. I knew very well that the Polish political leaders, colonel Beck and cohorts, held no illusions about Poland's ability to offer any effective defense. Nonetheless, they were bent on firing up the patriotic spirit of the thousands they knew would have to die in vain. Would history declare them patriots, or war criminals ?

As a result of my article, Karol Pienkowski, chief of the Polish Radio's foreign department, hired me as editor-broadcaster of French and English short wave programs. The salary was too good to turn down. I decided to postpone my return to America and give radio a try. I did not know it then but soon I would be "the voice heard round the world".

There was no time to go home. We ran straight from the bridge on the Vistula to our offices at the radio station. Here, first signs of panic. Some were crying. Humiliation, not fear. The violent noise of bombs and anti-aircraft guns penetrated our sound-proof studios. I had my own little cubicle that consisted of a desk with standing microphone, another mike overhead, two telephones, one with an outside line, the other for inter-office communications, an electric turntable and a small selection of recordings. Out of habit I tested the mikes. They were live. I phoned my boss for instructions. He had none. His voice was hoarse and strange. I went on the air to announce that Poland was at war and Warsaw under bombardment. At that point I had not the slightest idea what was going to happen to us, how long the bombings would last, whether we would survive or die. My own excitement was so great, my adrenalin flowing so fast, I did not really think beyond the job I had to do. That was all that mattered. It didn't occur to me to leave, to run for my life. I wasn't even scared. I would not be for many hours yet. Being on the air invariably gave me a feeling of power, as if the microphone was an instrument of command. From letters that our listeners had sent us in recent weeks we knew our short wave broadcasts were reaching as far as South America and even Australia.

The War Years

Until today, I had always painstakingly structured each broadcast hour in consultation with the news and editorial desks, submitting all texts to my supervisor and the "upstairs" censors.

Now, as the biggest story of my life was beginning to unfold, and the chance to tell it was mine, I didn't know what to say, where to start my regular opening words: "This is Warsaw Calling" would have to do. Nobody was there to guide or censor me.

For the first five days, a skeleton staff remained at work, inspired by the mayor of Warsaw, Starzynski, who spent hours on the air appealing to patriotism, exhorting all Poles, military and civilian, to resist the German invaders. Close to collapsing from exhaustion; his once strong voice down to a whisper. With a mixture of admiration and pity, I watched this ordinary man become possessed. He urged his compatriots to continue cavalry charges against German tanks, to fight the enemy in the streets, on every corner, until death. "To do less would be cowardly", he cried. To me it sounded like obscene madness. An unfair barter of life for glory. Were more corpses needed still to assuage the insolent,atavist souls of the already dead Polish heroes? The horsemen: nationalism, misplaced patriotism, Hail Mary already rampant; the fourth was still to come.

"Why don't the Germans cut us off the air? They must have reached our transmitters", I asked. "They probably monitor every word for their historical records and our agony feeds their superiority complex,I guess",someone said.

I had two powerful receivers in my studio and kept switching bands desperate to know whether anyone in the outside world could hear me. "This is Warsaw Calling". At one point Paris Radio acknowledged me. Then London. William Shirer, the American journalist-broadcaster had heard me and would record for the States. Overcome by emotion, drained of all strength, I fainted. My colleagues used smelling salts to revive me. Even as the building rocked and air blasts threw us against the crumbling walls, I felt nothing. Too spent to react, to continue broadcasting, I fell asleep at my microphone. When I awakened, nothing seemed real. My friends were just shadows of my fantasy, contorting under some evil spell. If I acted quickly, my confused mind said, I could still save them. I reached for my phone. Dead. I ran upstairs. The executive offices were deserted. I yelled something and a woman colleague rushed in. She already knew. The directors, including my boss, Pienkowski, and the editors simply ran away before the Germans encircled the capital. Probably, I later surmised, going over the Carpathian mountains to

Romania, the last escape route out of Poland. Two brave technicians, my female colleague and I were left abandoned, alone, to "defend the citadel".

It was to be a demonstration of my unintended, accidental and definitely involuntary acts of bravery imposed on me by fate, born of desperation and fed by soaring, bitter anger. I had to stay at the radio station because it was no longer possible to leave. By now tons of rubble had blocked all exits. We were buried, breathing the dusty air, choking, fighting the feeling of claustrophobia and with a gut-retching selection of food and drink found in the cafeteria stores: bars of milk chocolate, tea biscuits, apples and several cases of French champagne. We would diet exclusively on chocolate, apples and biscuits for the next eleven days. We never got to the Champagne.

I continued to go on the air. But, how many times can you say: bombs are falling? So I sang the Marseillaise instead. And I raved. Hadn't the French already declared war on Germany? Where were the English? They too had promised to come to Poland's aid, I shouted. Surely my America would do something, I pleaded. Did not General Kosciuszko fight in our War of Independence? "This is Warsaw Calling. Please, please help. This is Warsaw calling". I sang with a croaking voice while tears choked me. I cried, I screamed, I begged, I raved, I recited poems. I played Chopin's Funeral March, then his Étude Révolutionnaire. Like in a dream I could see my early school music teacher, Brother Florian, and feel the pain when his rod wacked my knuckles for every wrong note. Then, with no more tears, I sobbed.. I had been on the air for a total of 18 days and nights when suddenly it was all over. The thundering stopped. Warsaw had surrendered.

Somebody dug us out. We divided the station's cash. Our legs could hardly carry us but we still had to run and hide. Outside there was smoke, the stench of dead bodies and torn horse flesh. Barely alive, we made it to my female colleague's flat on the outskirts of the city. On the way we passed through entire sections of the city reduced to smoldering rubble.

The Poles had lost their entire airforce and the few anti-aircraft guns of Warsaw were silenced during the first days of the war. German Stukas bombed everything in sight, unopposed. It was vicious, deliberate mass murder of defenseless, panic-stricken civilians.

I knew that during the coming night I would have to leave Warsaw and try going east, away from the Germans, as they would surely kill me for all the insults I hurled at them on the air. Food and sleep would come later. Right now, above all, immediately, I had to find a change of underwear. Or die. We broke into a flat on the next floor. He must have been a real dandy. I left a note on his desk: "Darling, forgive me. I just couldn't resist your shorts. See you in Paris. Love, Wanda". I hoped my underwear benefactor shared my perverse sense of humour.

She shook me awake. "It's three in the morning and time for you to leave. Drink this", she said, handing me a cup of black tea. I vomited. An hour later, having successfully evaded German patrols I walked out of Warsaw and headed East. A peasant gave me a ride in his horse cart. He let me fill my pockets with carrots. Again I slept. Then I walked again. Sometime in the late afternoon, I saw them. A miserable bunch on foot. I joined.

He was like a wet limping dog that had been thrashed by a cruel owner within an inch of his life and now could only wimp. But this was a man or what was left of one. Shreds of a Polish cavalry uniform, unseeing eyes. He had fought gallantly until the regiment died, crushed by tanks. He dragged himself to Warsaw. That's where he lived. That's where his mind perished when he found his wife and small children burnt to nothing by a German incendiary bomb. Corporal Wladek, his batman, led him out of the city and now they were many miles from the capital, still in panic and going they knew not exactly where, but away, away from the Germans. Tadeusz, for that was the colonel's name, spoke not at all.

At night we could hear his own forlorn refrain of a Polish lullaby:

> The pigeons on the roof were not mine
> All the sounds belonged to others,
> I wrote my opera buffa at the age of nine
> If I only had some brothers

On and on, repeated and repeated again until our nerves went raw . To our pleading eyes, Wladek would only say: "my colonel used to write poetry and how can I stop a dead man ?"

We were twelve in number. A motley lot of escapees from hell, bound haphazardly together only by the common want to survive. Scrounging for food at night, keeping watch for German troops during the day, we hobbled toward the Russian-invaded part of Eastern Poland, not quite sure where this really was. We had heard the Russians were willing to help victims of German aggression. Tired and hungry, the chill of the night increased our misery. We were learning to hate each other. Then it happened. The colonel was dead. Wladek found him one morning with a cord round his neck, strangled. The faithful corporal shot himself through the temple. No, Tadeusz, you would not find brothers. You found an assassin instead. Now we were ten and one of us was a killer.

I had been taught and then persuaded -almost that is- by the elegant minds of my Jesuit teachers that while one can perceive the presence of even an abstract God, it is not possible to live inside the feelings or reactions of another human being because the distance between the separate realities of individuals is unbridgeable. Now I could firmly reject both tenets. The first as mythology, as the luxury that people use to make themselves happy, the second as a distortion in one's mind. God was nowhere 'round, and for the moment at least, I was living inside the feelings of another human being. Suddenly, I did understand anguish, share the blankness of the colonel's mind, Wladek's despair and even the killer's insanity. And all I could think of was neither godly nor complicated. It was desire for revenge.

We were sleeping on hay in a barn next to a friendly peasant's house. He had fed us cabbage soup the night before and gave us shelter. First the dogs' howling, then angry barking and jangling of chains woke us. Strong arms scooped us off the ground.

Within minutes we were searched, stripped of our few belongings and thrown in the back of a military truck.

We were in Russian hands now, just as we planned from the beginning. But reality fell short of expectations. Not quite friendly liberators, not ogres either. Just silent soldiers doing their job; clearing everybody out. We traveled on bumpy backroads, seeing no one. East, then southeast, till the sun was closing on the horizon. We could not tell the time; we no longer had our watches. Twice we stopped to "stretch" and they gave us hunks of black bread. At least we didn't have to walk. "Where are you taking us", we asked. "Uvidzim,we shall see" was the only reply.

We arrived at a railway junction during the early evening and were taken to what seemed to be a warehouse. There was nothing inside except rails and some empty barrels. They called us one by one, every thirty minutes. Who left, didn't come back. I was the last. A soldier threw me a blanket. "Sleep now", he said, shutting the huge door. I stayed awake till he fetched me in the morning. I washed at the water pump outdoors. He gave me an old brown shirt. It was clean. My own filthy and already in tatters. Across the courtyard we entered a two story wooden building. It was a school. I could see blackboards.

"Evgenii, what are you doing here? You are too young to be a spy." He called me by my first name. He must have seen my passport. They are not going to shoot me. These thoughts flashed through my mind. The weariness and fear left me. The officer addressing me spoke English well. He had barely an accent. A lilt really, the pleasant kind educated Russians can never quite get rid of when speaking a foreign language. I liked his looks. Closely cropped dark hair, about 35 years old, medium height, slim, a slightly crooked smile, white even teeth. The first friendly face and voice in a very long time. It all came pouring out. I couldn't stop.

The siege of Warsaw, the escape, the endless trek towards and away, the murder, everything. He didn't interrupt and didn't take his eyes off me. I knew it. I felt them. "That's enough, my young friend", he said, finally. "You will eat now and then rest. I shall call for you in several hours". I was too sleepy and tired to eat. The soldier took me to a small room, with a cot and washbasin. He showed me the toilet round the corner and left. I realized I was no longer a prisoner under guard. I lost the day because I fell into a restless but still deep sleep until the corporal woke me late afternoon. His name was Alex and he handed me my watch. It had been wound and said 5:30. "You are lucky the sub-colonel likes you, otherwise you would have been sent to Smolensk with the others". Thanks to my voice coach in Warsaw, Yuri Orlov, I could understand Russian. Professor Orlov came from St.Petersburg. When the Poles hired me as a foreign language broadcaster I had difficulty maintaining a steady voice pitch. After some minutes on the air I sounded like a castrato. It was a question of learning to breathe properly. Professor Orlov had the answer to that and many other things. He became a friend. Someone I could trust. I listened because he told me truths I had never even thought of.

"I must say, Evgenii that you are a very peculiar fish. I don't quite know what to do with you. You are an American, born in Pittsburgh, which is very far from where we are now. In practical terms our encounter takes place in no man's land. Poland but no longer Polish. Russia with no Russians. All because two powers that are deadly enemies strategically divided a defeated third country that will soon again become a bloodied battleground. You must tell me all you observed about the German military. Not locations or formations or armaments because we know all that. Tell me what you saw of their discipline, their attitude toward the vanquished Polish army, toward the civilian population. Anything you know of their psyche, their spirit. Do you think the Germans are really totally dedicated to Hitler?" (he pronounced it Gitler). I told him of my impressions from the brief trip to Germany with Tommy Whitehead. "One should, I said, make a clear distinction between dedication and fascination. All Germans are dangerously fascinated by the Führer to the point of accepting anything he says or does without protest, even when their inner conscience rebels. The majority is dedicated to Hitler, completely ignoring questions of political or social morality, And, I can tell you that until one has seen the German army, it is impossible to know what real discipline means. The soldiers I saw in Warsaw, in open military vehicles, facing each other four, six or eight to a side, looking straight ahead from under their deep helmets, rifles upright between their knees, were not men but machines. The same machines that kept bombing the city after all defense had long crumbled. No admiration for Polish heroism, no mercy for the vanquished. Just brutal contempt."

This was our third session. On the second day, he did a thorough job of grilling me, and since I was more than willing to bare my soul, he knew just about everything there was to know of my past, my mental development and spiritual leanings. The colonel, whom I heard another officer call "comrade Grigori", was a clever man, a subtle man of culture. It made me wonder his background. He told me he came from Leningrad where he was a member of the staff at the Museum of History of Religion and Atheism He also taught at the Krupskaya Institute of Culture and briefly had studied in Paris.

As ideas and concepts came to our minds, so did the appropriate expressions with total disregard of their linguistic origin. We spoke a mixture of Polish, which we both knew pretty well, French in which we were fluent and English where I had an advantage. Grigori would slip in a Russian phrase or two when it suited the occasion and I always seemed to understand.

One thing was very clear to me. Grigori had no illusions about the Nazis and their objectives concerning his Russia. "We could never trust the Germans. They invariably double-crossed us and while pretending to support the Revolution they encouraged separatist movements in the Ukraine and Caucasia. We agreed now to a non-aggression pact only because we must have time to prepare and to secure advance positions before their Panzer divisions strike. Hitler is a madman. Millions of Russians will die under the onslaught of his formidable war machine. We know that. He might even conquer much of our homeland, but only temporarily, because in the end we shall crush the invader."

Grigori was getting increasingly inflamed as he talked. "When you get back to America, tell your countrymen that old Russia has disappeared in smoke. The driving forces of Tsarist government: vodka, taxes and orthodoxy have perished along with the noblemen, the squires described by our Pushkin, Turgeniev and Tolstoy. We are no longer afflicted by what the Siberian peoples called "Russian sickness". "Colonel", I interrupted, "you are really not telling me anything new. We Americans are quite familiar with the changes in Russia since the Revolution but, as you know, we fear any regime born out of violence". "Evgenii, you had better watch your tongue. You are safe in my care, but others may be less tolerant of your amerikanski brashness. Let me tell you that your government practices political calumny and falsifies history. Your society is blind because it created a false world. And make note that individuals, even those possessing genius,develop only as rationally as the society that nurtures them. When it suits your purpose you mutate truth into the big lie. You Americans believe only in what you wish to believe. Your history books harp on the horrors of our revolution but not one word is said about the fact that during the first three decades of this century, which encompass the revolutionary years, Russian art was the most advanced in the world. Have you ever heard of Malevich, for instance?" Grigori's mention of this particular painter puzzled and astonished me. During our meetings in Warsaw, Professor Orlov had told me Malevich was considered a sort of prophet-holy man whose paintings invoked identification with religious faith and that Stalin "buried" him for not fulfilling the criteria of the prescribed Soviet ideology.

"Oui, Mon Colonel" -subconsciously I had slipped into French because I also remembered professor Orlov saying that some of Malevich's early paintings like "Floor Polishers" ultimately derived from Matisse's "Dance"-, I have heard of Malevich",and I told him what I knew. For what seemed like a very long time Grigori remained silent.

"You are right. The realist line imposed by the Party spirit stifled the creativity of such greats as the poet Mayakovsky, the abstract painter Kandinsky and writer-philosophers like Bulgakov. But that will also change." I was absorbing everything Grigori said. He had made some highly intriguing observations and certainly not by accident alone. Still, half of my mind was on his words "when you get back to America". For the first time I really believed he would let me go free. He interrupted my meandering: "did you ever know a Russian before me?" The question nearly brought tears to my eyes. "Yes, I said, I know another Russian and I told Grigori about my teacher, my friend and mentor, my starets, professor Yuri Sergeievich Orlov from St.Petersburg and Warsaw. Grigori just stared and stared at me while his fist tightened round a pencil till it broke in half.

Days were passing and I had become depressed. The comings and goings of military vehicles, the sudden frenetic activity when trainfuls of Polish military personnel under guard stopped at our railway junction, then periods of silence. Grigori's absences and changes in his mood were all getting me down. I had no idea what was happening in the outside world.

Very early one morning I woke up with a start. Something had clattered to the floor in Grigori's quarters. I got up to see. There was light in his bathroom, the door left ajar. A whiff of lavender. Grigori was on his knees. I saw him crossing himself. I was dumbfounded. Did Grigori only pretend to be a dedicated communist, an atheist? Something else struck me. He crossed himself not in the Russian orthodox manner but the catholic way, from chest to left shoulder first. How could that be? Quickly, I retreated to my room. Alex was nowhere around.

Grigori was missing for forty eight hours. He called for me the moment he got back. "You will be leaving for home the day after tomorrow. This means you will first return to Warsaw, obtain a German exit permit and head for France or Italy. We will take you as far as Biala Podlaska. There you will board a train toward Warsaw. Our people will be on the train to watch over you. They will tell you exactly where to get off. You will enter Warsaw on foot one half hour before curfew. Should you be questioned by the Germans where you were during the past several weeks, tell them you went to Otwock to see your friends, the Bendek family. There is Jadwiga, the mother, 35 years old. Zbyszek, the son, who is 14, as is his twin sister Zosia. The father, Kazik, is still missing. In case the Germans investigate, and this is not very likely, the Bendeks will confirm you were with them until this coming Friday. Understood ?" "Yes, Colonel. And I am very grateful to you, not only for all you have done for me but also for the things you told me". "Da, Evgenii. Much of everything is luck and luck may depend on timing. Your being here, seemingly straight out of nowhere, reminded me of a fable attributed to our great Alexander Pushkin. Listen to it carefully for it has much wisdom.

"Once upon a time a romantic swallow, visiting Moscow at autumn's end, noticed a remarkably handsome feminine figure sitting high on the Kremlin wall. Augustus-for that was the swallow's name-had never seen anything so beautiful and instantly fell in love. To attract her attention and prove his worthiness, Augustus would climb high in the sky, majestically glide in ever widening circles and suddenly swoop down to the Red Square in a daring dive, pulling out with only inches to spare." Grigori looked at me as if wondering whether I was listening. "I'm with you, Colonel, catching every word". He continued: "Alas, the object of his affection paid him no heed. Augustus could not bear to be so ignored and looked round for counsel from his elder brethren but they had already hastened south to warmer climates because winter was closing in on Moscow and frosty weather was not for swallows. Only the sparrows remained, but they just chatted endlessly and followed the horses. Finally, one day when he had great difficulty flying through the falling snow, the harsh scolding by two elderly spinster sparrows alarmed him. "Go south, you simpleton, go south before you freeze to death here." With a last forlorn look at his love, Augustus set his compass for the Black Sea and flew straight into a blizzard. On top of the Kremlin his black seductress retreated into her crow's nest.

Within a few miles Augustus realized he had tarried too long. His wings were icing. His breath was short. His heart pounding, he crashed onto a farm-yard. He knew the end had come. He fainted. A feeling of warmth restored his senses. A passing cow had mercifully buried him under an avalanche of her hot dung. In minutes he felt alive again. He stirred, then poked his head out of the cowpat. The farmer's cat lunged and gulped down poor Augustus".

"How did you like my story?" "Not very well. What's the point ? " "Ah, Evgenii, today you are less than bright. There are morals in the adventures of Augustus. Firstly, not everyone who craps on you must automatically be considered an enemy. Secondly, not everyone who pulls you out of a pile of dung is necessarily a friend. Finally, when you feel safe and warm, stay put."

I was anxious to leave, still didn't want "the day after tomorrow" to become today, for it would be hard saying good-bye to Grigori.

Warsaw - Vienna - Venice

I followed Grigori's instructions to the letter, entering Warsaw without mishap. German occupation forces had meantime issued strict orders to the civilian population. These were posted throughout the city. Nobody was allowed to leave Warsaw without a special pass issued by the Kommandantur. One could get shot for trying to get out without one. Our embassy was long gone. The Germans had ordered all diplomatic personnel to leave Warsaw by special convoy just before the main offensive on the capital. Anthony Drexel Biddle, our ambassador, was among them. He would have a lot to tell his good friend President Roosevelt. Many weeks prior to the outbreak of war our embassy had urged all Americans to get out of Poland without delay. I ignored the warnings. As far as I knew, no Americans were left in Warsaw. I had no one to turn to. Thanks to Grigori my red American passport was still in my possession. With it in hand, I entered the Kommandantur, explaining to the officer in charge that I was American and wished to go home. He stared at me for a what seemed to me an eternity, while I shook and perspired. Then he inspected what appeared to be a list of names. Would he know of my radio broadcasts ? Apparently not. Finally, he asked: "what in the devil is an American doing here in Poland". I stuttered some meaningless words. He handed me the exit permit saying:" Mit der Dummheit kämpfen Götter selbst vergebens". I recognized the quotation from Schiller and quite agreed with him. It meant: "With stupidity the gods themselves struggle in vain". Obviously, he felt some pity for me. I was a sight. When I smuggled myself back into the city, my friends gave me a sweater, some old trousers and a pair of boots several sizes too big, because my disfigured feet had swollen. I did not walk, I shuffled along. My bones stuck out despite the huge portions of potatoes and kasza I had devoured daily at Grigori's "schoolhouse." Coming into the Kommandantur I nearly fell. The German seeing my pathetic condition evidently decided I posed no threat to the Third Reich.

How to get out of the country? Which direction to go? I needed to get more rest. But where? My own flat was bombed out. The fire had destroyed everything, totally. I regretted most the piano and my books. I went back to my friends, also bombed out and occupying some unknown person's cellar. Since I last saw them they had been contacted by two strangers who desperately wanted to leave the country. One was Chuck Siegel, an American of Polish descent, fresh graduate of the Polish

Institute of Physical Culture. He would not tell us why he had to avoid all contact with the Germans and their appointed militia. I suspected he was on their list for acts of sabotage. The other, Rinaldo Wise, was a victim of abominable timing and a comedy of errors. I knew Rinaldo from the Polish radio where he broadcast programs in Italian. Born in Cairo of an English father, he came to Warsaw in a burst of patriotism inspired by his Polish mother, to apply for Polish citizenship. A couple of months before war broke out he got his wish and, shortly afterward, also a prison sentence for failing to report for military service. My boss at the radio told me about Rinaldo's misfortune. I managed to obtain his release through the intervention of a friend of mine, a high official in government. The chaos of war confused everything, leaving Rinaldo with no papers, no identity. All he had was initiative and enormous courage. Together, the three of us decided our best bet would be to head for Italy. Rinaldo assured us that once there he could arrange everything. A few years back he was a student at the University of Bologna, making friends with individuals who were now in high places, he said. Two nights later Rinaldo stole a car with German plates and markings, proposing we drive it to the Czech border. I told him he was mad and refused to go, fearing we would be caught within hours and shot on the spot. Rinaldo's favorite expression was "chi non rischia, non fischia" (He who takes no risk can't whistle or, to win one must take chances). "Are you coming?" Chuck was all for it. Finally, I agreed to join them in this mad, unconscionable, high risk adventure either because of physical and mental fatigue, or desperation, or simple need for companionship following my lonely ordeals. I just could not face being left behind. Surely, the Gods look after maniacs and fools. City checkpoints waived us through. Driving all through the moonlit night, mostly without headlights, we got to the city of Katowice on the Czech border without being stopped. We abandoned the car, hiding it as best we could at the railway station. We were in such a hurry to get out of Warsaw before alarm was raised over the missing automobile that stupidly we took no food with us. Now we were very very hungry. Across from the railway station we entered a small restaurant. We ordered sausage sandwiches. The waiter laughed. "The Germans have all the sausage". Then, hearing Rinaldo speak English to Chuck, he nervously pointed to the black uniforms of the SS entering the door. We left slowly through the back exit, holding our breath. What if they found the car? This was no time to be questioned.

We could see from the excellent map found in the car that we were more than 640 kilometers from Vienna and would have to travel through Ostrava in Czechoslovakia, now controlled by Germany, to get there. Austria was German too, annexed a year earlier, but our quickest, safest route to Italy. We got on the train buying tickets from the Polish conductor. I was the only one with any money. I gave him a large tip, one hundred Zlotys. There were no seats. We had to stand. My feet started to bleed. Luckily, nobody paid attention to us. Oddly, no documents were checked until the Czech-Austrian border and there only perfunctorily. I kept looking at Chuck. He acted unconcerned yet I knew that, just like me, he was choking with fear. There was little reason for us to be so terrified. This was not the war zone, we had tickets and our passports were in order. It was all because we were thieves on the run. Still, that damn German car did get us to the border. Rinaldo was nowhere to be seen. He reappeared only when we reached the Vienna railway station. The Polish conductor had hidden him well.

We found the American embassy. A consul received us. His name was Herbert Fales. On hearing his first words of greeting I passed out. I woke in bed at the consul's residence quite ill, with a high fever and an abscessed throat. The consul was a very kind man, obviously worried about me. He got me excellent medical care. When I felt stronger he gave me Steinbeck's "Of Mice and Men" to read. I thought it awfully depressing. Chuck and Rinaldo kept urging me to get well so that we could continue our journey. The consul agreed. "The sooner, the better". He also told me he had sent a despatch to Washington about me. During my illness I must have talked a lot. He gave us all some money, saw that we get safely on the train. I would never forget this fine gentleman Herbert Fales, United States consul in Vienna.

Vienna - Venice

The fast train took us Vienna-Graz-Udine-Venice. A spot of trouble in Udine, the Italian border, involving undocumented Rinaldo. However, with his perfect Italian he convinced the border police to let him through. I found this quite surprising because in Fascist Italy discipline was not to be trifled with. In fact, just minutes later I saw an elderly Italian woman being fined by the conductor for boarding the train without a ticket. When she threw the receipt on the floor he called the train police. The poor lady was taken off the train at the next station in tears. I asked Rinaldo who had witnessed it all "what on earth did you tell them?" "It's not what I said to them, it's what I showed them". He let me see a photograph. It was of a group of smiling young men surrounding Mussolini. Right next to Il Duce stood Rinaldo.

My thoughts went back to that exhilarating day in Rome where I had traveled two years earlier hoping to see the man who created the Fascist Party. The party with the nationalist, syndicalist, anti-communist policy whose leader did so much to help Franco in the Spanish civil war. I was a fervent admirer of Il Duce and applauded him that day in Rome when he addressed the spellbound crowds from the balcony in Piazza Venezia.

Now we were nearing the city of Marco Polo. Later renowned for its schools of painting, the Palace of the Doges and so many other magnificent creations of man. Venice, the inner sanctum of genius. We found a small bar-trattoria with rooms for rent above. The owner's name was Gianni. He presented us to his wife, Mimi. I was an opera buff since childhood. I couldn't believe it. Here was my Mimi, so I just had to be Rodolfo. Without thinking, I recited: "Aspetti, signorina, le dirò con due parole chi son, e che faccio, come vivo. Vuole? Chi son? Sono un poeta. Che cosa faccio? Scrivo. E come vivo? Vivo. In povertà mia lieta scialo da gran signore rime ed inni d' amore". My surprise recitation from *La Bohème* brought down the house, such was the enthusiastic reaction of Gianni and his customers. A few phrases from Puccini and from several other operas was my total knowledge of Italian. When the applause died down, we confessed to having no money. "Don't worry" said Mimi, "I shall take care of you. Ci penso io". And so she did, together with Gianni and their friends. These beautiful, wonderful, generous, crazy Italians looked after us, fed us, spoiled us by letting us sleep late under warm soft, immaculate eider downs, then bringing our breakfasts on a tray. They told us stories of old and of new Venice, asked us about America, laughed with us and taught us naughty songs. They took us in gondolas on the canals, pointing out famous sites and palazzos. It was all tonic for our souls. When our money arrived from America they wouldn't accept any of it. We all cried when the time came for us to leave for Genoa where the pride of Italy, the magnificent transatlantic *Rex* waited to take us home.

We had to leave Rinaldo behind. I did not expect to see him again. How would he manage, this man without a country? I worried a lot about that. But then, suddenly, we were in the port of Genoa, nearly a different world. My thoughts automatically jumped to the other side of the Atlantic, to America.

Genoa - New York (Rex)

It looked like half the population of Europe was trying to board the Italian luxury passenger ship, the *Rex*, about to sail out of Genoa to Naples, then New York. It was possibly the best, most certainly the safest transatlantic vessel to travel on. If there were any German Man-0'-War or submarines in the Atlantic, they would not attack a vessel of an ally, the reasoning went. No one doubted that the invasion of Poland was only a prelude in the German quest for European domination. Ugly reports of ever increasing persecution of Jews in Austria, of concentration camps in Poland, and Mussolini's increasingly belligerent speeches were spawning germs of mass hysteria.

Fortunes were being offered for cabin space, sold out long before. The line's offices were besieged by bribe-itching fists clutching wads of dollars, hoping for a last minute cancellation. Mounted Carabinieri intervened over and over again to disperse the crowd. Chuck and I were lucky. Our passage had been secured by the American consulate. Our continued good luck saw to it that our dining room companions were garrulous, uninhibited wits. The cultured Julius Lewitanski was a well known jeweller from Warsaw. He had changed his name from Lewy, not a very original switch. It didn't fool the Germans. Diamonds were far more persuasive. Not one to be outwitted, Julius had his relative in New York make suitable arrangements with the American aunt of a high German official who promised him safe passage out of Poland. He even managed to take some stones with him. He kept them in a black velvet pouch. Julius could not resist showing them to us. He beamed when I introduced Chuck. "Another Jewish boy saved", he exclaimed. Chuck nearly swallowed his spoon. With his dark curly hair and prickle beard he could have been thought Jewish and with a name like Siegel it seemed obvious. Actually he was born Szczygiel, a Polish name one had to sneeze to pronounce. That was why Chuck's father, tired of being constantly teased, went to court and got himself a new one, not realizing it sounded Jewish. Julius pretended not to believe the story. "I'll bet you a diamond he's circumcized" he said one evening at dinner. The big, broad, bulging with muscles Chuck merely grinned before grunting: "You know where you can put your diamond". Julian's riposte "I've done it before, I can do it again" surprised me a bit. Julian was always so decorous.

So here we were: a Jew who had a Polish "catholic" name - Lewitanski- a Polish Catholic with a Jewish name -Siegel-, and last but not least the eponymous René, Lesueur, a French professional tennis coach from Bordeaux whose name meant "sweat". He had been coaching the Italian Davis Cup team and told us about the phenomenal Palmieri who played only forehands, by switching his racket from hand to hand. I could not help wondering what this ambidextrous tennis champion did with a fast ball at the net.

When I was not busy in my cabin making copious notes, trying to recall in detail recent happenings, faithfully recording all that Grigori had said to me, I repeatedly attempted engaging Julius in discussion. His hedonistic, rakish mind intrigued me. How did he feel, this middle aged childless widower, losing the only world he knew? Did he have the guts to start all over again? Could he, would he be happy in America? I asked Chuck what he thought. "Eh, you know how Jews are. They always wind up on top".

Julius was hard to draw out. He would tell jokes and toss out quaint Jewish metaphors, avoiding serious talk. Until one evening when I caught him on deck. The Atlantic heaved. The wind was cold. We stood against the rail. Julius talked about himself. He was a contradiction, he said. A Hasidic Jew, intellectually primed since his school days to protest against authoritarian rationalism, to rely more on faith and emotion than on reality and reason. He once truly believed that man could approach God through prayer and worship, though he condemned religious enthusiasts "The inhumanity of Warsaw drained me of faith", he said. "My heart turned to stone". I felt that Julius wanted me, was asking me, to tell him that what he said about himself was not true. That he would live again, believe again. I could not. Our disparity in depths of suffering would not let our minds touch. I deplored the fact that I had not yet gone through sufficient mental calisthenics in life to be able to follow his theology. Could I possibly lighten his disillusionment with my own ingenuous brand of iconoclasm? "Believers, I told him, transgress moral law, restating the ontological argument for the existence of God by accepting the Cartesian bogus syllogism "dubito, ergo cogito, ergo sum". In their overweening conceit, believers are so sure of having found the truth they no longer doubt, no longer search. That is hubris, ultimately causing the transgressor's doom", I sentenced. "Be an agnostic. Be humble. Admit that God is unfathomable, that nothing can be known about the existence or nature of God. Is not humility superior to conceit, Julius?" He was too sophisticated to be led into my blind alley from which there was no escape except surrender. Obviously amused by my amateur sophistry, he patted me on the shoulder and said "I enjoy being superstitious".

In the early morning haze the skyline of New York looked like the jagged caried teeth in the lower jaw of a Dinosaur, more intimidating than friendly. U.S.immigration officials were on board checking passports. A very tall fellow, about my own age, stood in the line just ahead of me and Chuck. He carried a pair of long skis. "Did you cross the Atlantic on skis?" "Well, not really, but I brought them all the way from Cracow" said Mat Gluchowski. A New Yorker, he was visiting relatives in Poland when war broke out. As soon as trains were running he reached Venice via Budapest and Zagreb. No German exit permit, no delays, no hunger, no fear. He only worried about his skis and looked like a man coming back from vacation. We thought of throwing him overboard.

On the dock, I retrieved my small suitcase. The customs man looked at the meager contents. He had seen poor immigrants before. He didn't even notice my soft, brown, very handsome Borsalino hat I had purchased in Venice.

I was home at last. Chuck gave me a fast good-bye hug. His parents whisked him away. I was alone. Twenty years old and sorry for myself. It didn't much matter really. I would be catching the train for my home town that same night.

Chicago - New York - Chgo

The Chicago Daily Tribune, isolationist, anti British platform of its publisher, Colonel Robert R.McCormick, ran headlines like:

"Moscow Orders Reds to back Roosevelt".

The William Randolph Hearst press printed a jingle:

"The Red New Deal with a Soviet seal
Endorsed by a Moscow hand
The strange result of an alien cult
In liberty loving land".

As early as October 1937 Franklin Delano Roosevelt sounded warnings against "the epidemic of world lawlessness" reminding America that in 1931 Japan invaded Manchuria, in 1935 Mussolini took Ethiopia, in 1936 the Spanish Civil War began, with one side supplied by Russian arms and the other by Nazi equipment.

Isolationists derided Roosevelt as an alarmist and as late as July 1939 the Republican Senator Borah declared in Congress that there would be no war in Europe.

The America First Committee advocated pacifism and isolationism, its ranks filled with Anglophobes, anti-semites and reactionaries. America's ambassador to London, the whiskey made millionaire and vitriolic Anglophobe, Joseph Kennedy, to whom Roosevelt referred as "my ambassador", advised the president: "stay out because England would lose the war".

Roosevelt was not easily swayed but fearing a possible victory in the 1940 presidential race by his opponent Wendell Wilkie, who told his audiences that if they voted for Roosevelt it would mean crosses for their sons, FDR included in one of his addresses a phrase written by his speechwriter Robert Sherwood: "Your boys are not going to be sent into foreign wars", Roosevelt won again. His third term as president.

America saw and heard but still was not prepared to act. Austria, Czechoslovakia, Poland, Norway, Denmark, The Netherlands, Belgium and France had all fallen victim to Nazi aggression .

The Chicago Daily News and its radio station with the call signal: "This is WGN, the Voice of the People, Chicago", -the WGN stood pretentiously for "World's Greatest Newspaper"- never stopped advocating non-intervention in Europe, sharply influencing public opinion in Illinois and other mid-western States.

When I embarked on a lecture tour, in this climate so hostile to my own views, I felt like Sisyphus condemned to push a rock to the top of a hill, only to see it roll down again short of the top . My agent was a crackerjack writer-promoter, John Marshall Ziv, who contacted me after reading an interview I had granted to a magazine of my home town, Oak Park, a few weeks after landing in New York.

I spoke to many different audiences. I had nearly forgotten that Americans were a nation of joiners. Rotary Clubs, Kiwanis, Elks, Lodges of every description, circles, associations, civic, amateur, academic, professional. Name it, I was there. Also, of course, high profile organizations of national, even international repute such as the Chicago Council on Foreign Relations. High, low or middle, the majority of the listeners, while applauding and sometimes gasping at my personal adventures, would turn deaf at any suggestion of America's active involvement in a "foreign war". Moreover, I kept getting the distinct impression that speaking of the German war machine, its destructive power fed by the tremendous German industrial capacity, was seen as propaganda designed to frighten Americans, rather than alert them to danger. I think I can take credit for the first use of "military-industrial complex" in describing Hitler's Third Reich. A Chicago newspaper columnist, Irving Phlaum, accused me in print of being a German propagandist. I thought this was very nice of him since his article instantly doubled my fees. But, I was bitter in my lonely role as advocate for military intervention and felt an intense and distressing experience of meaninglessness, of an existential vacuum.

The only kindred soul on the lecture circuit at that time was Otto von Habsburg whose dynasty supplied dukes and archdukes of Austria, kings of Hungary and Bohemia, ruled the Holy Roman Empire and sat on the throne of Spain. In flawless English, this trim, handsome young man spoke of the rape of his own country and of Europe by Hitler. Alas, the decent, reliable, obtuse, intellectually absolutely unthreatening midwesterners, were meat and potato men, not the least interested in the problems of foreign lands. They came to see the archduke, to be able to tell their friends they shook hands with royalty, not to heed him.

Looking out the window of my agent's office in the Merchandise Mart building on Wacker Drive in Chicago, I could see the offices of the German Consulate. I felt it ironic I should be on the landmark property of the Kennedy family just when this new idea on taking some action against the German-American Bund came to my mind. The Bund was recruiting volunteers to help organize pro-German rallies across the country and generally spread propaganda for the Third Reich. I asked John to get me an appointment with the "morgue" of the Chicago Tribune. There was little there about the Bund but I did learn that the German Consul General was Dr.Krause Wichman who had arrived in Chicago only recently. This meant he had to be a solid member of the Nazi Party.

I had no difficulty getting an appointment with the good doctor as he had read about me. He greeted me with the courtesy and manners of a well bred German. He seemed anxious to hear my impressions of the Blitzkrieg in Poland, commenting that since then several other countries had surrendered "to the invincible German armies". Would I be interested in going to Berlin to work for the Ministry of Propaganda there? He could arrange for me to get a challenging assignment. This was one trap I was not falling into. I told him I did not speak German and would therefore be of little value. Could he, instead, give me an introduction to the German-American Bund? Yes, he could and he would. After asking me when I would be free to travel to New York he phoned the Bund's headquarters there to expect my visit before the end of the week and gave me his visiting card with a note on the back in German. It said: "Kurt, be nice to our friend".

For the next three days I kept phoning the Chicago Field Office of the FBI, unable to get past the switchboard. "If you are not reporting a federal crime and don't know who you want to talk to, I can't put you through, can I?" Finally, special agent Devereux agreed to see me.

Before I was able to explain the purpose of my visit he had already asked me a dozen totally meaningless questions about my lecture tour, told me what a wonderful job the FBI was doing and asked what my plans were for the future, now that I was back in my "native land". I noticed he had a clipping of Irving Phlaum's article about me on his desk. It could not be called an auspicious start for what I hoped would be my "special mission" for the FBI. I got him on track only with considerable difficulty. "What are your thoughts about my idea and do you have any immediate instructions for me on the procedures I should follow if and when I am on the inside of the Bund"? "Well, he said, we will arrange for a special agent from the FBI New York office to meet you next Tuesday in front of the Metropolitan Museum of Art at 10 am." I would recognize him as he would be carrying an umbrella and a newspaper under his arm. "What is all this charade for", I asked. "That is the way we do things round here"."Won't your agent be conspicuous with an umbrella if it's not raining?" "Don't be facetious". "And yes, you will travel to New York by Greyhound bus". "Close to 1000 miles by bus? You must be crazy", I protested. "You will attract less attention that way". "But I'm not hiding from anyone". "We know what we are talking about. Go by bus".

As I was leaving his office, he returned to me Krause Wichman's visiting card, instructing me to enter the drugstore on the ground floor of the building, order a Strawberry Sundae at the counter and wait. Bewildered but obedient, I did just that. A few minutes later an odd looking individual sat down next to me, putting a folded newspaper between us. He looked round, pointed to the newspaper and quickly left. I found $200 clipped inside the newspaper. I never figured out why I was given this money in the first place or why was it not simply handed to me in Devereux's office a few minutes earlier. When I got home and began analyzing the situation, I decided that either I myself was going daft or our FBI agents were dangerous comedians in disguise. Before I even started they had already committed three serious blunders. One, they delayed my departure for New York by five days after I told them of my agreement with the consul general that I would be leaving by the first direct train. Two, there was no need whatsoever for me to travel by bus, the cheapest transportation available. It would take me much longer, be dreadfully tiring and, should anyone be monitoring my movements, cast doubt on my financial status just as I was about to angle for a high profile but unpaid position with the Bund. And three, there were two very visible holes in Krause Wichman's visiting card, screaming loud and clear it had not been kept in my wallet but pinned to a file. Sure enough, after waiting at the Bund's reception desk in New York for an hour, they told me Kurt was not available. Could I possibly come back in three weeks? After returning by train to Chicago, I sent special agent Devereux a pair of roller skates.

Windsor - Canada - Liverpool - U.K.

I leapt with joy on receiving the postcard. It said: "bring me some woolen socks. Rinaldo". I remembered giving him my uncle's Chicago address, but when we said goodbye to each other in Venice I never expected to hear from him again. All of a sudden he was right next door, only about 160 miles away, in Windsor, Canada.

His sense of humour was still intact. The "bring me some woolen socks" was a reminder of how we trekked for so many miserable miles together with only the tops of our socks in one piece, the soles torn to bits, toes sticking out, until we found haven in Italy.

It was also a reminder of our hunger, our laughter, our tears, the rhythm of the lagoon of the Adriatic, the marvelous company of our hosts Gianni and Mimi who explained to us the impressionistic brush of Tintoretto, the asymetrical dynamic compositions of Tiziano and taught us to thrill at the sight of languishing, drunkenly tilted gondolas with their many secrets.

Rinaldo, never lacking in ingenuity, made it to England, joined the British forces. With the rank of sergeant he was despatched to Canada to recruit for the Royal Air Force. The town of Windsor was buzzing with anxious anticipation of military action. It was jammed less with Canadians than American volunteers from every state of the Union. After

The War Years

Rinaldo told me how tough things were in England, how every man was needed, I caught the volunteer fever again. Two months earlier, in Chicago, I tried to enlist in the U.S. Army. It was my day of infamy. The medical board classified me 4F which meant I was not qualified to carry even a broom in American forces. As we were not at war, our military doctors were being very selective and while they found nothing radically wrong with me, I was underweight and certainly no competition to Tarzan. In Canada, the medical board was far less severe. If you were not in a wheelchair or in coma you were good enough to serve in His Majesty's forces. I signed up with the RAF under my mother's maiden name to avoid directly breaking American law. My relatives and my agent went bananas when I phoned them in Chicago about my decision.

Before I got used to my ill-fitting airforce uniform, they packed us off to England. We sailed from Halifax on board the very overcrowded *Newcastle*. The seas were rough but nothing compared with what awaited us in Liverpool. German bombers had already been there more than once. The harbour was a wreck, a giant cemetary of sunken ships. It was cold and rainy and windy. We were ankle deep in mud. The barracks drafty and dirty. The food, mostly watery Brussels sprouts, unbearable. We complained about the lack of proper nourishment, about the filth, the garbage spilling over in the kitchens, the system of pretending to wash dishes by simply dipping them in barrels of cold greasy water, the time wasted in queues just to get into the overcrowded mess hall. It did us absolutely no good. The Sergeant Major simply yelled louder at us in the language of Lancashire we could barely understand. What we North Americans found most infuriating was the damn imperturbable stoicism with which our English colleagues seemed to accept it all without a single complaint. To us they would mockingly say: "Don't you know there's a war on?" Yea, we thought, but how do you expect to win it sitting on your duffs in the mud? At the time we still did not know, how much we were to learn from the incredible British. Then came Blackpool where we were individually billeted with local families. I could readily understand why the name "Blackpool", but much less how its people managed to be kind, generous and full of good-natured humour.

Still, it all became a bore when we languished without organized activity for several weeks. Finally, postings. For me, the EFTS (Elementary Flying Training School), then AFTS (Advanced FTS), where I would get my first taste of real discipline from the fabulous Scot, Squadron Leader Calder. During this period of intense training there was little encouraging news from home. Barely a few glimmers of hope were beginning to appear for the small number of American interventionists who argued that if the dictators were not checked, America would be their next victim. In his third presidential campaign Roosevelt attacked the Republicans for joining hands with the Communists whose leader in America, Earl Browder, still cried: "Not a cent, not a gun, not a man for the imperialist war".

Significantly though, with foresight Roosevelt declared: "something evil is happening in this country when a full page advertisement paid by Republican supporters of isolationism appears in the *Daily Worker*, the newspaper of the Communist Party".

In the "Four Freedoms" speech to the U.S. Congress, after winning his third term, he advocated the loan of war materials to Britain. A glimmer of hope? Perhaps. Right then it sounded more like Maréchal Bosquet's description of the Charge of the Light Brigade: "C'est magnifique, mais ce n'est pas la guerre". (It is magnificent, but it is not war).

We in Britain were doing the real job. The kind of stuff that would make the difference and which we would later hope to banish forever from our minds.

Scotland

We had crashed in the snowy Grampian mountains of Scotland. I was in pretty sad shape when they brought me to Dupplin Castle. Fleeting moments of consciousness and darkness, mixed. I heard an orderly say: "watch it mate, he's one of our Yanks". I was floating somewhere again and dreaming. I saw Squadron Leader Calder, my commanding officer way back at the Advanced Flying Training School. The orderly had brought him back to me with his: "one of our Yanks". Calder was a Scotsman. Big, tough and loud. A fine officer and a man we all respected. He had issued an order that all "USA" shoulder patches were to disappear instantly. How would the hospital orderly have known I was a Yank if I had obeyed that order?

Drifting again, I saw the astonished look on the Squadron Leader's face when I told him that wearing nationality designating shoulder patches was not against "King's Regulations" and if he was going to insult us, we would all march into town, drop our pants and parade half naked. Calder knew I had not the slightest idea what the "King's Regulations" had to say in the matter and he could have thrown me in the brig right then and there on any number of charges. But, he also knew that there were over one hundred Yanks in British uniform at the base. I had counted on his being fond of Americans. When we first arrived he noted the presence of a group of Texans and remarked "Ah, Texas, our most loyal State". He rescinded the shoulder patch order. Now I was in a British hospital where someone had called me "our Yank". I tried to say something but couldn't. A nurse whispered "now, now"and wiped off my tears.

It was a long haul. I lost track of time. Not of pain though, or of the nausea induced by large, frequent doses of sulpha drugs.

Apart from injuries, I had serious infections and pneumonia. Nothing seemed to help but at least I was conscious now and grateful for the near constant presence of my guardian angel, the young fragile, honey blond titled lady who insisted on anonymity when she turned Dupplin Castle into a military hospital. When I could no longer stand the pain she tightly held my hand. When despair seized me, she talked to me about duty and honor and sacrifice and reward and her beloved Scotland. Against all odds, she kept me alive. Then, one early morning there was a group of people round my bed. The Matron gave me an injection. Many followed. Only weeks later did my benefactress tell me in strict confidence that I had been administered a new and not yet officially available drug called penicillin. She had somehow managed to get it for me. It was the second time in the war that British heart and initiative saved my life. There was a humorous moment during my period of convalescence provided by John Swensen, the Swede from Mankato, Minnesota, who occupied the bed next to mine. We had talked quite a lot and he wanted to give me a souvenir before I left the hospital. Taking a small case from under the bed, he started unwrapping a small object from what I took to be white tissue paper. On closer look I realized it was not tissue but a good old-fashioned British Five Pound Note. He wouldn't believe me until the doctor making his rounds confirmed it. "Yiminy", he cried, my buddies and I found a load of this stuff during the evacuation from Dunquerque. "You know what we did with it? We used it for toilet paper. I'll be able to tell my grandchildren that during the war Grandpa took some awfully expensive craps". "You bet" I said, looking at the miniature Mannekin Pis statue of a little boy peeing into a Brussels fountain-Swensen had just given me. "At twenty dollars a crack, it sure was a pretty fancy deal".

They posted me to St. Andrews to rest and wait for my discharge papers. The British called it being "invalided out of the service". It was a boring and frustrating time. From my room at the Marine hotel I watched squadrons of American bombers flying toward targets in Germany. The rumble of the RAF returning to base at daybreak would often waken me. I could also see the golf course, and just beyond, the bright red capes of the university students on their daily walks near the cliffs above the angry waves of the North Sea. The University Vice Principal, whom I approached, agreed to let me address them. I gave three lectures under the title: "The influence of astro navigation on geopolitics". Half serious, half tongue in cheek I theorized how new discoveries in technology would change the map of Europe after we, the Allies, won the war. On my part, I learned that the noisy stomping of feet on the auditorium floor did not mean derision but approval. I guess my listeners sort of liked me. Once, on a drive, I got a glimpse of Princesses Elizabeth and Margaret, in Scotland to escape from the bombs shattering London

London - Washington - Luxembourg - London

When I came to London as a civilian, after being discharged from the Royal Air Force, my first job was with the BBC as night editor. It all happened through a rather odd coincidence when I accidentally ran into an old acquaintance while dining at an Indian restaurant called Veraswamees in Swallow Street. He was the same man who gave me my first job at Radio Warsaw. His name was no longer Pienkowski. He now called himself Wagner. I felt not inconsiderable resentment toward him for having deserted me without a word when the German invasion of Poland began. I also wondered why he had changed his name. I was even more curious, but never asked, how he managed to get me hired so quickly by the British Broadcasting Corporation. In wartime Britian it was wiser not to ask unnecessary questions just to satisfy one's curiosity.

At BBC's Bush House my British bosses kept me very busy not only writing and broadcasting but training me in the art of political propaganda. They first introduced me to and then, apparently getting a nod of approval from even higher authority, had me formally join a select group of wizards responsible for the formulating of psychological warfare directives. Occasionally they invited me to White's for lunch, their jackets pipe-ashed, breaths alcoholic, intellects sharp, resolve fixed. These middle-aged backroom boys, with university honours from Berlin, Munich, Leipzig or Heidelberg, who years earlier tentatively espoused, more often exposed, derided and denuded Heidegger, Hegel, Schiller,

Goethe, sarcastically challenging the allegorical statements of Wagner's Nibelung gods, giants and dwarfs on the corrupting effect of lust for power to a game of strip poker or counterfeit chess, knew precisely how to unfold every quirk of the Teutonic-turned-Nazi crazed soul, now relentlessly drowning it in ridicule over the airwaves of our clandestine transmitters and through underground newspapers circulated in occupied Europe.

Their less subtle, more secretive colleagues in a related group, devised Machiavellian radio messages designed to inject deadly Weltschmerz into the livers of the German military men.

"Did captain Hans Luber of the Fifth Corps stationed in Darmstadt know that his wife Emma, resident at Nr.5 Bahnhofstrasse in Dresden, was sleeping with the handsome lieutenant Wilhelm Hebbel?" The remarkable thing about these tidbits was their accuracy in every detail. Much later, I discovered that this type of personal information about German officers was being furnished by Allied agents working under the direction of the secret American intelligence office in Berne, Switzerland, operating there in violation of the country's neutrality laws but, remarkably, never shut down by the Swiss.

The American Office of War Information (OWI) in London wanted to hire me. The BBC would not let me go. A compromise had to be reached. Three nights a week I would work at the BBC, the rest of the time with my compatriots. A murderous schedule. I was bound to become a basket case, my friends warned. Actually, I enjoyed every minute of it. It was not all work. The marvellous thing about Londoners was that despite the bombs, the wreckage, the daily death toll, the hardships of rationing, the horror of it all, they were not going to let "damn Jerry" get them down. So while cursing the exploding rockets,we applauded the inspiring melodies of the songstress Vera Lynn, the bawdy humor of BBC comics ("if it's laughter your're after Trinder's the name"), went to marvellous West End theater, joined so called bottle clubs where you were supposed to bring your own booze but actually bought it under the table from management.

We listened religiously to the BBC evening news, to Winston Churchill's inspiring speeches, laughed when told "the trouble with Yanks is that they are overpaid, oversexed and over here" for we knew it was said with affection because all of us were in this struggle together. Yes, the marvellous thing about London, no, about the British, was that no matter how tough it got, no matter how much they bled, it never entered their mind that England could lose the war. Victory was always theirs and at hand.

Irving Berlin put on a show for us: *This is the Army*. We gloried in it. The rhythm, the humor, the melodies, the lyrics, the sense of timing, the costumes, the dancers were all sensational and strictly American. For some mysterious reason, the British with their superb legitimate stage, their great actors, playwrights, beautiful women, fine musicians, could never produce a musical show worth a damn.

Robert Sherwood, the American playwright and President Roosevelt's speechwriter ("Your boys are not going to be sent into foreign wars") who was on the board of the OWI, came to London to present his play: *There shall be no Night*, starring the famous American acting couple Lynn Fontane and Alfred Lunt. This time he had the right message, earning applause.

A young actress in the cast, Muriel Pavlow, was the most enchanting creature I had ever met. I could not get her out of my mind. But, it was forbidden fruit, so for many years after I would admire her on the London stage, where she had become famous, only from the remoteness of a forlorn spectator.

One morning as I walked into my OWI office at Inveresk, Celia, my secretary, motioned to a parcel on my desk, saying: "a messenger brought it for you a while ago. I had to sign for it". The flat package, neatly wrapped, had the label of a well known department store in Oxford Street and was marked "gift ". What struck me immediately, was the way it was addressed. Below my name it said: "U.S. Office of War Information, Intelligence Unit, Inveresk House. Though not entirely complete, good enough to reach me. However, the puzzling and startling part was the inclusion of "Intelligence Unit". This designation existed only in internal confidential documents, never openly used.

I shoved the parcel into a drawer, forgetting about it in the rush we inflicted upon ourselves each morning with our remarkable aptitude to create perpetual chaos. There were just too many people trying to be useful but getting in the way. Late that evening, still in the office, I opened the parcel. The note inside said: "Evgenii be careful". I got nervous shakes. There was only one person in the world who called me Evgenii.

The documents were signed Russian military reports on the executions of thousands of Polish army officers, shot in the back of their heads, with dates, names and ranks. Their common grave could be found in the Katyn woods near Smolensk. There was also an eyewitness statement in Polish, signed:" Lech Witkowski, Colonel Polish Army". An attached note explained that Colonel Witkowski managed to escape to neutral Sweden and was interned there. What was I to do with this package of political dynamite, I wondered. And, how could I explain having it? I could see myself in a straight-jacket if I told my superiors that Selfridges, that nice London department store, had sent it to me wrapped as a gift. Would anyone believe me a Russian officer had it delivered to my office? Could this whole thing be a plant instigated by the devious Soviet Department of Disinformation in order to compromise Grigori? The matter boggled the mind. I would have to reflect before doing anything. The gruesome documentation was complete, very convincing. Also, I was sure Grigori would not lie to me. I could still remember the trainloads of Polish military personnel under Russian guard stopping at the railway junction where I was temporary prisoner in the schoolhouse. And Alex. Of course. It was Grigori's batman Alex who told me I was lucky the colonel liked me because otherwise "you would have been sent to Smolensk with the others".

This, I felt, was going to be one helluva nightmare to handle. Not that the story of the Katyn forest was entirely new. Intelligence services of the Polish government in exile had repeatedly accused the Russians of this wholesale murder. I suspected that the British wanted to keep the lid on this matter. As long as the Soviets were fighting the Germans they were valued allies, so "don't rock the boat". As simple as that William Gladstone, British P.M. and statesman observed a hundred years earlier "nations do not have permanent enemies, nor do they have permanent friends. They have only permanent interests."

The British usually knew what they were doing but I wondered whether we Americans knew who our enemies were, or for that matter, what our true interests were. Would solid documentation and eyewitness accounts make a difference? I doubted it. I didn't dare take the damning parcel home with me. I stuck it in my secretary's out tray, under a pile of papers. Two days later, after much agonizing, I submitted the Katyn documents to my bosses through channels, without comment, but earmarked for our Department of State. It was a mistake. The dossier fell into the wrong hands and earned me a suspension. My personnel file now had a note: "pending clarification, suspended from official duties for pronounced anti-Soviet sentiments". This was pretty scary. The Communists in State seemed awfully sure of themselves. Luckily, I had a few friends there. In London, my chief editor, Dr.Zbigniew Grabowski, whom I trusted completely, confirmed what I had heard from my own Polish sources in London, that a clique of communists had infiltrated our information services, including the Voice of America. They had reason to believe, they said, that a certain Irena Balinska was among the main operatives. I knew her by name only from a number of cabled communications we had exchanged through BBC official channels. She had persuaded the policy people in Washington to shift control over Polish language broadcasts from me in London to studios in New York. The program content instantly changed, becoming a crudely transparent paean of praise to the Soviets. The real damage to the morale of the Poles was being inflicted by insidious statements that the United States could and would have only limited influence on the political future of their country. My London staff was enraged. So were my colleagues in the Psychological Warfare Division and the BBC where I still kept my first London job.

War or no war, I had to personally see my influential friends in America before matters got totally out of hand. My bosses at BBC granted me leave without hesitation. To get air transportation, my trip had to be classified as official business. This involved pulling some strings, so there was no way to keep my trip secret. The opposition was ready. When I landed in New York, immigration officials kept my passport. Without it I would not be able to return to England.

In Washington it was an uphill fight. Some thought me suffering of paranoia. Others knew I was right, but immediately took pains to stress their inability to intervene, to take any action at all. They made no attempt to conceal fear of political backlash that could detrimentally affect their miserable careers. The cowardly anonymous threatened me by phone. "You bastard" they'd say, we will get you". But, there were also some important members of the Senate who listened, deeply concerned. A very wonderful lady in Washington, Mrs. Ruth Shipley, Chief of the Passport Division, had a new passport delivered to me at the Westbury hotel in New York. Air passage to London had also been already booked for me.

Back at my desk, I had my hands full. The BBC job was no joke and certainly not part-time as originally conceived. I had to spend more and more hours on matters related to Allied intelligence. In my second job as chief of a political section in the OWI I was, among other things, responsible for the preparation of operations of the future U.S.

Information Service at our Warsaw embassy. For these and other reasons I tried to avoid being transferred to Supreme Allied Headquarters-SHAEF-Luxembourg following the Normandy invasion. However, the brass thought differently and before I knew it I'd been had. I fudged my official orders. Instead of taking the military air transport direct to Luxembourg, I first wangled a ride with the British to Portsmouth to try and find out what happened with my friend Tommy Whitehead. I had a bad feeling. Two years earlier during one of my RAF leaves at "Snoxhall", the country home in Surrey of the Marks family, we were all listening to Prime Minister Churchill's emotion-charged announcement on the fall of Singapore. He spoke of a "far-reaching defeat". I could see that Julian and Nancy Marks were shaken. Their son John was with the British Navy somewhere in the Far East and they had not heard from him for a long time. I myself felt seized by an overwhelming sensation of personal loss. I knew something terrible had occurred.

My hosts, alarmed at my sudden pallor, gave me a brandy and sent me off to bed. In my nightmare Tommy was drowning.

"Snoxhall" had become my haven, my paradise in mufti from the very first day Nancy Marks picked me up at the Cranleigh railway station and introduced me, the unknown American of the Eagle Club, to the warmth and luxury of their handsome rambling house. I had many days there listening to the wry, sometimes cutting humor of the pipe sucking Englishman, Julian, cherishing the gentle kindness of his American wife Nancy, admiring the attractiveness and invigorating spirit of their daughters Nancy, Joan and Susan. For years after, I would catch myself humming our favorite tune "Deep Purple". It belonged to the intimate happy and courageous moments we shared amidst a bloody war that was won thanks to people like the Marks family.

In Portsmouth I saw Tommy's mother. She told me Tommy had joined the navy and was killed by the Japanese when they took Singapore.

Shaef - Luxembourg

> FROM GENERAL MCCLURE, SHAEF, TO USINFO-NYK. CLEAR
>
> REF OWI PERSONNEL ATTACHED TO PSYCHOLOGICAL WARFARE DIVISION.
>
> EUGENE VAN DEE, EDITOR OF BROADCASTS TO DISPLACED PERSONS, FOREIGN WORKERS AND PRISONERS OF WAR.

THE ABILITIES OF MR. VAN DEE IN THIS BRANCH OF RADIO LUXEMBOURG'S ACTIVITIES PERMIT US FOR THE FIRST TIME TO INSURE PROGRAMS OF HIGH STANDARDS,A HIGHLY IMPORTANT FUNCTION IN VIEW OF THE CURRENT SITUATION AMONG DISPLACED PERSONS WITHIN GERMANY" END.

My first assignment for SHAEF in Luxembourg was to organize radio broadcasts in the Polish language and then also in Russian directed at the thousands of displaced persons and Soviet soldiers taken prisoner by the German army, later liberated as the Allied forces advanced. I needed a literate group of Russian and Ukrainian editor-broadcasters. I thought there would be a myriad of candidates to chose from. Wrong. I interviewed perhaps as many as one hundred potential candidates brought in from liberated POW camps. More accurately, I *tried* to interview them. The moment I mentioned "radio" they became paralyzed with fear, refusing to work with us.

"Having been taken prisoner by the Germans we are already condemned to die, they told me. "The NKVD will get us all. You ask us to further contaminate ourselves by doing dirty propaganda for you. Go to the devil, but please do not send us back". The key words, revealing it all: "don't send us back". The Allied Command had agreed to "repatriate" Soviet military personnel found by allied forces in German POW camps. The war was not yet over, continuing to take its tragic toll on friend and foe alike.

We, the Western allies, were contributing to the additional slaughter of Soviet soldiers with each carload we delivered to Soviet lines. Stalin who in fits of paranoia had murdered so many of his closest political collaborators in Moscow, now added tens of thousands of his own soldiers accusing them of treason. Mere "exposure" to Western capitalist influence in a POW camp, spelled automatic "internal exile" to places of no return. Instant execution for the luckier ones.

On two occasions, the military trucks I had ordered prepared to transport Ukrainians to Soviet lines were destroyed by fire the night before scheduled departure. It was easy to find those responsible but realizing there was no way for them to escape their awful fate, our conscience would not permit us to punish them on the spot. How perversely we treated our conscience. By consigning these thousands to hell we were no better than the obediently blind guards at German concentration camps shoving prisoners into gas chambers. But who were we to defy the mighty Stalin?

The obstruction of Churchill's vision by Roosevelt, Eisenhower and Marshall would prove to be the century's greatest disaster.

Eventually, I got my Luxembourg radio staff together. The Polish end was no problem for I had the best to select from, all eager to work. When it came to Russian broadcasts, count Tolstoy would have been proud of me even though I did wonder how many Soviet soldiers were able to appreciate the elegance of their native tongue. For lack of ex-prisoner volunteers, I had recruited Russian emigrés living in Belgium since the revolution. We modernized and vulgarized the language as best we could by monitoring and then copying Moscow's broadcasting style.

The Voice of America wanted me to include live broadcasts from the front lines so I became a war correspondent as well. After a half dozen crazy visits with a recording unit close to battle lines and one particular incident where a bursting shell threw my jeep into a ditch, I decided to give up further heroics. Instead, I turned chicken. From the relative safety of my Luxembourg studio, hooked up with army headquarters, I merely relayed to New York the official bulletins. When I heard my own brave voice returning to Europe, phony battle sounds in the background, it became clear to me that nobody gave a damn where I happened to be located as long as it sounded right and I could say the Allies were moving forward.

Edward Stettinius earned me my very first on-the-air blooper when twice in a row I fluffed the line: "the United States Secretary of State Stettinius". A ghost voice broke in with: "just call me Eddie." I thought that was funny. Our censors did not.

Yes, but there came a time when the Allies were not moving forward but retreating under the counter attack of Marshal von Rundstedt in the Ardennes. He had penetrated deep into Belgium, pinned down American forces in Bastogne, his tanks nearing Luxembourg. This final German offensive was called the Battle of the Bulge. It scared the daylights out of us. At the radio station we had no proper defense but were determined not to hand over the facilities to the Germans. Explosives were set to blow up the whole place. Fortunately, it proved an unnecessary precaution.

On one sunny but still chilly afternoon, after the final collapse of von Rundstedt's offensive, I was lying on my back in the garden gazing at the wisps of passing cloud when my friend, the talented pianist Edward Kilenyi, punched me in the stomach yelling "the Hun is here". Indeed, as

I looked to the end of the park, I could see two tall slim figures in long black leather coats approaching from the forest. Walking slowly, backs ramrod straight, heads high, boots polished, faces grim, the German generals were coming toward us alone. Kilenyi's brain was faster than mine. "They have come to surrender", he said, hardly able to contain his excitement.

This situation called for higher military authority, I thought. But who could accept the surrender of generals? The answer came to me nearly instanter. It would have to be, positively, absolutely beyond any doubt, our own colonel Rosenbaum.

Forget that Rosenbaum was not a real colonel. Not even a real corporal. Like all civilians on detached service with the armed forces he had been given a "simulated" military rank, plus army uniform to prevent him from being executed as a spy if captured by the enemy. He certainly did not look very military. With a somewhat protruding belly, of just below medium height, corpulent Rosenbaum, director of the Philadelphia Symphony, an aesthete, probably a bon vivant as his witticisms testified, was about to accept the surrender of two senior German officers, their ultimate humiliation. This was an opportunity not to be missed. We made sure the generals got his name. They saluted like marionettes, proffered their pistols, said nothing. I watched as their aristocratic necks turned crab red with anguished anger. A sight to behold. In a loud voice Kilenyi said: "Am Yisrael Chai" -The people of Israel lives-.

Later, Rosenbaum and I talked about what we called "the afternoon of the generals". "I rather enjoyed that, he remarked. It was *gebrauchsmusik*-the composer's obligation of providing music for functional use-but, sadly, only a pizzicato in the long tortuous German symphony. Did you notice their cheeks? "Of course, the typical "V" dueling scars of Heidelberg University". "Yes, regular army Junker breed. We will give them VIP treatment, a perfunctory interrogation before sending them back to their estates. There, they will begin writing memoirs to tell their sons and grandsons how gallantly they fought for the Vaterland, losing the war only because of the madman Hitler and the anti-German conspiracy of the Jewish American military industrial complex". What a pity, I thought to myself, not to have been able to turn them over to the Russians.

Supreme Headquarters on the Continent had no further need of me so I went back to my London office of OWI. I would now make the final preparations to join the U.S.Department of State at our embassy in Warsaw.

It would turn out to be an extraordinary and painful experience. I remembered Poland's beautiful, joyous capital from the days I spent there before the war. Then, this city of a million inhabitants formed part of the romantic three-city European playground: Vienna-Budapest-Warsaw, where ordinary citizens enjoyed just being alive and the great, slightly madcap and exuberant bravura tenor, Jan Kiepura delighted midnight crowds singing operatic arias from the roofs of taxis.

When I returned to London I was shown a cable my superiors had received from the Department of State. It was anything but encouraging. It read:

> AMBASSADOR LANE SAYS IT WILL BE IMPOSSIBLE TO TAKE VAN DEE IN WITH HIM TO POLAND SINCE HE IS BEING FORCED TO LEAVE MUCH OF HIS OWN STAFF BEHIND IN PARIS. HE HAD A CABLE FROM HARRIMAN IN MOSCOW ADVISING HIM THAT ONLY ONE BUILDING IS AVAILABLE IN WARSAW FOR OCCUPANCY AND THAT ONLY A MAXIMUM OF NINE PEOPLE COULD BE ACCOMMODATED AT THIS TIME. HARRIMAN SAID THAT ONE BUILDING ONLY HAS RUNNING WATER AND THAT FOOD AND SUPPLY SITUATION CRITICAL. HE SUGGESTS RESPONSIBILITY FOR ENTRY INTO POLAND BE LEFT LARGELY WITH VAN DEE AND TO KEEP IN TOUCH WITH THE PARIS EMBASSY. BLOCHMAN.

As ambassador Lane left it up to me, I decided to depart for the Baltic port of Gdynia as soon as I found a suitable freighter to transport the large quantities of materials and equipment I had stockpiled for my Polish operations. The prospect of entering the city that was eighty percent destroyed frightened me. First, at the beginning of the war, there were the German stuka bombers and artillery. Later, the retreating Germans dynamited Warsaw block by block with their customary precision, killing over half a million people while the Soviet troops calmly watched from across the Vistula river and did nothing to help. Moscow wanted the Germans to kill as many Poles as possible. Was that really in Moscow's mind? Did the Soviet army deliberately refuse to come to Poland's aid? I knew the answer and the answer was yes. I knew because I was there. Sort of, that is. My British colleagues at London's Inveresk House were alarmed. They had reports that despite their repeated appeals for calm and patience, the leader of the Polish underground, general Bor-Komorowski intended to call a general uprising to liberate Warsaw from the Germans.

He told London's secret couriers the time was right because German armies were already crumbling in defeat under the merciless attacks from East and West. Also, that Soviet troops were nearing Poland's capital and would undoubtedly assist its liberation. How terribly wrong he was.

The Polish Government in London twice sent special couriers to the Underground Army hoping to persuade Komorowski to postpone the Warsaw action until a commitment of assistance was obtained from Moscow. The couriers were never heard of again.

I was still in charge of our special shortwave broadcasts and tried to apprise the Poles of the dangers they faced. The sending of coded messages to the underground was routine. They heard, they acknowledged, but as they were Poles, they ignored all warnings.

Chapter 2

Warsaw - Paris - Rome

Warsaw - Konstancin

It was a bitter cold winter evening. My wife and I were driving from Warsaw to our newly rented villa some 25 miles from the city, It was very dark and the road icy. The tyre chains did not stop the car from dangerously sliding sideways on curves. It made me nervous and added to my fatigue. Half way home we saw the bright lights of a restaurant and decided to stop for a glass of tea. The place was nearly empty. As the waiter greeted us, we could hear two young Russian officers arguing near the entrance. Both were cuffing a boy of about ten. This looked like potential trouble and I thought of leaving. Too late. Noticing my pretty wife, the officer who I could see had the rank of major, staggered over to our table, obviously having had a few, and sat down. He slapped a pistol on the white table-cloth. His companion, a captain, followed holding the youngster by the scruff of his neck.

My wife whispered "how do we get out of here?" The two Russians were now beginning to crowd us, moving their chairs closer. The major reached for my wife's hand. "Don't touch my wife, I said, or I'll..."

The words died on my lips. The major roared with laughter, pointing to the gun in front of him. Terror seized me and I had difficulty breathing. The waiters, all Poles, realized danger was ahead when the second Russian began shouting obscenities and demanded more vodka. Behind his back a waiter was signaling me, pointing to a window. We were on the ground floor. He was telling us to make a run for it. Another bottle was put in front of the major and a calm voice speaking Russian asked him whether he would like to personally instruct the cook what delicacies to prepare for dinner. It would all be "on the house", he added. "Da, bring the cook here", the major shouted.

The same calm voice replied: "but you must choose the fish and the meat yourself in the kitchen". The major lifted himself, made a few steps then turned back to grab his pistol. Answering the waiter's persistant beckoning, he finally disappeared behind the kitchen door. By a stroke of extraordinary luck the captain just then decided to go to the toilet. That left only the lad and he was on our side. We dashed for the window. It was unlatched. We tumbled out, head first, onto the icy ground. My wife screamed in pain. The car was on the other side of the building. We ran stumbling, falling, up again. We made it. I could not get the key into the lock of the door. It was frozen. For once I was glad to be a smoker. The indomitable Zippo lighter did the trick. I punched the starter once, twice. The damn engine wouldn't catch in the fifteen below zero cold. There was shouting behind. The two Russians were approaching fast. They fired shots. My fingers numb, I tried again. The engine caught. We drove like crazy. My wife cried. We did not sleep that night.

I said nothing to my ambassador. He would not have known what to do. A few days later, I told the story to Nicolai, the smooth, English speaking attaché, of the Soviet Cultural Mission. I complained bitterly about the lack of discipline among Russian soldiers and used a few pungent Russian words Grigori had taught me. We were at a cocktail at the British embassy. An English colleague heard it all and gave me a disapproving look. I didn't care. I was angry beyond words. He was right. Relating the incident to Nicolai I had mentioned that the Russian major boasted to me about his ability as a veterinarian. I wished I had not revealed that detail when at our next encounter, the same cultured, smooth attaché, smilingly informed me that he had the veterinarian and his companion arrested and shot.

My nearest and dearest neighbor was Hedy. She lived in a tiny, two room house containing only a few objects of her former opulence. Until the Russians came she owned a beautiful home in Konstancin where I now rented a villa. They didn't bother stealing anything. Swinging on the crystal chandeliers they crashed them to the marble floors, slashed the paintings, smashed the mirrors, built fires on precious carpets, shot out the windows. In their war dance of ultimate triumph over the decadent Polish bourgeois, they defecated from the balconies and set the place ablaze, leaving behind only a crying shell. They forced Hedy to watch. For many years she had been married to a wealthy American, Maurice

Pate. Appointed head of the U.N. Children's Emergency Fund at the end of the war, Maurice paid periodic visits to Poland, always imploring Hedy to return to America. Invariably her answer would be: "That's impossible. How could I live in luxury when my countrymen are being persecuted?" The same unalterable blind stubbornness that afflicted the three Polish naval officers who travelled aboard the cargo ship with me from England to Poland knowing their chances of remaining free citizens were very slim. They had served with the British Navy. Because of that they were now marked men in their own country. During our ocean trip I kept asking myself what possessed these men. Megalomania? Joan of Arc syndrome? Or was it the traditional Catholic masochistic attraction of martyrdom? I saw the Communist police arrest them when the ship docked at the port of Gdynia.

Hedy had a young admirer, Erik, who looked after her the best he could with his limited means. It was a touching companionship of two survivors. One day I ran into Erik in the corridors of the hotel all foreign missions were using as temporary offices. I had heard from mutual friends he was in really bad straits so I handed him a fifty dollar bill saying that I had received it in the embassy mail for Hedy. Just then two individuals came round the corner and quickly headed in our direction. To my amazement Eric stuffed the bill in his mouth and swallowed it, eyes red from the effort. The secret police took him away. A Pole caught with foreign currency could get shot. Eric was lucky. They had no evidence. He was released after a week. He came to my villa at night to tell me about it. His face was badly bruised. I forced upon him a few Polish Zloty bills before he retreated in the dark. One had to be very careful. The ears and eyes of the secret police were everwhere. An incautious inquiry about a friend could lead to his arrest. The secret police, commonly called "Bezpieka" were like trained dogs following a scent. Any contact with foreigners automatically made Poles suspect and even the most circumspect were subjected to constant abuse.

For more important embassy receptions we would hire the handsome Prince Czetwertinski as maître d' hotel. Knowing he was fluent in five languages, the Secret Police ordered him to apply for the job. It would enable him to eavesdrop and report on conversations between diplomats. Naturally, he immediately told us all about it. We were delighted to give him the job. Until the war the Prince owned vast country estates as well as properties in Warsaw. Among them the luxurious hotel Bristol. Now, no longer young, in a different world, Poland's new rulers allowed him to wash dishes and serve at tables in the partly rebuilt hotel he once owned. His bearing was an inspiration to old staff members. "If the Prince can take it, so can we" they would tell me.

He had also a regular day job from which he could not escape. Beginning at four every morning, five days a week, he delivered sacks of coal to government offices. That was his punishment for being a member of the aristocracy. He dutifully reported to the dreaded Security on everything he managed to overhear at our diplomatic receptions but it was our "special team" which made sure he always had something of interest to relate. The team's members were the most extraordinary collection of hard bitten poker playing diplomats any country had ever seen. Poker was the reason they became friends in the first place. Bored beyond belief in devastated Warsaw, with nothing to see and nowhere to go, thrown together in the only available building, the hotel Polonia, where all diplomats worked and slept in cramped quarters waiting for their embassies to be restored, cards were the Holy Grail. The poker players' "dean" was His Excellency Pao-Yii, ambassador to Poland of Nationalist China. His hands were those of a five year old. We called him "Baby Hands". We liked Pao-Yii. He was both erudite and witty. He could quote to us from the Analects of Confucius, the Bible, George Washington or any modern poet we wished to name. Seeing the depredation of the Polish people he visibly suffered. "If the Kuomintang fails to stop Mao-Tse-Tung, he will enslave six hundred million Chinese and that will be a lot worse than what is happening to the Poles", he'd sigh.

"Baby hands" was outweighed one hundred pounds or more by his towering, fun loving, politically savvy Russian wife, Genia. She was a bit too open-faced to excel at poker but nobody could beat her throaty contagious laughter. Genia feared the Communists and she hated them. Then there was Osvaldo Pombo, the young Argentine attaché, a dedicated Peronista, who pretended to have only skirts on his mind, while in reality doing an expert job of political analysis of developments in Poland for Buenos Aires. By chance I knew that, with his government's approval, he secretly furnished Argentine passports to prominent Poles who were in danger of being arrested. The fourth "regular" and a master of finesse was His Excellency Hassan Bey Nassr, Egypt's envoy to Poland and member of the Egyptian Society of Political Economy in Cairo. Suave, charming but inscrutable, Hassan kept his political views to himself. The final component of the poker group was a young lady from Vienna, the greatest habitué of them all, who, it was said, came out of the womb tightly clutching a deck of cards in each hand, never to let them go. Altogether, a bunch hard to beat in any game. When I proposed an ad hoc conspiracy to mock and confound the Security Police and their Russian bosses, they accepted with glee. At one formal cocktail Hassan, in an animated but conspiratorial sotto voce conversation with our First Secretary, several times referred to the "Zugzwang Plan", making sure that Prince Czetwertinski was within earshot. Soon afterward Nicolai, to whom I relentlessly referred as the "vet exterminator", invited Hassan to a Russian dinner, evidently hoping to loosen his tongue with vodka, then pump him about the "plan" which he called the "Zingzang Initiative". Hassan, the Egyptian fox, enjoyed the game equivocating until Nicolai gave up, provoked and angry. He was no match for the sophisticated Hassan. Poorly briefed as well. We knew that the Russians kept up-to-date and very detailed profiles on all foreign diplomats in Warsaw. Had Nicolai bothered to check, he would have known that Hassan Bey Nassr would sooner take poison than reveal anything to a Communist. Also, that Muslims don't drink alcohol. Obviously, he was not familiar with chess either. A player would have recognized the word *zugzwang*, the meaning of which is that the next move, any move, is bound to bring disaster.

"Zugzwang" bounced round the diplomatic corps, quoted back to us in various versions from the "Zwieback Protocol" to the "Zigzag Compact" for several weeks so that eventually my ambassador guessed the truth but evidently thought it wiser not to inquire too deeply into the origin of the matter. He may have even been amused at the discomfort it caused the Russians. We, the grand conspirators, smirked quite marvelled at the mayonnaise minds of the men from Moscow. But, when we tried another canard, through the mouth of Osvaldo, about "special agent Cadmus", it didn't work. Either the Prince got cold feet, purposely neglecting to refer what he had heard or else the Russians knew a bit more about Greek mythology than we suspected.

Warsaw - Kielce

An anonymous caller told me Jews were being massacred in the town of Kielce, about 160 km South of Warsaw. As the embassy's Information Officer, I hastened to alert the many American press representatives, who were then in Poland because of a forthcoming political referendum, of the pogrom. We piled into cars. By the time we reached Kielce it was all over. Scores of Jews had been battered to death with wooden spikes torn from fences surrounding their dwellings. Others thrown to their death from high windows. Men, women, children slaughtered without mercy. We were all in shock. Could this be happening in Poland where, as everyone knew, 90 percent of the prewar Jewish population was killed by the Nazis? Three million in the death factory of Auschwitz alone. Why? Who? "Ritual murder by Jews of a catholic child, that's why", someone yelled at us. "We all did it to them", said another. How had this depraved superstition about ritual murder by Jews survived the centuries, to surface again in what one thought to be a reasonably enlightened society of postwar Poland, was beyond our powers to understand. As the story unfolded, we learned that a young boy had indeed been thought missing the night before the pogrom. He decided to sleep over at his aunt's house but forgot to tell his mother who, by early morning, became hysterical and accused the Jews of kidnapping him.

In the car, returning to Warsaw, I told the traumatized journalists travelling with me about the pained humor of one of my Jewish friends who once remarked there was so much anti-Jewish propaganda at the Warsaw university he attended that he wondered how he managed not to become antisemitic himself. "Why then, I asked, should we be so surprised at what happened yesterday in the the small town of Kielce"?

The American ambassador called a press conference referring to the Kielce murders as "an unfortunate but perhaps understandable incident". The journalists were first stunned, then outraged by the ambassador's abominable choice of words. Reporter's telegrams went flying. Washington cabled me press quotes and reaction-feedbacks within forty eight hours. The rash judgement and vindictiveness of the American press shocked me and the entire embassy staff. Arthur Bliss Lane, our ambassador, had been under tremendous strain for months. He saw the cancer of communist rule destroying the Poles and he, the guardian of democratic principles, the official representative of the great United States could not do a damn thing about it. He cared and the pain was strangling him. Now, our own American press was out to ruin his good name. The "Kielce Incident", as it later became known in relation to Bliss Lane, was one more example of reporter arrogant callousness. Through the eyes of such wisemen the Western world watched events in Poland, vision obscured.

The three men of Yalta: Roosevelt, Churchill and Stalin had "settled" the Polish borders and agreed upon the Russian zone of influence in Central and Eastern Europe. The Poles, who had fought with distinction on all fronts from the Battle of Britain in the skies to Tobruk and Montecassino, had been shamelessly betrayed by those whom they had helped save. How long would it be, they wondered, before the Communists totally controlled Poland?

Homer Bigart, Flora Lewis, David Lawrence, Larry Allen, Sidney Gruson and other luminaries of American journalism were fast in and out of Poland, stopping over just long enough between flights to get a foggy bearing, describe it all in three hundred words or less, sagely predict tomorrow, then dash off in search of another headline story. Only rarely were they given time to think. Then, they could actually be quite good.

Warsaw - The Brits

His intimate friends called him Bill. The rest of us referred to him simply as H.E. To the Polish government he was His Excellency William Cavendish Bentinck, British ambassador. It is said that nothing ever surprises British diplomats because they can always find a precedent for whatever might occur. Call it historical diplomatic experience. H.E. had it. His antecedent, Lord William Cavendish, British Governor-General of India a hundred years earlier, had it. It ran in the family.

H.E's Warsaw Head of Chancery, John Russell (later Sir John), the only son of Sir Thomas Russell Pasha, also had it. Bentinck and Russell were assisted by a staff of well prepared, highly motivated and very tough professionals. Before being sent to Warsaw, all members of the British embassy were meticulously briefed on what to look for, whom to watch out for. From intelligence records they had to memorize facts, figures and faces. They knew who the friends were, who the agents and double agents were. Their lives could depend on such careful briefings. Among the sharpest observers was John Russell's Greek wife Aliki of Athens (né Diplarakos) who also threw the best diplomatic parties.

"A thousand voices, each telling a story, can be heard", H.E. would say at his staff meetings. Go to concerts, sports events, attend mass, mix with shoppers. Observe, listen, listen again. Try to identify methods of intimidation used by the Security Police. Find out what the Russians do to render the Poles mouldable, more pliant. What sequence and combination of physical, psychological and intellectual forces are being applied? How do the victims resist brainwashing? Is the Soviet political hierarchy in Poland changing?" The list was long, the purpose precise. "Find out as much as you can about your enemy, how he thinks. But remember: Our Polish friends must never be exploited. Don't offer political opinions. Instead, whenever possible, nourish their morale. Tell them they have not been forgotten, only temporarily mislaid in an unpredictable maelstrom of history. Tell them that the power of the weak lies in their capacity to endure the persecution of the strong and that Poland must have no more dead heroes.

I still had my special British pass from London, with no photo, just my name and an illegible signature scrawled on a small green piece of cardboard. It was the most important single document ever given me. I never tried it, of course, but at the time it was given to me I nearly believed it would have permitted me to see even Churchill. Now I used it to certify myself with the British embassy, constantly pestering my friends there with questions. Mostly they obliged me, sometimes not.

In contrast, the American method was to "play it by ear", one day at a time. If you were tone deaf, all the better. You would not hear the cries of the anguished. "Set up listening posts, organize networks, promise support. When they hit a trip-wire and get caught, damn them and forget them. It's the name of the game. There are always more where these came from".

Even such obscenity could have perhaps found some rationale, had it resulted in the implementing of serviceable policies. But, by the time so called intelligence input went through the razor sharp analytical brains of experts, only non sequitur sausage emerged. Were they all idiots? Not by a long chalk. It was the much practiced principle that if you don't know the answer, obfuscate or blame somebody else. Sadly, the field men devoted more time inventing justification for their existence than on gathering intelligence.

There was only one American in Poland at that time who knew what was going on, what to do and when to do it. His name was Leon Dayton. Officially, he was head of the American Red Cross.

Warsaw

I tried to remember exactly what Grigori had told me about interrogations. "You must avoid looking your interrogator straight in the eyes for more than a couple of seconds at a time, or he will think you are challenging him, trying to stare him down. Don't look up in the air. It will be taken for a sign of arrogance. Don't look at the floor. It will be seen as a sign of your fear and he will pounce on you like a cat. "Well, I remember asking him, "where IS one supposed to look?" "At his left or right earlobe and, if he is one of those who likes to show off his determined profile, look just slightly above his head. Count slowly to four in your mind before replying. Under no circumstances attempt to answer a question with a question.

Don't smile unless your interrogator believes that what he just said was particularly amusing. Don't twist your hands, it's a sign of nervousness. Don't cross your knees as it will affect your physical balance. Stay mentally alert but try to relax your muscles by letting them go limp, individually in each part of your body. No matter how many times the same question is asked, give the same answer, changing only a word or two so that it does not sound rehearsed. All this applies to routine interrogations. However, once they put you under the bright light, you can forget all I told you. It will mean you are not considered merely a suspect but a definite source of vital information. You might as well start talking and save yourself the pain of torture."

The two of them had picked me up that morning as I parked near the office. I knew immediately they were from "Bezpieka"-Internal Security-because they all dressed alike. Loose jackets to conceal the guns and flared trousers, so wide at the bottom they covered their shoes. They were polite. "Please come with us". It would have been useless to argue. The black, low slung Citroen drove us across the river.

"Co wy robicie tu w Polsce?" His Polish was that of the poorly educated person. He was testing me. I pretended not to understand. He repeated in heavily accented English: "what are you doing here in Poland?" "I am with the American embassy". "We know, but what is your job?" "I am the information officer". Too late I remembered another bit of admonishing advice from Grigori: "never volunteer information even when you are convinced they already know the answer, because it gives them a lead to further questioning". I had just violated that principle by describing my embassy function. When you feel frightened it paralyzes your mind and it is not easy to remember everything. He jumped in: "ah you collect information, yes?" It was not a question. It was a statement. Damn him, I thought. He scribbled something in his notebook.

It was nine in the morning when the Security men brought me in. Now it was nearly two in the afternoon. I was getting very tired. They were giving me the weariness treatment. Many questions in rapid succession: "Who are your Polish friends? Do you like girls? Do you go to church on Sundays? What schools did you attend?" Then they would ignore me, ask no questions for a quarter of an hour or so. That was the silence treatment to make one sweat.

"May I go now?" I asked. Grigory had told me that in every interrogation there is the right psychological moment to seize initiative."If they appear to have run out of questions and you have not given them any compromising information, ask to leave. "Of course you can go. You are not a prisoner but a friendly American". "Thank you. May I have my passport back, please?" The number Two man left the room, returning after a few minutes. He whispered in the ear of number One who turned to me saying: "We are very sorry, but your passport is in another department which closed for the day. It will be returned to your embassy in the morning". My heart missed a beat, then thumped so loud I thought they would hear it. Of all the advice Grigori had given me, the most important one was to do everything possible to avoid getting separated from one's documents. Without them, in hostile territory, you had no identity, no defense, no recourse, no hope. You simply didn't exist. I protested: "You know very well it is against the law to be in the streets without papers. Besides, my ambassador would be very angry if I left my passport behind".

Why the game with my passport? They were trying to intimidate me, but I had them there because I knew they would not keep it. In a police state everything must be done by the book. Blind obedience to regulations, unthinking discipline is a conditioned reflex.

And the book said that the personal belongings taken from a detained individual had to be recorded in every detail. I saw the ledger the moment I entered the interrogation room. Each item they took from me was laboriously examined and entered. The process was exceedingly slow because in some instances they were not quite sure what they had found or what name to give it in the ledger. My membership card to an English club had them puzzled. "Co to jest?" What is this, one asked the other. My uneasiness increased. There are few things more frustrating or dangerous than trying to reason with ignorant men. "If you must be interrogated, Grigori told me, pray for an intelligent fellow".

Bureaucracy has its good points. Entries in the ledger were written proof of my detention and interrogation. Records could not be changed without top level clearance. This happened very seldom. My inquisitors could only add to the entries: either "suspect detained indefinitely" or "suspect released, personal belongings as listed above returned".

They escorted me to the sidewalk, handed me my passport and an envelope with my other items and even waived down a taxi. I didn't really think they had any intention of arresting me or making me disappear. Still, could one ever be absolutely sure about that? If Security decided to ignore the rules and had me picked up again a few minutes later by a squad from other headquarters, without any documents, winding up nameless somewhere in a Kamchatka prison, who would ever find me? But then, as long as there were two of them, neither trusting the other, I had a built-in safety factor. I counted on it. In the taxi my knees suddenly began to shake and I felt like vomiting. When Security pulled me in, I was sure they were on to something. Something important, like our plan to smuggle Mikolajczyk out of the country. Head of the Polish government in exile, he had come from London at Allied insistence to join the so called "Coalition" in Warsaw. The Soviets would have given me the Order of Lenin for this information, More likely, if they had even a hint, I would have been put under the bright light. The Soviets were already poised to kill Mikolajczyk. Why did the Allies risk his life so unwisely? We should have known that what was done to Poland at Yalta could not be undone in Warsaw.

When the Security people asked what I was doing in Poland, I had a giddy-nervous reaction. It was the same question I had asked myself as well as other members of our embassy any number of times. What were we doing exactly? Nobody seemed to really know, except that we were supposed to be diplomats. The directives from Washington were vague or contradictory. When I pointed this out to ambassador Bliss Lane at a staff meeting, he sarcastically asked: "do you think you are smarter than the State Department?" What he did not know, or, more likely, refused to openly admit was that the State Department and particularly its Eastern European desks were riddled with communist sympathizers or outright Moscow lackeys. The very same breed that managed to get me temporarily suspended in London following my disclosure of the Katyn papers. Now they were doing their best to filter despatches coming in to Washington from our Eastern European missions and then, in a variety of ways, "bend" directives issued by the office of the Secretary of State.

As I would soon find out they were not quite finished with me personally either. Their new attack and a very dangerous one occurred several months later when the Department of State sent a cable to the Warsaw embassy advising I had lost my citizenship by joining the Royal Air Force. I should surrender my passport immediately, it said. I was stunned. The Security Police had undoubtealy intercepted the cable and must have thought us mad for it was not even coded but sent "clear". The ambassador was livid over the message itself and the outrageous breach of government procedures. My personal friends in the Congress protested to State and to the White House, pointing out that thousands of American citizens had served with British forces during the war. The British ambassador to Washington wrote a letter to State in which he said: "I am obliged to express my dismay and distress that an American who came to our aid in time of need should now find himself so unfairly penalized". He added that Americans joining British forces were not asked or required to take oaths of allegiance to the Crown. The U.S. Immigration and Naturalization Service refused to yield replying that while perhaps not required, Van Dee may have insisted on doing so. Could he prove he did not? Bureaucratic stalemate. It did prove that somebody had done an unusual amount of digging to find record of my service with the Royal Air Force, since I had enlisted under a different name.

I felt confident that my friends in Washington would prevail. But how long would it be before the Polish Security asked me: "Passport have not? This country what manner arrive?" The thought was blood-curdling. While congressmen, State Department and Immigration officials, as well as my personal attorneys were all engaged in mutual recriminations, a veteran American vice consul in Warsaw found the solution in a law which said that citizenship could be restored by taking a new oath of allegiance to the United States. Old Glory in the consul's office looked awfully good to me when I took that oath. Now all I had to do was convince the Polish Security Forces it was all a case of mistaken identity, State Department bungling or a hoax and that my citizenship and diplomatic immunity were never in doubt. That would put everything right, wouldn't it, Mr. Secretary? Balderdash!

When rich Americans make heavy contributions to party coffers they are often paid in ambassadorships. Not required or even expected to possess any knowledge of international affairs or of the country where they are to serve, these spurious ambassadors, who are personal representatives of the American president, hinder intelligent foreign service career officers in their work, circumvent official channels to communicate half-baked political analyses direct to the President and repeatedly cause seizures at the Department of State.

When the multimillionaire Stanton Griffis arrived in Warsaw replacing Arthur Bliss Lane, his first diplomatic initiative was to instruct the factotum attaché, Walter Schwinn, to install high-powered loudspeakers and "blast them away". A destitute polish family had surreptitiously moved into a small building being renovated for the consular section. Walter was a very decent chap and resented the assignment. But, he was a career man and knew his Foreign Service catechism well. The bottom line: "dont think. If you think you might err. One mistake and you will be out; better let the other guy take responsibility". For Walter not to be in the Foreign Service was unimaginable, so he mutely followed orders. The children cried all night, their eardrums bursting from high-decibel blasts of Sousa's marches. After 48 hours the family fled in terror. The intrepid Americans had recaptured their precious territory.

Warsaw's diplomatic circles talked about it undiplomatically. Nick Charles of the British Embassy said to me, over a drink: "You Americans are incorrigible, always assuming that excellence in a few things excuses incompetence in everything else". And Nick was one of the kind ones.

Griffis distinguished himself in many different ways. He could chase a secretary round his office faster than a man half his age. That was his usual morning exercise. Sometimes he even netted a fish. The British ambassador's car was a conservative Humber. The French drove their Citroens. The American ambassador arrived with his twin, made-to-order Chrysler stretch limousines, bar included. They were the biggest personal automobiles Detroit ever produced. .

Not that Griffis was all bad. He meant well. He showered gifts on his staff. No one could question his high sense of patriotism and duty. It was just that he never suffered from cultural agoraphobia-the fear of empty spaces of the mind. On the contrary, he collected them. His horizon was totally dominated by a Stonehenge of giant dollar signs.

Shortly after the high-decibel eviction of squatters incident, I jumped ship, leaving the State Department for two main reasons. First, the Department was not keen on extending my appointment since I protested too much and too loudly for someone who had gotten into the Foreign Service through the back door. Believing myself to be mostly right, I was not about to mend my ways. Second, because an offer from the American film industry to become its manager for Poland was my Deus ex Machina. I would be my own boss and the pay was better. It also meant giving up diplomatic immunity. This worried me. I could not forget the recent act of sabotage aimed at me personally by the seemingly indestructible clique of communist sympathizers operating within the Department of State who hated my guts.

Warsaw - Brussels

Flowers and candy will do just dandy, I thought to myself when it was announced that Mrs.Radkiewicz would come with me to Brussels. She was the managing director of the government motion picture organization, Film Polski. She was also the wife of Poland's dreaded Interior Minister, boss of the secret police.

The agreement the Polish government signed with our Motion Picture Export Association provided for the Poles to freely select the movies for distribution in their country from the vast backlog of Hollywood titles. As it was not practical to ship hundreds of prints into Poland, we arranged for selection screenings to take place in Brussels. Mrs.Radkiewicz pulled rank, appointing herself the official selector.

Brunette, in her late thirties, of pleasant demeanor, not hard to look at, she had a pungent sense of humor as I found out when the day following our arrival in Brussels she pointed to an individual in the hotel lobby. "See that scarecrow? He is Russian. Here ostensibly to protect me, actually to spy on me. My husband is their first deputy in Poland. I was trained in Moscow but still they don't ever trust us completely". I was amazed to hear such a risky statement uttered so casually.

I was in charge, had plenty of spending money and a free hand to run the project as I saw fit. With some malice aforethought I chose the best hotel in Brussels, the Metropole, arranging for my guest to be installed in a luxury suite. There were large bouquets of flowers delivered each morning as well as ribboned boxes of chocolates which I knew she could not resist. Belgium is the delight of the gourmand. We joined the happy glutton club with unabashed enthusiasm, frequenting the finest eateries in town. She enjoyed every moment of it. And she talked a lot.

It was a new experience for me. I had never before been exposed to wide open windows of unrehearsed pain, protest and the anger of a communist, except for Grigori and he was an enigma, probably not a communist at all.

She saw Polish society divided into disconnected layers. The thinnest, the most transparent, represented by the intelligentsia whose self-anointed duty it was to advance intellectualized theories on what other Poles ought to do for their country. Then, the priviligentia, the upper bourgeoisie solely interested in the accumulation of material wealth and to whom patriotism belonged in Sienkiewicz historical novels. Finally, "the dumb, sullen, uneducated, unthinking working class, easily controlled, always ready to charge the invisible enemy with pitchfork and shovel".

"Yes", she said, "in the distant past Poland had great writers, painters, poets, composers, but not one single decent political thinker in generations. And now, it is a nation driven by passion alone, spawning only dictators and priests".

Her opinion of Americans was even less flattering. It came straight out of a communist primitive handbook on capitalist society.

"You Americans never developed any political or social theory, never had any strategy. But, of course, if you don't have a policy you don't need strategies. While we communists are trained to have infinite patience, to plan years, even decades in advance of anticipated developments, you people make ersatz analyses, attempt to solve a problem by tomorrow morning, thus littering the landscape with corpses of your trusting followers. You promise, you cajole, you wave the American dollar under their nose. Then, in your abysmal arrogance, you sacrifice them without remorse. In intelligence work, you are ignorant fools. We track down many dissidents in Poland by shadowing your people. They make the contact. We make the arrest. You still count on individuals whom you thought your agents during the war but who really worked for us then and continue to do so now. Your so called networks are invaluable sources of information to our services. I don't mind saying all this because the deductive capacities of your intelligence people are those of the mentally retarded, so you will never be sure whether I told you the truth or whether I lied.

Not only did I hate to hear these tirades but had to pretend I didn't understand half of what she was saying. Inside I quaked because with each word she jabbed a raw nerve. What I had to unravel in my mind was whether she was baiting, advising or warning me.

I wanted to ask her how she felt about the torture by her husband's secret police of the Poles who returned to their country after serving with British forces. Why had they broken the bones of and drove to mental derangement Ted Bujak, the fighter pilot ace who had the special privilege of wearing an orange scarf with his blue RAF uniform because he earned it with his Distinguished Flying Cross and Bar. The goons leaving him crippled forever, demented, begging for food in the streets of Warsaw where he would have died had it not been for the British ambassador who found and saved him. I wanted to ask but I was too much of a coward. For eight days we screened an endless stream of American movies until our heads and eyes ached. The final selection made, we returned to Warsaw.

Warsaw - Lodz

They worked in three shifts of eight hours each. Two men crews, virtually never varying the routine, always ready to jump into their black Citroen cars to follow me. The secret police squads were invariably composed of young, physically fit, well armed individuals. Though inherently aggressive, therefore always dangerous, few of them had much formal or professional training and were, in effect, predictable amateurs. I felt confident that if an unarmed confrontation occurred, I would have little difficulty outwitting them.

I directed our motion picture business for the whole country from two offices: my headquarters in Warsaw, where I employed a staff of five and a regional one in the industrial city of Lodz, some 100 miles from the capital, responsible for accounting and publicity.

In Lodz, my "guardians" installed themselves in the Grand Hotel where I stayed when in town. Predictably and conveniently they could watch my office windows from across the street.

In Warsaw, as soon as the Motion Picture Export Association entered into agreement with the Polish film monopoly, the Security Police made sure that a retired Polish colonel was assigned as my assistant to watch me and report on my activities. The colonel was a decent fellow of some culture. From the beginning I realized he hated spying on me, though he was obviously afraid to openly say so. It was sad and pathetic to watch him suffer. Like so many of his countrymen, the poor colonel was caught in the merciless vise of communist control. Most often their acceptance to collaborate arose from the conviction that somehow, somewhere, in one fashion or another, the feigned acquiescence would not only save their life but provide opportunity for acts of undetected sabotage, not realizing it could never turn out that way because the communist apparatchiks controlled their every move directly or through their Polish, Moscow trained trustees.

In a reign of terror there were few possibilities of sabotaging the powerful. On the contrary and more tragically, many a patriot found himself forced to contribute to his country's degradation by obeying Party orders, only to cry out to his masters at the end of the day and in the deepest of human agonies "thank you for letting me stay alive."

I played games with my secret police angels, varying my travel routine between Lodz and Warsaw, suddenly departing near the end of a crew's shift. It raised havoc with their schedules. I saw their confusion and anger from my window each time my driver, Stefan, brought up the car to the hotel entrance, purposely making a show of loading my suitcase, just after I had informed the less trustworthy members of my staff I would be leaving for Warsaw at a later hour. I knew that someone was faithfully reporting everything I said in the office. My phone lines were bugged. I could only count on the loyalty of my driver. Stefan, a young man in his late twenties, he was devoted to me and hated the communists with passion.

Lodz was a grimy, sad, depressing industrial town which before the war had the largest and wealthiest Jewish population of any Polish city. Under German occupation the Jews were carried off to gas chambers, to the furnaces, the firing squads. After the war,the few who survived witnessed only apathy and neglect of governments, of churches, of nations that closed their gates so that refugees from the holocaust could not enter. One of my poster designers in Lodz, who was Jewish, once observed: "many events in Jewish history are too terrible to be believed, but nothing in Jewish history is too terrible to have happened".

Very rarely I would venture out of the hotel in the evenings, even though I was tempted by the many bars and restaurants. The streets were dangerous after dark. One sleepless night, I wandered across the street to a bar in the arcade leading to my offices, longing for a shot of good Polish vodka. It would brace me, I thought. I got the shock of my life instead. There in the bar, talking to my "angels", with my female accountant Basia on his knee, was someone whom I knew to be dead. With the nom-de- guerre of Jerzy Slowik, he was London's much decorated courier-liaison with the Polish underground, four times parachuted into German-occupied territory, always miraculously making his way back to London with important intelligence information. He had a charmed life, we said, admiring his guts. Then, on the fifth drop, our Special Service Unit lost him. Reliable sources reported Jerzy had been killed by the Germans. Evidently not quite. Here he was in Lodz. It suddenly became clear to me why some key Polish operatives working for London had been caught and armament drops meant for the underground fighters intercepted by "Red Cells". Slowik was a double agent, a traitor to the Allied cause, all along working for the communists. His appearance right under my nose both mystified and terrified me. My presence in Lodz must have been made known to him and he was too good, too well trained to be careless. Did he want me to run into him? Sure that he had not spotted me tonight I left the bar in a hurry. I did not want him to know I had seen him. I needed time to think, to get a grip on myself.

The next several days were one long nightmare. I kept looking over my shoulder wondering if Slowik had perhaps assigned his lover Basia to get me. Did she carry a gun in that large purse of hers? Or would it be a knife? Trembling would seize me. I could feel the sensation beginning with my toes, slowly crawling up to my neck, lifting my scalp, hurting my eyes. Sudden visible danger I could handle. It made one's adrenalin flow, kicking in automatic reflexes. This was different. This was uncontrollable paralyzing terror. A full week went by before I calmed down sufficiently to begin thinking rationally again. After all, why now? I had been identified by the secret police even before I stepped off the ship that brought me from England to join the staff of our embassy in Warsaw. They knew all about my activities in London. So really, why now? Still, I could not get rid of the gnawing fear. I decided to tell Daniel. And, the man in Prague had to be informed of my discovery without delay. He would know what to do.

Daniel Laroche was trained to hide behind ingenious protective covering, the kind circus clowns have. They are so full of colour, so foolishly amusing, the public sees them only as harmless jesters. Dan was hired and sent to me by The Man in Prague to handle my publicity department. He was fat, wore large horn-rimmed glasses. He puffed and wheezed, constantly wiping perspiration off his brow while tripping over three Chow dogs he kept on tangled leads.

The posters, the press releases, the point of sale displays, the articles and everything else designed to promote sales came from the brain of a master. He knew and used every gimmick in the book. When a movie was "dying" he would secretly hire hoodlums to break the cinema's display windows, pay others to create a phony anti-American demonstration, then call for police assistance, and alert reporters who were on his payroll to cover the incident. Had publicity been his chosen profession he would have made a fortune anywhere in the world.

Dan was allocated a very generous budget. He travelled a lot, visiting cinemas round the country, talking to the managers, the press, buying drinks for one and all, playing the generous fool. Only The Man in Prague and I knew that during the war Dan served as an explosives expert with the Maquis in underground France and that the "clown" had a degree in Slavonic Studies from Cambridge University.

Lodz - Olomouc - Warsaw

I just had to get to Czechoslovakia soon to see the Man from Prague who was taking a cure at Green Lake Spa, near the city of Brno. It would be a long 250 mile ride from Lodz. But, if I managed to cross the Polish-Czech border on Friday morning, I thought I should be able to get back to my office not later than Sunday night by driving a bit fast. Nobody would miss me, provided I could somehow lose my secret police shadows.

"Easily done" said Dan. "First we shall travel to Katowice which is very near the border. There I'll arrange for a special showing of the Bette Davis movie and you will present some awards to local cinema managers. On the following morning, not too early so that heavy traffic is already moving, you will take off like the wind in your souped up Ford on the Cracow highway, turning off somewhere behind trees, letting the police buggers go right past you. A u-turn will head you straight for the Czech border, while the cops going in the opposite direction try catching up with you all the way to Cracow". Dan's scheme worked. No problem losing the Security boys. No Czech visa was required at the Czech border. "No contraband? Safe journey". Nearly too smooth to be true.

I knew it wouldn't last. At Green Lake it was altogether a different story. I presented my reasons for wanting to leave Poland with what I thought was admirable skill and logic, talking through most of the night. The Man from Prague would have none of it. He was one of the toughest dialecticians I had ever encountered. This was not the time to panic, he told me. Moreover, there were important matters for me to handle, not the least of which concerned our pending agreement with the Polish National Bank for the release of substantial sums of our accumulated Zlotys in favor of the Warsaw branch of the world-wide Jewish organization, the Joint Distribution Committee. I knew that the JDC was the only hope of survival for the remnants of Poland's Jews and that my presence in

Warsaw was critical to the prompt conclusion of negotiations which I had already initiated with the Polish authorities. I could not argue any further with The Man from Prague who had his priorities straight and the authority to impose them. Besides, I would be learning a lot more about the fascinating world of international finance. "I 'll stick it out, I promised, for as long as I can".

Before saying good bye, obviously as a good humour sweetener, The Man insisted on telling me that motion pictures were the greatest invention since the wheel. "You invest a certain amount of money in a film production only once. After that you just have to make prints and collect box office receipts from all over the world for years and years to come." This over-simplification amused me and I departed on a higher note of optimism.

I had stayed much too long. Time was getting short. I shot out of Green Lake promptly losing my way, winding up on the main road toward the industrial town of Olomouc. Approaching the outskirts at high speed I could see, a couple of kilometers ahead, the Saturday crowd of soccer fans drifting out of the local stadium. A motorcyclist, with companion aboard, stopped at the edge of the road, evidently waiting for me to pass. Then, changing his mind, started to dash across. His bike stalled directly in front of me. I had no time to stop. Two bodies went flying over the roof of my car. When the ambulance arrived, one man was dead, the other had a broken leg. The Czech "kriminalka" police arrested me.

A doctor bandaged my badly hurt knee and my sprained wrist. I found myself in a nice, clean cell. The bars on the window sent chills down my spine. I waited for someone to begin questioning me. No one appeared. I could hear the phones ringing somewhere near. Slowly panic started choking me. Two hours later they brought me a sausage sandwich and tea. I tried to sleep. I was in very serious trouble, I knew, but it bothered me less than the image I could not shake from my mind. That of the young man lying dead in the road. The effect of the doctor's injection was wearing off. The throbbing and sharp pain now spread through all of my bruised body. With it came a degree of lucidity. What in the devil made me come to Czechoslovakia and then get lost near Olomouc of all places? They, the police, were bound to ask me whom I knew, where did I spend the previous night. Who was I anyway? I waited hour after hour for someone to talk to me. Nobody. Absolute silence. My throat ached. My head was splitting. I did not look forward to a long period of hospitality in a Czech prison. Under no circumstances could I involve The Man from Prague. I wondered what my friends, my staff in Poland would do if I failed to turn up in the office on Monday. I feared someone would report my absence to the American embassy. The last thing I needed were embassy inquiries with the Polish foreign office. The bigger the diplomatic noise, the greater importance an incident assumes, the worse it gets because an ever increasing number of people are involved creating waves. Human behavior is mixed in motivation, but its consequences are often beyond our anticipation and control. Two persons I knew had crossed into Czechoslovakia, Dan and my driver Stefan. Would they talk?

It was Monday morning. They brought me a sumptuous breakfast. With effort I managed to drink the tea. No one had yet interrogated me or even mentioned the tragedy of the car accident. At three in the afternoon a senior officer accompanied by a stunning female in uniform entered my cell. This is it, I thought to myself. No accusation, no trial. Just a firing squad. They did not speak, but motioned me to follow. In the courtyard stood my car. Not a trace of damage. It was completely repaired and painted. The female officer smiled at me. "We are quite efficient" she said. "Drive your car to the Polish border. I shall stay with you. My colleague will follow". I still had no idea what was going on. All I could tell is that she had a beautiful pair of legs. I could not help staring. Her sitting close to me seemed to anesthetize all my pains. She flirted with me in silence. At the Czech-Polish border she spoke briefly with the guards. Then turning to me: "Congratulations. You have some powerful friends but though your eyes flattered me, you must learn to keep them on the road". Before I could ask who, why, where, she had changed cars and was gone. She would be hard to forget and a long time before I found out the why, where and the who.

It was late night when I got back to my villa near Warsaw. The police car was parked right in front. Two friends from the embassy were dozing in the living room, apparently hoping I would soon appear. They told me that the embassy had initiated inquiries about me with the Polish foreign office and that Stanton Griffis had telephoned ambassador Reinhardt in Prague, asking him to do the same with the Czechs. What I feared had occurred. Someone lost patience and talked. Fortunately, my "powerful friends", the beautiful lady in uniform referred to and whom I still did not know, were able to intervene and save me before our diplomats "set things right". But for this fortunate timing I might have rotted in a Czech jail for a very long time. Naturally the ambassador could not have known of the bizarre twist to the events and I had to be thankful for his willingness to act so decisively on my behalf. I expected the roof to cave in on me when I went to see him. But Griffis was Griffis, thus his sole comment was "don't chase broads across borders". No one ever accused him of lack of initiative but to come up with such a delicious alibi for me required constructive imagination as well. I would stick with his version.

In Lodz, my accountant Basia had crying spells. While I was away, someone wired explosives to her fiancé's car, blowing Jerzy Slowik to smithereens.

Warsaw

I had been expecting trouble for weeks. My accountant Basia's hostile attitude had alerted me. The suspicions round her lover's death were eating at her. I knew that sooner or later the secret police would succeed in putting two and two together. They were short on brains and a plodding lot but had infinite patience and kept meticulous records on every move we made. Once they decided to pounce, it would be too late to avoid catastrophe.

My assistant, the Polish colonel, was showing definite signs of nervousness. From the first day he entered my employ I made him switch to American cigarettes, keeping him well supplied. His own left a terrible odor. He got to like the Old Golds, Camels and Chesterfields. These last several days he was lighting up every two minutes, leaving burning butts everywhere and I could smell alcohol on his breath in the morning. This was most unusual so I knew the secret police was about to pay us a visit. I could see that the colonel's constant pacing and fidgetiness was getting on my driver's nerves. Stefan never asked questions, never offered comment but his face would light up when I sought his advice on even the most trivial of matters. I trusted him implicitly and now felt very tempted to take him into my confidence but as much as I needed a friend and a vigilant ally, I rejected the notion,not wanting to place him in potential jeopardy. Nobody could be expected to withstand the "screws" of the secret police. If you knew, you talked. Once you admitted you knew but failed to immediately inform them, death by torture was the result..

I had sent Daniel officially to the Baltic port of Gdansk on a publicity junket. Our records said so. In fact, he was at the other end of Poland, near Cracow, awaiting a signal from me. Unless alarms went off, leaving the country was not a complicated matter. I needed to create a smoke screen, a plausible reason for his sudden disappearance so that the secret police could close the case and not pursue it any further.

Three months earlier we had arranged for a young woman to pose as Dan's wife and join him in Warsaw, allegedly from the town of Bialystok. She was a buxom blonde, always dressed to kill, wearing plenty of make-up. Not too loud in appearance, just fancy enough to make people wonder whether she was a lady or something less. Nobody suspected her of being a decoy. It was now time to use her talents.

She arrived at the office in the early morning, screaming and wailing that Danny had taken all her jewelry and money and borrowed large sums from her friends allegedly to conclude an important business deal. The previous night, she said, tears dripping, he phoned bidding her farewell.

The colonel and I rushed for our office safe where we always kept a good deal of money. There was nothing there. I had emptied it earlier. We called the police demanding the immediate arrest of our crooked employee. The American embassy chimed in saying a clerk had seen Daniel take some official government stationery which he might use for fraudulent purposes.

The police grilled Daniel's wife over and over again. She was a good actress. They went through our files, asking a million questions. From my office they phoned their colleagues in Gdansk. They were drowning in show-efficiency but it was evident they really couldn't care less. The con had worked. The police were now sure Daniel ran away because he did not want to go to prison for larceny. Who had the time to look for petty thieves?

A friendly man of the cloth telephoned Cracow for me. Our inimitable publicity genius got to Paris via Vienna and Zurich. He sent me a postcard signed "Daniel Boom".

Warsaw - run Augustus

Everything the British ambassador, Cavendish Bentinck, admonished his staff to watch for many months earlier, was now coming to pass. With earlier agreements between London, Washington and Moscow ignored, unilaterally abrogated by the Soviets, non-communist Poles had no further say in anything concerning their country or their own existence. Communist apparatchiks were now in total control. The Red noose no longer strangled slowly but cut deep into the flesh of freedom, blood dripping. Arrests were routine, deportations regular, pretense of political compromise derelict, last vestiges of hope sequestered. Despair took permanent lease on Polish lives.

I was now able to see Mrs.Radkiewicz on business matters at Film Polski only occasionally. My visits were obviously being sharply curtailed either by her own design or by higher authority because "they" no longer trusted her. She herself had told me when we were in Brussels: "Remember that in order to avoid rot in our communist society, everyone must always remain suspect, never allowed to feel totally safe". When I asked how long that kind of society, skewered by unending fear and suspicion -no questions allowed- could avoid self-destruction, her answer surprised me. "For as long as the capitalist world continues to exploit the working man". She knew this was not worthy of her intellect and that I would mock her for the transparent cliché. In fact, I remembered daring to say: "that's cat dirt".

Our film business broodingly continued at a constantly reduced pace, making room for Soviet productions. It was less and less healthy for Poles to be seen entering a cinema showing American movies, even when these were ridiculously mutilated by the censors.

That particular morning Stefan picked me up at my country villa earlier than usual. I had been sleeping badly or not at all recently, kept awake by imagined noises and real fears. By seven o'clock we reached my office. Nervous boredom would soon set in. There was little to do. I had cleared out most of the accumulated film money through a series of not entirely legitimate yet government-condoned transactions with the Joint Distribution Committee and other organizations.

My wife had gone to the United States to take advantage of a law permitting alien wives of Americans working for U.S. companies to obtain citizenship without prior residence, provided the husband remained abroad during the naturalization process. The Motion Picture Export Association in New York gave her legal assistance in the filing of required documents and within thirty days she received her American passport. It was the fastest official granting of citizenship then on record. Though immensely pleased, I still had serious misgivings about her returning to Warsaw. There was something evil in the air. Were they going to arrest me? I did not think myself a sufficiently important personality to be brought to public trial. Besides, they would have a difficult time proving anything despite the ample dossier I knew they kept on me since my days in London. On the other hand I no longer enjoyed diplomatic immunity, so anything was possible. Perhaps they would just quietly knock me off.

As I looked outside my office window into the garden below, I drifted into fantasy-land. With the eye of my conceit-stricken imagination I saw myself insolently addressing an enormous courtroom filled with Russian generals. I cowed them. I told them what I thought of their communism. I was William Jennings Bryan. No, not him. Bryan was a windbag and an ass. Make it Oliver Wendell Holmes. When I completed my oration all the fancy epaulettes fell off. The generals were now mere corporals.

The slamming of the entrance gate brought me back to reality. The blustering hero vanished. I was frightened, losing my nerve, accepting that if they arrested me, held my little daughter hostage, put me on trial, I would tell them anything they wanted to hear.

My phone rang. A familiar voice I remembered so well said: "Evgenii! Remember Augustus. Don't tarry". The line went dead before I could say anything but the message was clear. Grigori told me, ordered me to leave Poland immediately or I would be nabbed by the cat just like Pushkin's swallow.

The moment danger was identified, clear in focus, a change in me invariably took place. The sudden rush of adrenalin kicked in my conditioned reflexes. Fear vanished. Calculating cool took over. I was lucky too. It was a Wednesday -the day the embassy plane routinely arrived from Berlin to deliver mail and supplies-, leaving with the diplomatic pouch and whatever else the embassy wanted to send out. Take off would be at 2 in the afternoon which meant I had over four hours to get myself organized.

I instructed Stefan to drive alone to the American embassy garage and tell "Penny" to requisition a new carburator. Stefan took meticulous care of my car and knew I didn't need any carburators but he would ask no questions. I told Stefan to get back to the office as soon as he could deliver my message.

Penhollow, known as "Penny", would do what was necessary. It had all been carefully prearranged. "Penny" was one of those extraordinary individuals you hoped would be at your side if you ever got caught in enemy cross-fire. A military man on detached service with the embassy, he was officially in charge of vehicles and transporation. I liked him from the moment I saw his muscular figure and friendly grin when he came to pick me up in sub zero weather, at the Baltic port of Gdynia where I had just arrived from England with a full boat-load of cars and supplies for the embassy and no dock help in sight. "Penny" organized things instanter, then drove me to Warsaw across the vast deserted areas of East Prussia, brutally ravaged by the Soviet army; its entire German population forcibly deported, leaving not a soul in cities like Königsberg or a single chicken on the farm. It was an eerie and foreboding experience.

Only a few persons knew that during the period I was still on the staff of the American embassy, "Penny", at great risk to his life, had personally smuggled Mikolajczyk, the former Polish prime minister, out of the country right under the nose of the security police. The largest limousine ever produced in America had served a purpose after all. A true hero, Penhollow deserved a medal for his dedication and bravery.

I knew that this morning, as soon as he got my message, he would go to the "secure" cubicle in the office of the American military attaché, Colonel Tom Betts, to tell him my moment had come and that I absolutely had to be on that day's flight to Berlin. Tom was a highly competent and courageous intelligence officer whom nothing could faze.

Meantime, from my office where all lines were still bugged, I put a call through to the embassy doctor fixing a 1 o'clock appointment for my daughter. I made sure my colonel watchdog,who arrived a minute or so earlier, could hear me. Then I took most of the cash from the safe, leaving a receipt and a bye bye note for my accountant Basia, hoping she would have a heart attack realizing I was out of reach. That is, if things went well for me.

Stefan was back. I asked him to drive me to my Konstancin villa "slowly and gently." I didn't want the people in the black Citroen behind us to get the impression I was in any kind of a hurry.

At the villa I would go through an emotional crisis. For obvious reasons it was impossible to tell my wonderful friends, Joseph and Maria, the couple I employed as cook and butler, that I was leaving the country and not coming back. Whatever justification existed for my action,it was still a rotten thing to do to them. What would happen to them ? Where would they go?

For over thirty years they had served the princely Czartoryski family who fled abroad when the Germans invaded Poland. A few months after I arrived in Warsaw, an Italian friend, the young principessa Maria Pignatelli, sent them to me. Joseph was a superb butler-maître d'hôtel. At formal dinners we communicated exclusively by eye signals. A glance and Joseph knew exactly what to do. He dictated the rhythm of courses.

He could intervene in a "crisis" with utmost subtlety. He mixed the best of cocktails, knew his wines and could drift in and out of the salon completely unnoticed. His manners were impeccable. Superior, I often observed, to those of many of my diplomatic guests. A fine judge of people. A single flutter of his eyebrow told me everything. I had great respect for Joseph.

He taught me a lot. And Maria? Well, sweet Maria was just the best cook in the whole country.

I sent Joseph to the hothouse to cut some flowers "for a lady at the embassy", I said. While he was out, I ducked into the servants' quarters putting money into the pocket of his dress jacket. He would find it later when preparing for my arrival from the office and the cocktail hour.

I could take no baggage, nothing at all. If I did, the Citroen kings would certainly notice, to later accuse Joseph and his wife, probably the gardner as well, of "prior knowledge", that damnable charge used by the secret police, always impossible to disprove.

Two German pistols stared at me from the desk drawer. I had forgotten all about them. Bringing arms into Poland was a criminal offense, a real dumb thing to have done. If found by the police, Joseph and Maria faced long imprisonment. I had to remove the Lugers from the house without attracting attention. I slipped them into the double cover of my tennis rackets. The bulges looked a bit odd, nothing more.

My six year old daughter was out with her governess for a walk in the woods. They were due back momentarily. Not more than ten minutes had elapsed since Stefan and I drove up to the house. It seemed to me much longer. Where were they? I was impatient, nervous, trying to show no emotion. My daughter Karen ran into my arms. "I'm exactly on time, not a second late", she said. I had phoned from the office when to expect me. Really to make doubly sure the eavesdroppers knew I would be taking my daughter to the embassy doctor. I dared not look back. Maria and Joseph would see my pain. We drove past Hedy's cottage without stopping. Hedy did not need to be told. "Our lives are but one continuous betrayal" she once told me.

Stefan drove down the ramp of the embassy garage, quickly jumped out of the car, saluted me and ran off. He knew he would not see me again. His salute told me he approved. I handed my tennis rackets with the concealed Luger pistols to Penny. I was sorry to lose them. They had special meaning to me having belonged to the two German generals whose necks were so red when they surrendered to colonel Rosenbaum in Luxembourg.

We switched to a different car, exiting at the other end of the garage. Nobody followed. The embassy service plane had its own tarmac. Papers in order, we got past Polish security. The young captain looked me straight in the eye and wished us a good trip. The Warsaw bureaucrats had not yet sent any signal about me. The Dakota took off. From my bucket seat I could see the cargo compartment filled with crates and parcels of all sizes, bearing APO (Army Post Office) addresses. Each week, embassy employees were sending home, at government expense, furs, jewelry, oriental carpets, antique furniture, paintings, even a grand piano on one occasion, and other priceless items acquired from impoverished Poles at a fraction of their true value, then paid for in cheap Zlotys bought with dollars on the black market. "The Scavenger Club", as I called them, were doing a brisk business.

In Berlin, I reported briefly to Major Epp of the U.S. Army intelligence. He would advise The Man from Prague. There were no further regular commercial flights that day to England but I was able to charter a small private aircraft which later that evening landed us at an airport near London. We felt safe at last.

Three weeks later I received a call to visit the American embassy at Grosvenor Square. Gerry Keith, the chargé d'affaires from Warsaw had brought news for me. Polish Security raided my villa and my office, missing me by some 48 hours. Stefan was badly beaten, teeth knocked out, but released. Princess Pignatelli got my message and would do her best for Joseph and Maria who were thrown out of the villa, questioned and also set free after a week in prison. Nothing had been heard from other members of my staff. The most curious and gratifying information Keith gave me came from our military attaché, colonel Tom Betts. The message he sent me, worded in a manner only I could understand, was that the morning following my departure he received warning to get me out of the country in a hurry and that he knew the warning came from Mrs. Radkiewicz. Flowers and candy? Maybe.

London - Paris

The past is a foreign land. They do things differently there. This was London, not Warsaw. Here, I did not have to keep running just to stay in one place, like Alice's enemy the Red Queen.

Still, the city depressed me. Very little rebuilding had taken place since I left nearly four years before. When the noise of bombings still echoed in one's ears, the empty lots, the craters where homes and offices used to stand could be accepted as inevitable scars of war. Boarded-off empty craters that no one noticed any more, neglected open spaces, overgrown with tall weed, were now lamentable signs of British weariness and dejection.

My euphoria was rapidly wearing off. Long drugged on tension, my nervous system craved excitement, new action. Instead, I was a jobless prisoner of boredom seeing life, once again, from the unstimulating viewpoint of a sack of potatoes. I soon found out that London had not much need for my nebulous talents. On the other hand I didn't feel ready to return home to the States.

An unexpected phone call from New York quickly dissipated my melancholy. John McCarthy, vice president of international operations for the Motion Picture Association of America was on the line: "Our two European directors, Frank McCarthy and Rupert Allen are returning to America. Would you like to go to Paris as deputy to the new European chief Gerald Mayer?"

I had heard of Gerry Mayer from my British colleagues. He was a close friend and wartime collaborator in Switzerland of America's "super spy", Allen Dulles, who headed the Office of Strategic Services (OSS), the forerunner of the CIA.

"Yes, Mr. McCarthy, I know Paris pretty well and would very much like to work in France. When do I start"? He gave me ten days to report to the association's office at 21, rue de Berri, the Herald Tribune Building. My luck had not abandoned me. Neither had Irving Maas, my friend and erstwhile boss at the Motion Picture Export Association. I knew he had to be behind the Paris job offer. I already owed him a lot and this new job was a real plum. I would be working for and with the finest business brains in the motion picture industry. Not to mention Paris.

Memories creep up on one. That evening, still exhilarated by my good fortune, I remembered the five year old boy, Eugene, dressed in a black velvet suit with lace collar, wearing buttoned patent-leather shoes, stomping bravely along the Champs Elysées, swinging the ultimate badge of elegance, his cane, when suddenly, it went flying down the street under the feet of fast moving strangers. "My cane, he cried, my cane".

Through teary eyes he saw his mother smiling at someone standing above him. "I'm sorry I kicked your cane, the young man said. I really didn't see it. Cross my heart. Here it is". Eugene noted he was black, very tall, wore a most elegant red and blue checkered vest and a gleaming smile. Before Eugene could say "thank you", he disappeared down the street.

"Maman, how did the man know I was American? He spoke English to me. "Hurry now", Maman answered, "Walter is waiting for us at the hotel". Eugene didn't like Walter. He did not like him at all. Who was he anyway?

That evening Maman took Eugene to the opera. After the first act he already decided the French were the fastest, the best builders in all the world. No one had ever told him about revolving stages. But, what he would always remember best of Paris was not the Eiffel Tower, or the Louvre, which frightened him, or even the beautiful Jardin des Tuileries. It was Le Tombeau de Napoléon. Its blue light embraced his innermost feelings and would never let go. It was perhaps because the prism-like cut glass windows in his father's Chicago study would, at the right time of day, throw the same kind of hazy blue light round the bronze bust of Napoléon Bonaparte. Eugene loved his father.

Chapter 3

The Golden Years

I was in Paris again, the city of never ending magic. It attracted the world. The painters, the writers, the hacks, the aficionados. The famous, the inglorious, the has-beens, the never-have-beens. The wicked, the cruel, the pimps and the kings, the beautiful and the horrid. Generation followed generation to learn, to copy, to envy. The French let them all admire the glories of France but never to partake in the finest treasure of all: her honour.

In less than half the time it took the German blitzkrieg to overrun Poland, the French surrendered to the Third Reich whose armies end-turned, at Sedan, France's Eastern frontier fortifications, the Maginot Line. Ominous Sedan, where in 1870 the French surrendered to the Prussians in the Franco-Prussian war. Then they fought. This time German newsreels would show the *poilu* running for his life, with a bottle of wine instead of a rifle in hand.

Now, after Germany's defeat, France was humiliated. Her pride begged for mercy where no mercy could be granted. The shadow of Pétain fell long. To be French was no longer épatant. The wicked, the ugly, the vain and the celebrated, the overt, the covert, the center, the right, the real and the phony were nibbling away at the tricolour with the sharp teeth of self-indulgence.

Distorted perceptions of guilt and glory, of sacrifice and pity, fear and courage, want and need joined to cast on all the pain of virtuous chagrin. "Je me trouve dans une espèce de souricière dont il ne serait pas possible de s'échapper", my newest friend, Marcel Achard told me. It really was a mousetrap from which it seemed impossible to escape. De Gaulle resented the Americans for allowing him to "liberate" Paris when all the French knew the battle was long over. He would not forget the Casablanca conference where Roosevelt said of him: "Yesterday he wanted to be Joan of Arc, now he wants to be Clemenceau", which made Churchill laugh and General Giraud blanch. The Germans would forever remain the "sacré boche", the English "carroteurs", the French "collaborateurs" and "cochons". "Dieu merci, one heard, the Russians didn't get to us. " But they did. Beginning with the French underground during the occupation and through the battles of liberation, to and beyond The Fourth Republic, communists directed by Moscow had their way in France. Then there was also Algeria, French territory for over one hundred years, now beginning guerrilla warfare against the French in Africa,terrorizing Paris with plastic explosives, before any referendum on the status of Algeria was even contemplated. Ben Bella, the Algerian nationalist imprisoned by the French, was spinning intrigue and plotting murder from his cell.

Military conflicts were far from over. In French Indochina, Nationalist Forces set up the independent republic of Vietnam and a grim, hopeless war was on. France was not a happy nation. At home, doubt, mistrust, moral inquiry concerning collaboration with the enemy would never end because no one risked defining it on either a personal or national level.

A beautiful lady I got to know well and profoundly respect, argued that if mere projection and displacement could turn anything into anything else, why bother trying to give morality an intellectual justification. "All of us were collaborators, she said. The *poules* and the women of high society. The butcher, the baker, the candlestick maker. It was a question of survival. What do you Americans think of Pétain? Was he a collaborator or a hero? Would holding on to his personal past glory justify sacrificing a million French lives? Did patriots escape abroad or remain in France? Give me answers to these questions and you shall have not the Légion d'Honneur, which our government has bestowed on half of the swine in France, but my embrace and my undying gratitude because I too am confused. But remember that men and parties are either heroic or ridiculous and not so much in themselves as in their reactions to circumstances. Mon ami, bear in mind that any rupture in the correlation between the subjective and the objective becomes the prime source of both the comic and the tragic in life, in politics and in art. When the French Revolution was entering its decisive stage, the most eminent of Girondists was suddenly degraded to a lamentable and ridiculous figure next to a Jacobin. But it was the Jacobin, Robespierre, who instituted the reign of terror".

I met her during the first major negotiations I had with a French labor union. Its members, the "dubbers", were the highly specialized people who substituted their voices on film soundtracks for those of English-speaking actors, synchronizing lip movement to perfection. Always the same dubber for a particular actor. As a result, the moviegoer "knew" the voice of Gable or Stewart or Grable or Crawford who sounded as French as Jean Gabin or Michelle Morgan. To suddenly use different voices was unthinkable. The public would howl insults. The union was now demanding wage increases American film companies could not afford but hesitated to flatly turn down.

She was on the opposing side, this young and beautiful actress. "I am to give you a message", she said during one break when we were alone. "You should propose the creating of a special school for dubbers, financed jointly by our French union and the American companies". It was an ingenious suggestion. The thought we might hire and train a new set of dubbers scared the union. We renewed the old agreement virtually without change. Who gave her the message? She would not say, but I had a hunch. I made friends with this enchanting actress-combatant-philosopher. On one week-end I would accompany her to the Pantin area of Paris, next to the dilapidated working class district of Courbevoie. She moved constantly, gravitating to where she could do most good, with her money, her encouragement, her love for the dejected, the underprivileged, the poor. We would take an apéritif together at obscure bistros. A Pernod for her, a fine à l'eau for me and smoke the Gauloise Bleue, a cigarette only a Frenchman could inhale without spitting out his lungs.

The communist press kept attacking me. I became nearly fond of one recurring phrase: "the perfidious lackey of Hollywood, this shameless American propaganda machine". It was so resounding in French.

I was devoted to this lady who loved France because she understood what it was to be French, and who despised the French because they did not. She honoured dedication and sacrifice because she was a communist, and had faith and compassion because she was a Jew. Her name was Simone Signoret.

I think it is called living in the fast lane. That we did indeed. We worked hard to maintain peace and unanimity among ten unequal-in-size albeit comparable-in-competitiveness film companies. No mean undertaking. When we negotiated with foreign governments or with labor unions or film trade associations, each one of our ten members received identical representation and treatment. Metro-Goldwyn-Mayer or Fox or Paramount got no advantage over Warner Brothers or Allied Artists. The united front, born of careful design, gave us extraordinary bargaining powers in all foreign markets.

We labored strenuously but we also played a lot. Parties, stars, enchantment, one night stands, excitement were there but only as tinsel. Ninety percent was hard work. The film business is a colossal, fast moving, constantly changing world-wide industry. The American general managers for Europe of the ten major film companies had many years of international experience. Out of their Paris headquarters they ran large organizations of specialists through networks of offices located in each and every large city of Europe. They traveled extensively, knew of the competition's every move. Experts in sales techniques, in marketing, public relations, accounting, banking, and last but not least, in the art of subtle diplomacy, they were managers par excellence in an immensely rich, cutthroat business. Our job in the Motion Picture Association was to represent the companies in all types of negotiations. We had to try and prevent government legislation and any other measures that could adversely affect their operations. With constant advice from company managers, the Association-MPAA-concluded major import, financial and distribution agreements with France, Germany, Belgium, Holland, Spain, Turkey and Italy. Germany was in the hands of the remarkably talented Mark Spiegel who eventually took over the European office in Paris. As vice president of the International Association of Film Producers, I was also involved in copyright conventions, the approving of film festivals, international motion picture coproduction norms and the like.

All of us had friends, connections, influence, social standing and sometimes also enemies. It came with the game. We were paid well, lived even better. In Paris, all our company business luncheons were held at Maxim's. When our favorite chef there left, we switched to the Ritz. Where else.

Large, efficient multilingual organizations operating in many countries inevitably attract the attention of intelligence services hoping to use them as cover for their agents. Experience had taught American film companies that sickthink paranoia is the intelligence community's occupational disease which can only spell trouble. We ignored all approaches.

We had our own commercial information network of friends whom we secretly called quarks. In France, members of the Inspectorat Générale de Finance, all top graduates of the Ecole Nationale D'Administration. In Spain, the Opus Dei, an organization at the heart of the Catholic Church. Italy was in a category of her own. Italy always is. There is a dictum that it is not what you know but whom you know that counts. There is another adage, attributed to Lord Falkland, that when it is not necessary to make a decision, it is necessary not to make a decison. I was especially fortunate regarding the first and never failed to attend to the second. It saved me from committing dangerous blunders of judgement.

All of us had been affected, in one way or another, by the war, so it was not difficult to accept the old Scottish motto: "be happy while y'er leevin, for y'er a lang time deid" and not because we had minds through which winds blew. We carried with us the reflected glamour of Hollywood. Doors opened. Women flocked. We savoured, we dissipated, we thrilled. From the races at Longchamps and lunch in the Bois de Boulogne, to nights at the Lapin Agile, La Nouvelle Eve, Eléphant Blanc, Crazy Horse Saloon striptease.

We vaulted from La Scala, to the Roland Petit Ballet, across the Côte d'Azur, and La Costa Brava, Monte Carlo, the Quartier Latin, the Louvre, Montmartre, the Santa Città Vaticana, the Expressionists, the Impressionists, the Existentialists, the everything. It was incredibly exciting.

Paris

We called him Maxime the Fox. He was the Paris representative of *Variety*, the American trade paper, bible of the entertainment world. Baron Maxime de Beix, in his late sixties, was what the French would refer to as a "roué", a cunning, calculating rake. He knew Paris and the Parisians inside out. The fact that he represented *Variety*, automatically provided him a passe-partout. He was everywhere, invited or not. Few liked him, many feared him as the most consummate of gossips. I thought Max a sad relic of a kinder world, a survivor vainly hoping to be recognized at least as a has-been. When I told him about the cocktail party I was planning for a few key government officials, sprinkled with show people and some Paris glitterati, Max implored me to invite his good friend Maurice Chevalier. For a moment I was taken aback because the French had labelled him a collaborator who performed for the

Germans under the occupation. Now, in still bruised but culturally reviving postwar Paris Chevalier was socially ostracized and refused professional engagements. Personally, I tended to believe the French were looking for scapegoats, hoping to conceal their personal sense of guilt by striking out at the celebrated. Still, I hesitated. "Max, I said, Maurice is a controversial figure. If I, as representative of the American film industry, invite him to an official party, there might be more than one highly placed nose out of joint. What will I do then?" Max looked at me with what I thought signified contempt. It made me think again. Could I possibly help the "legend" to rekindle his career by such a simple gesture as inviting him to a party? Emotionally, I was very much in favour. Professionally, I knew I had to be careful because some of the people who were blackballing Maurice would be my guests. My job was to make friends, not offend French sensibilities. I stalled Max and phoned Maurice Bessy, one of the editors of the magazine *Le Film Français* for advice. "Go ahead, by all means invite him. Some of your guests will have temporary stomach cramps, that's all. Chevalier is a real tough *gars* whose stage appeal and talent will bring him right back to the top very soon". I considered Bessy the keenest, the best informed newspaperman in town. We knew him also as a friend of American film companies. I asked him to come to my party. He had to go out of town that evening. I gave Maxime de Beix two invitations.

Their arrival was announced when the party was already in full swing, champagne flowing. This was Max's expert timing to catch everyone relaxed, guard down. Sadly, his stratagem failed. The moment Chevalier entered, a near hush fell over the room. Just long enough to sound like a clap of thunder. Max was nervous and pale. I shuddered. Hostile eyes of icy resentment seemed to focus on Chevalier. My illustrious guests were not prepared to pardon and accept Maurice. They would probably not forgive me either for what they undoubtedly perceived as a deliberate insult on my part. I was witnessing cold, studied, deliberate, biting rudeness meted out, as only the French at their best can do, to a once applauded, now held-disgraced compatriot. I looked at all these bigot bigwigs of the film and theater world and the smug government officials searching for a sympathetic face, a touch of empathy. Then I saw France Roche, the young, beautiful and very talented reporter for the country's best show business magazine, *Cinémonde*. She was talking to Maurice, then laughed as if trying to attract attention, before slowly moving away to watch him over the rim of her glass from across the room with sadness in her eyes. This was a gracious gesture to Chevalier, a snub to the rude. I didn't know what she had said to him but it must have been nice because that familiar broad smile briefly lit up his face. I felt grateful. Maurice bid me a hasty au revoir. Max scurried unhappily after him.

The following Monday Max came to my office at an early hour. This was unusual because he never went to bed before three in the morning. Normally he came in after lunch dozing off in my office armchair. My secretary repeatedly timed his naps and they lasted precisely 33 minutes. We never could figure out how he did that. This time he was wide awake, upset and obviously very angry. "Your damn cocktail party, he said, will cost me my friendship with Maurice. Did you have to invite all the worst bastards in Paris?" "Wait a minute, Max. You saw the invitation list and had no objections. Why blame me?" I stopped right there. I could see that Max was distraught, on the verge of tears. "You really don't understand, do you, Max began. Maurice was never a collaborator. Sure, he performed in Germany but it was in a French prisoner-of-war camp. He was less culpable under the occupation than Jean Cocteau or Colette or many other celebrities. He is the same Maurice Chevalier who was awarded the Croix de Guerre in the First World War. True, he was a convinced Pétainiste because like the Maréchal, he saw more merit in saving lives than in sacrificing them. Some warped people even accused Maurice of antisemitism. A shameful lie. I know that at great personal risk Maurice saved the life of his constant companion, Nita Ray, and she was Jewish. Have these rotten cochons of the performing arts already forgotten the infamous all -French *Commissariat Général aux Questions Juives* at Place des Petits- Pères that sent so many good men and women, Jews and gentiles, to their death in German concentration camps? Should the French women who gave birth to over 80,000 illegitimate children of German soldiers all have their heads shaved, be further humiliated and expelled from our society for collaborating with the enemy?" Max carried on for a long time. He started to cry. There was nothing I could say or do to calm and console him. He was only too right. Everyone knew of the racist, anti-semitic acts of persecution committed under the French government of 1940-44. A government which was not imposed by the Germans on the unwilling French but one appointed and given full powers in 1940 by the freely elected French parliament. Could one forget that in two days during the summer of 1942 the Paris police arrested 13,000 Jews, including 4,000 children and sent them off in cattle trucks to German extermination camps? Or, that of the 75,000 Jews deported from France under the Vichy government, fewer than 2,000 survived? Was that unwilling collaboration with the German "final solution" -the extermination of all the Jews-, or an independent purely French-bred inhumanity? Max somehow managed to survive the period of the war. No one was able to discover how or where. Later, when *Variety* gave him a credible identity, he began appearing at important functions invariably accompanied by at least two very young, beautiful girls. One of them revealed to me the secret of his attraction. Too old to be a sex menace, he told them, and with no heirs, he would leave them his entire fortune. Max didn't have a dime to his name.

For a short while Max had a deputy at *Variety*. He fired him. "Couldn't write worth a damn, you know", he said to me. However true, it was a lucky turn of events for Art Buchwald who, with his customary unabashed chutzpah, promptly talked himself into a job with the Paris Tribune to begin writing the column *"Paris after Dark"*.

Was it a sample of Hollywood showmanship or of ridiculous extravaganza? The ingredients were risible: a Jewish producer presenting his version of France's national heroine Joan of Arc-the Maid of Orléans-casting his wife Joan Bennett in the title role, staging the film's world première at the resplendent Paris Opera House,and hiring the Garde Républicaine,with their glorious uniforms and shiny helmets for extra effect.

We reminded Art Buchwald not to wear white socks with his tuxedo. He was capable of doing just that. His way of cocking a snook at the glitterati. Art was a snob of a new species. We saw him as a sort of homespun, demi-tasse philosophical fusion between shrewd opportunism and the existential belief that man must oppose his hostile environment to become what he has not been. Not quite appreciated by the French, with whom he had little communion, this quintessentially American persifleur would shape his own destiny and in the process wave his wit gaily about. His sense of humor could be paradoxically waggish as when he allegedly approached a Paris uniformed policeman politely asking him, with a straight face and abominable accent, "Monsieur, parlez vous français? Adding "quel dommage" -what a pity- when the perplexed flic nodded his head.

Art's companion was a young lady whom I called Irish Ann. She was as delightful and high spirited as only an Irish girl can be. Seeing them together reminded me of someone's observation that America, the great receiver, embraces some new ingredient from every culture to arrive within its borders. Among them Jewish irony and Irish poetics. Ann and Art did not seem to really fit together,yet they were a perfect match.

The opera house was bursting at the seams, crowds forcing their way into the foyer, shoving aside the wooden barricades. The huge chandeliers exploded with light. Bejeweled women holding on to their penguin attired escorts floated up the carpeted stairways. I waved to the distinguished director of the Paris opera, Monsieur Favre Lebret. He ignored me. The week before, I had unwittingly committed a major faux pas. The beautiful prima donna he brought to a reception left early, with me. Lebret felt I had brazenly "kidnapped" his adorable soprano. Actually, it was nothing of the sort. In fact I knew she felt offended that I dropped her off at the hotel immediately after she told me that Spyros Skouras, the indomitable president of 20th Century Fox and one of my super bosses, was her great friend and sponsor. I liked her but I liked my job better.

The gala at the opera was a social success. The film itself a flop. In his inimitable arhythmic bebop style, Buchwald left no survivors. "The movie was such a bore, he wrote in his next day's column, the leading lady slept right through the entire performance". The producer, Walter Wanger, threatened to sue, then challenged Buchwald to a duel. Having the right to choose weapons, Buchwald picked 15th century armor, with heavy halberds. The Bois de Boulogne was agreed upon as the field of combat. Time:six in the morning. Buchwald let the rumor fly that Charlie Chaplin would be one of his seconds. The exchange of challenges and insults carried forth in the press for a number of days, keeping Paris readers highly amused. His readiness to blithely tease the ludicrous, disregard intimidation from any source including his own ego, and laugh at himself with self-effacing humor were among Buchwald's most appealing traits. "Listen, he said one lunch time to me and Charles Torem. I let people believe the big scar on my leg came from a bayonet wound suffered when serving with the marines, but I really got it escaping from the enemy over a barbed wire fence". Charlie Torem, Harvard man, member of the distinguished law firm in Paris of Coudert Frères, and a fine friend, didn't even pretend to believe Art's fairy tale. Neither did I but we liked him for telling it. Buchwald never said things malicious in his column. The Joan of Arc critique was no exception. The drollery gave Walter Wanger and his movie considerable publicity. Art did not mean it to be one-sided. Riding on its coattails Buchwald had shrewdly crafted for himself a shot at notoriety.

It was at about that time that Art asked me whether I might be interested in helping him finance the book he was preparing to publish. Naturally, I turned him down. Naturally, I never stopped regretting it.

There were three women in Paris, -mes trois Simones-metaphorically speaking, who strongly influenced my outlook on life. The first was an actress, the second a philosopher and the third an attorney. The actress Simone Signoret, told me all there was to know about redundant ethics and about the historical anatomy of a political "canard". The philosopher, Simone De Beauvoir, Sartre's soulmate of many years, taught me that knowing where you are is not much use if you don't know where everything else is.

Jean-Paul called De Beauvoir "that stubborn unyielding, opinionated cantankerous bitch". I quite agreed with the opinionated and unyielding. Cantankerous on occasion and, from what I could observe, especially when he got long-winded about the ungratefulness of mankind in his regard. She would then accuse him of despicable self pity and call him a "boscard"-parasite. Knowing her mind was equal to his,he forgave her all insults and while they appeared to interminably argue and disagree on nearly everything, they were intellectually close to indivisible. I had read his *L'Étre et le Néant* and *La Nausée*. Probably they were accessible only to better minds than mine. Was it Heidegger gone toxic? Kierkegaard turned atheist? The prostitute, the deserter, the lesbienne incarcerated for eternity without salvation in Sartre's *Huis Clos* offended and revolted me. When he discoursed, I struggled to decipher his meanings, could only guess where he intended to go. Simone knew how to express her thoughts in a direct, open and at times brutal but unmistakenly clear fashion. Where his *La Nausée* stressed the absurdity of life and the disgust it inspires, Simone wrote that old age rather than death was to be contrasted with life. "Old age is life's parody, whereas death transforms life into destiny". In comparison Jean-Paul sounded to me not only beyond reach, but obscene. All liverish hues. Was his health partly to blame, I asked Simone. "He cannot see well and his heart is constantly bothering him. But, it is his disgust with the absurdity of life, how people can stand with integrity in a world of betrayal and subjection of individual needs that oppresses him". She gave me a copy of his *Les Mains Sales*. "You will understand better after you've read this".

Only once did I attempt to inject my idea of humor in talking with Jean-Paul and regretted it instantly when his silence made me understand that he was not at all fond of my favorite writer, Miguel de Unamuno. I expected rather the contrary, thinking Sartre would have found affinity with don Miguel, the philosopher, precursor of existentialism, the author of *The Tragic Sense of Life*. It was when Jean-Paul tried to explain to me the sense of damnation suffered by the personages of his play *Huis-Clos* that I stumbled so badly, quoting Unamuno's irreverent comment: "el teatro, esta escuela de vulgaridad". He refused to speak with me for the rest of the evening. I ran for cover to Simone. She scolded me. "You should know better than to quote one thinker to another. His own mother wouldn't get away with it. Jean-Paul has always resented Unamuno's duality of both philosopher and humorist. He thought don Miguel's *Amor y Pedagogia* unworthy of a serious writer because he himself would have been incapable of inventing a character like Fulgencio Entrabosmares. Besides, too many critics have said that Sartre was influenced by Miguel de Unamuno which is a slanderous lie of course. Never forget that Jean-Paul est un animal très méchant. Quand on l'attaque il se défend".

Simone de Beauvoir was different from anyone I had ever known. She had a natural, intuitive awareness of human turmoil. Not merely an observer, she was a participant, standing deliberately exposed where life hurt and destroyed, refusing to take refuge or seek isolation. Simone, with the perfect consciousness of near psychic perception, could reach inside my brain to predetermine what it could absorb before infusing it. If she felt it was too weighty a concept she would say "you are still too arriéré - too backward- for this. You might suffer from overload". She would then talk to me instead about contemporary literature, the French symbolist movement -Verlaine, Mallarmé Rimbaud- that initiated the explicit to implicit statement and the parallel accomplishment in the impressionist school of painting,my personal passion. Through her I met Marcel Achard, playwright, author of *Domino*, who in turn introduced me at a Cannes film festival to "Framboise", that dynamite French liqueur that smells so delightfully of rasperries and then goes straight for your groin.

Though I may have seemed hindered by intellectual awkwardness, Simone did manage to impress upon me how important it was not to try to extract from a person virtues he does not possess at the expense of neglecting to cultivate those which he has. Quickly, inevitably I became her mesmerized intellectual slave and felt dejected when the time came to bid her adieu. Where did she come from? What was this sensitive, courageous being doing surrounded by stuttering, narcissistic phobiacs of this world?

The attorney? Well, until I was introduced to her I always asked: if it is true some women are equal to men, why is it that I never had the good fortune to meet one? And, didn't all intelligent people agree that the best feminine movement remains that of the hips? I liked to quote from Queen Victoria's letter to Sir Theodore Martin where she said: "God created men and women different-then let them remain in their position".

Unexpectedly, my inherent, uncompromising faith in the inequality of the sexes, the incompatibility of career with femininity, with blissful pregnant marriage, was being seriously undermined. I did not know her well but I would see and listen to "my third Simone" at meetings on complex legal matters affecting our film business in France.

Our corporate attorney, Pierre Gide, cousin of the writer André, and no newcomer to the legal profession, deferred to Simone's grasp of intricate laws and her instinct for the politically prudent. Her mind dazzled us. It clicked away as fast as the beads on an abacus in the hands of an Armenian rug merchant. All along her intellect seduced us no less than her feminine allure. There was no rivalry, no competition between the two. Male colleagues, whether in the legal profession or in politics, where she was making a name for herself, did not think of her as an intruder on their domain. I made a real jackass of myself when after one meeting, all agog, I mumbled to her: "if I ever meet another woman like you I shall marry her career". It made her laugh. "I think I know what you suffer from. It's the American feminophobia syndrome. In contrast, it never occurs to a Frenchman to question the equality of the sexes. This enables him to accept a woman's success without fear. At the same time to look at her curvaceous body and say: Vive la Différence. Try it some day". It would have been unseemly to argue with Madame Simone Veil, Maître Veil, even though I did not know then that she would be a cabinet minister twice during the Mitterrand presidency.

Cannes

The Cannes International Film Festival is always held in late Spring, just as the mimosa is blooming all along the Riviera.

Inside the festival palace, near the French public relations stand, I noticed Kirk Douglas talking with Ann Buydens, a beautiful young lady from Belgium, who represented Unifrance Film, the public relations-publicity arm of the French film industry. I knew Ann slightly, only as a colleague in the same business. One could not help being captivated by her dignified manner and quiet natural charm. French friends told me that she had gone through very difficult times during the war. Perhaps that was why I could see that her eyes had shades of hurt in them.

I very much admired Kirk Douglas as an actor. In my own "classsification" he had a strong-fibered poignant personality in whatever role he played, similar in resonance to Burt Lancaster and Anthony Quinn, though I suspected he was more of a sentimentalist in real life. I did not know him personally and could hardly walk up to him to say: "You had better be nice to Ann" so I resisted the impulse and crossed my fingers. A few months later I saw them together again at the Venice film festival. It looked serious. The hurt in her eyes was no longer there. I felt happy for them. How serious? Ask one of their sons.

An American film producer's representative approached me in Cannes. "Since you are vice president of the International Association of Film Producers, familiar with the intricacies of co-productions, would you be willing to assist us in putting together a project involving the well known French film man Jean-Pierre Berger?" This was not quite within the scope of my usual duties, so whatever I accepted to do would have to be on my free time, which meant between midnight and eight in the morning, but as Berger was a fine French producer and the American group came to me well recommended, I decided to give it a shot.

The festival's hospitality committee had Berger staying at the Martinez hotel. I phoned him there, explained the project in general lines, inviting him to the Carlton to meet the Americans. All went well and after three days of hard bargaining between the respective lawyers, involving millions of dollars on both sides, the contracts were signed. The same evening at dinner Berger asked why he had been selected as coproducer since he had such limited knowledge of movie making. "After all, he said, I made my money in pharmaceuticals and don't really understand much about your kind of business". Everyone tried to laugh it off, pretending not to believe him. Still, it was not said in jest. It turned out I had gotten hold of Jean Paul Berger instead of Jean Pierre Berger. Not related, they were both registered at the Hotel Martinez. Perhaps Jean Paul didn't know too much about films but largely due to my advice on international coproductions both parties had in hand an ironclad, virtually unbreakable contract. When the wrong Berger made his dinner announcement, it flashed in my mind that I was about to be skinned alive by my compatriots. I escaped only because these well known names were afraid that if the story ever got out they would forever be the butt of

Hollywood jokes. However, one should never discount the possibility of a miracle occuring. Some months later I was told the film was completed well within budget and that advances on distribution assured its financial success. The experience proved, once again, that just like in any other endeavor you can be a good producer if you have a team of professionals working with you.

Paris

We were in a Paris taxi. Eric Johnston, one of his Washington assistants, Griff Johnson and I, having just left a meeting with the European managers of American film companies where Eric, with Griff's help, had gotten muddled a couple of times in connection with our Italian business, confusing the main issues, then warned by his uncanny instinct, getting back on track, actually managing to sound both profound and witty at the end. A true artist belying Lincoln's maxim that you can't fool all the people all the time.

Griff, an economist by training, was a nice unpretentious chap who kept his intellect well hidden, his fears wide open. Strangers were anathema to him; a serious encumbrance in international negotiations. Eric said of him that he made the impression of a man who was always afraid someone would steal his breakfast.

I was sort of glad that Johnston and Johnson, for a while there at the managers' meeting, sounded unsure of themselves in discussing our Italian business, because I had been trying for some time to convince the companies my moving to Rome was a practical idea.

The final decision belonged to Eric so now I turned to him and said: "Let me make my base in Rome and within eighteen months I shall remove virtually all of the screen quotas on American films coming into Italy, reduce the amount of dubbing and various other onerous fees by half and get every dime of the companies blocked Lira converted into dollars on an ongoing basis". Considering the poor state of the Italian economy it seemed nothing short of reckless to speak of transferring millions of dollars each year to the United States, or to expect the super tough Italian film trade associations to reduce their premiums resulting from our film distribution. We rode in silence for several minutes making me wonder whether Eric had any intention of responding. He finally nodded, saying: "Okay, Rome is yours. If you accomplish what you promise, I shall triple your salary ad infinitum". Eric did not realize that his "triple your salary ad infinitum" was straight out of Sam Goldwyn's book of malapropisms, but I could hardly afford to burst out laughing. Fractured English or not, I had Eric's word. Griff emitted one of his peculiar noises, a combination of a wheeze and a snort, the closest thing to an opinion one could expect from him. I took it for scepticism, a natural reaction of this highly circumspect man. What really annoyed me though was his and Eric's total lack of curiosity as to how I intended to reach these seemingly unattainable goals. I let it pass because I had no intention of even alluding to my "secret weapons" or the strategy I meant to employ. Some of my colleagues did not err on the side of either perception or discretion and an inopportune leak could vitiate my elementary, albeit rather unchaste schemes for Italy. Also, I was still in shock of disbelief after the appalling result of a confidential conference of potentially profound political significance for France and the United States which took place a few days earlier in a quiet Paris hotel room.

When the meeting was originally suggested by general De Gaulle's homme de confiance, through the intermediation of the French Centre for Cinéma, I explained to Eric that monsieur Leduc had no direct connection with the French film industry but as a graduate of the École Polytechnique, he represented France's political élite-the "ruling club". It was therefore obvious, I said, our French visitor would have weighty matters to discuss.

The handsome, elegant Monsieur Leduc was clearly startled to see the man he had just addressed as "ambassador", unceremoniously take off his jacket and stretch out on the sofa, hands under his head, even before mutual salutations were completed. I was stupefied. Eric's behavior was entirely out of character. His good manners and social grace were usually beyond reproach. Mr.Leduc pretended not to notice. In immaculate English he began speaking of the deteriorating Franco-American relations, General de Gaulle's dislike of American dominance of the Western Alliance, about the increasing influence of the French Communist Party. He touched upon the trauma of French society shamed by the Vichy years. "France, he said, this immense human being with a will, character and pride of her own, that Marcel Proust wrote about, always acted as midwife to history and now again must heed her destiny. What should the leaders of France and America do to arrest the tides of mutual distrust, before they cause irremediable damage?" Monsieur Leduc's passionate eloquence left no doubt he was speaking on behalf of Charles de Gaulle. Le Général was proposing a top level Franco-

American conference, counting on Eric, the confidant of American presidents, to carry his personal, highly important message to our Secretary of State Dean Acheson or, perhaps to Truman himself. I looked hard at Griff. He too must have realized we were witness to history in the making, an electrifying experience we would long remember. I could hear reverberating in my mind Leduc's emphasis on France's "will, character and pride of her own" and "now France must again heed her destiny". Our boss either feigned deafness or, in fact, understood absolutely nothing. Leduc's confidential mission ended in an ignominious miscarriage when Eric's only response was to ask him when the French government would allow a higher import quota for American films. Monsieur Leduc never lost poise, just visibly paled. He thanked us for the meeting, then said "bonsoir", meaning adieux-that's that-, instead of the customary "au revoir". I accompanied him to the lobby, clumsily attempting to explain that Mr.Johnston had not meant to be discourteous. "Monsieur", Leduc replied, "a gentleman is never unintentionally rude."

The experience confirmed my ever growing fear that many influential individuals, accepted in our society as intelligent, perceptive luminaries were, in reality, intending dupes of sham intellectual "gavage", expertly cribbing from their holophrastic idiot cards, to impress other presque arrivés, but hardly ever listening or understanding what was happening round them.

I thought to myself how unfortunate, how horribly distressing it was that my Paris boss, Gerald Mayer, this impeccably mannered, consummate diplomat, on whom the French had bestowed the Légion d'Honneur in recognition of his wartime intelligence work, had taken ill just before we were asked to meet monsieur Leduc. Gerry would have instantly known how to respond to Leduc's political suit and carry it forward, either himself or through the good offices of his close friend Allen Dulles where it would have been acted upon with political acumen instead of the Rin Tin Tin complex.

A few years later France opted for her own "force de frappe" -atomic striking power-, and after that De Gaulle pulled France out of the military structure of the NATO. Would that we had listened to monsieur Leduc with a keener ear.

Paris - Rome

Having persuaded Eric Johnston and the European managers I would perform a few miracles in Italy, I had to get down there very soon. I felt elated about living in Rome. France would always remain my first love in Europe but, as far as the motion picture business was concerned, the French ministries as well as trade associations were administratively synchronized to the point of tedious boredom. The well trained technocrats yielded a point to us here and there, never straying too far from the "règlement", leaving little room for innovative changes in the basic clauses of our film agreement with the government. "Clean as a whistle but rather unimaginative", John McCarthy used to say of them. The French did not lack in imagination. Not by a long chalk. It was just that for any number of good reasons they insisted on a protectionist policy in order to revitalize their own cinematographic industry.

For me it was time to seek change, my euphemism for excitement. I knew where to find it. It prowled the banks of the Tiber. However, I would not be really breaking my ties with Paris, merely shifting the emphasis to a country that had cunningly invented a unique life style. One to be explored and envied perhaps but imitated only at great risk.

In Paris, my lovely playmates were bound to forget me once I started missing our Thursday trysts. They were models for the French fashion house of Jacques Fath, then king of the French haute couture. Their dressing rooms faced the garden terrace of my small suite at the Queen Elizabeth hotel. Uninhibited, in their naked innocence they would sometimes wave to me across the narrow courtyard. One late afternoon a plastic bomb, planted by Algerian terrorists, exploded in the neighboring bar, shaking the hotel and the Fath studios. The girls looked panic-stricken. I waved a wine glass motioning them to join me. Half an hour later Adrienne, Vida, Sabine and Françoise were drinking champagne in my suite. Coquettish Adrienne started it all. "Let's play shades" she called out. "Not shades, silly. The English call it charades", said Vida. The girls generously "adopted" me. From then on, every Thursday, we played the French version of charades. My lovely nymphets were insatiable. I got to know them well.

It occurred to me that before departing for Italy, I should perhaps introduce them to my colleague, Michael. Quickly, selfishly I changed my mind realizing that once they met him I would be put out with the trash the next morning. I was no match for this handsome economist raised in the diplomatic circles of Canada where his father had served as ambassador of Greece. Soon after he joined the Paris staff, our executive secretaries Yvonne Favarger and Paula Azarian began referring to him as the "D'Artagnan de Montparnasse". They liked Michael's Parnassian subtlety, his contempt for the pedestrian, the facile control he wielded over even the most intricate business problems. His charm instantly captivated the opposite sex, so one could easily understand why women saw in him the irrepressible, romantic hero of the Dumas novel. This mousquetaire, Michael Sakellaropoulo, was not only daring but endowed with an elegant and sophisticated mind. It pleased me to think that in the absence of our chief, Gerry Mayer, our nerve center for Europe, the Paris operation, would continue to have the advantage of Michael's exceptional skills.

Just as I was about to take leave of Paris, cracks began showing at the top echelon of the MPAA. The ambitious vice president for international operations, John McCarthy, was grating some egos that should have been stroked instead. He wore a Harvard tie, had married rich, projected the image of a beau geste hero, though with the slightly rough-round-the-edges brashness of the innocent abroad, waived his flair and talent breezily about, all along incensing the already smoldering resentment among the envious. In his zeal for life's greater effervescence, he did not hear the aborigines sharpening their spears.

My curiosity periscope went up when I learned, by chance, that John's European expense records were being scrutinized. He was spending a good deal of money on travel and the entertaining of government officials, at times perhaps rather grandly, but the public relations results more than justified the drawing of comparatively negligible amounts from our otherwise non-transferable local bank accounts. Suspecting some form of mean internal intrigue that needed to be thwarted, I phoned John at the New York office to let him know something odd was afoot, not realizing an indiscreet third party had listened in on our conversation. There had never been any wire-tapping or deliberate eavesdropping at MPAA offices. It was just my bad luck and stupidity. I should have called him at his Connecticut home. One day this mistake, born out of friendship, would weigh heavily against me.

My first offices in Rome were at Piazza Navona where the intimidating men of the Bernini fountains stared into our windows. I did a fair amount of gazing in the opposite direction, taking in what was happening at the many sidewalk cafés and restaurants. One early evening

The Golden Years

I spotted several of my Italian friends, among them the ubiquitous Baron Belisario de Mattheis, engrossed in animated conversation with a very handsome female, who, I thought, strongly resembled Clare Boothe Luce. Dropping all pretense of formality -in Rome do as the Romans do-, I sat down at their table causing no discernible reaction. Too late I realized the person commanding all this attention was one of the beau monde's most intriguing personalities, the ebullient Diana Cooper. It was not my finest hour. I listened with mounting perplexity to her superbly witty, unrelenting, gossipy sniping at Rome's finest thoroughbreds, catching only that most of them were involved in some kind of incestuous relationship with each others cousins.

Paucity in mental agility thwarted my attempts to keep up with the zigzagging butterfly logic of this delightful creature. It did not really surprise me. I already knew that her husband, Duff, and many intimate friends had long proclaimed Diana Cooper undisputed world lightweight champion of the non sequitur. Her most devoted admirer, the writer Evelyn Waugh, lovingly referred to her speech pattern as "eccentric idiolect". From a chance remark she made as we were all saying arrivederci, I learned that my old friends of the Warsaw "panic" era, John and Aliki Russell were now with the British embassy in Rome. I was anxious to catch up with them hoping they might offer further qualified interpretation of the events that led to my leaving Poland with such uncommon haste. I was to run into Lady Diana soon again in the sparkling setting of Venice.

One of my first office visitors was John Perdicari, correspondent for the *Hollywood Reporter*. The big, hulky, hoarse-voiced, never to be intimidated Johnny was a born sentimental do-gooder. "Have a problem, tell Johnny, he'll fix it pronto". "Want results? Tell Johnny. He'll deliver". Thriving on controversy, never taking no for an answer, he made Italian government officials cringe and run for cover when provoked by their officious do-nothingness.

Johnny took an immediate liking to John McCarthy, cabling laudatory despatches about him at every turn from Rome and Paris. That was good but it was also bad. Useful here, disastrous there. Everybody who was anybody in show business read the *Hollywood Reporter* with the morning coffee. Some specific powerful persons suffered excruciating pains of spleen whenever McCarthy was described as the "real brains" behind the international success story of the MPAA. I feared the pains would have a cumulative effect, but my attempts to cool Johnny's exuberant "hurrahs" were all in vain, no matter how hard I tried.

I turned Johnny down at first, when he suggested I ask Giulio Andreotti, the Undersecretary of State, to award McCarthy an Italian decoration. To start with, I had always disliked the very idea of medals. They reminded me of Russian and banana republic generals, not to mention organ grinder monkeys. It also seemed to me that to approach the government official who had the final say in all matters involving our multi-million dollar film operations in Italy to solicit a decoration lacked dignity. I knew the Honorable Andreotti to be a very tough-minded individual with an aversion for trivia. His critics referred to this dour, quasi monastic political protégé of Alcide de Gasperi, Italy's first postwar prime minister, as an ardent disciple of the Machiavellian creed that evil acts of the ruled justify evil acts by the ruler. No flatulence here. I was more than a little surprised when he agreed to receive me. He knew how very much I disliked and openly criticized his director general of the film office, Nicola De Pirro, a pompous leftover from the fascist hierarchy when Mussolini's favorite medium, motion pictures, was under the strictest of Party controls, so he could hardly be fond of me. Moreover, he virtually never dealt with foreigners direct, leaving it to his subordinates. I suspected it was because he spoke no foreign language. In my case he would have no need for an interpreter. Ignoring persistent misgivings and only to appease the raging bull Johnny, at the last moment I added the matter of McCarthy's decoration to my agenda.

I watched him with a mixture of awe and envy. Exactly my own age, Andreotti was light years ahead of me in accomplishments; already the leading strategist of the Christian Democrat Party elite, deciding the political future of his country.

"Would you be kind enough to enlighten me why you believe the Italian government should bestow an onoroficénza on Mr.McCarthy?" The tone and phrasing of the question reflected Andreotti's typical biting irony. I had more than one answer for him, and if he thought his cleric teachers were good at turn-table, double-think sophistry, he should have met mine. But, I was here to praise Little Caesar, not to bait him. It would have been wrong to antagonize this rising star of the Christian Democrat Party which the United States and the Catholic Church had embraced as the only available effective antidote to social instability the Communists were so successfully fomenting. How the buffoons of postwar Western leadership managed to spawn in Italy the largest communist party outside of the Soviet Union from a background of fascism, was something no one would ever comprehend. Things went wrong because we were ignorant, greedy, dishonest, impatient and selfish. Also, because we thought we were better. I was not prepared to make further contributions to the already existing monumental record of American clumsiness by arguing about baubles, so I said nothing further.

I told Johnny to find another ally, referring him to my friend Baron de Mattheis of the Interior Ministry. Surprisingly they succeeded where I failed. McCarthy got his medal. And, as I feared, there was no limit to the rancour this basically innocuous sideshow provoked at MPAA's high command. John Perdicari just kept shooting his silver bullets over the horizon, woefully oblivious of whom they might wound. He was like the proverbial Russian bear crushing his human friend's face with a mighty blow, while only meaning to brush a bee off his nose.

Venice - San Marino - Rome

This was one of the duller Venice festivals. Our own films in the competition were far from brilliant and even the Italians had nothing extraordinary to offer. I could not help thinking that the lack of excitement was a sad commentary on this normally grand international event, to the success of which we had all devoted so much time, money and creative effort. During the past several years, I had been called many times to the stage of the festival palace at closing ceremonies and collected a total of 23 Golden Lions, Venice's top awards, on behalf of American actors, actresses, directors, producers and other talented cineasts.

The only exuberant burst of applause we got this time was on opening night. Just as we alighted from the limousine in front of the festival palace, hundreds of fans in attendance, klieg lights aglow, flash bulbs exploding, the beautiful star on my arm lost her panties. Daintily stepping out of them, she never lost stride, just smiled. A nimble photographer made a great show of arranging them in his breast pocket. White, they went well with his tuxedo. The crowd howled with delight.

After the movie performance, Bud Ornstein wanted to go to the Gritti Palace hotel where Elsa Maxwell, the ingenious professional party organizer for the société blasé, had invited us to meet the duke and duchess of Windsor. I was against going, pleading fatigue. Bud, whose chronic devotion to the beau monde had no limits, insisted we make an appearance, at least for Elsa's sake. It was a boring affair, with roughly fifty guests milling about, while the famous couple seemed to sulk in the far corner of the terrace. The duke did not offer to shake hands. Gwen, Bud's wife, was not about to curtsy to her countrywoman, the duchess. One might say it was a draw. We quickly moved away to join the stunning madame de Felcours, a friend of mine from Paris days. "Eugène, she said to me. Quelle déception. He is completely colourless and the poor woman a sort of unfulfilled Emma". "Amanda, aren't you being a bit cruel?" "On the contrary, I was magnanimous", she replied.

On the way back to the Lido in a motor-boat, I told Bud and Gwen the story of my favorite "Irishman". In Paris, I used to take my Irish Setter, named Sheriff, for a run in the Bois de Boulogne. One early morning, with no one about, I let him off the leash. Moments later he was romping round two other dogs on short leads, which I took to be schnautzers. Their owner was swatting away at my dog with a riding crop and probably hit him on the nose because Sheriff froze, then lifted his leg and peed on the aggressor's checkered trousers. Horrified, I tried to apologize. The man never said a word or gave me a glance. I was clearly at fault but this dog beating brute was infernally rude. I turned to Sherriff and said: "My boy, you are the only fellow I know of that ever peed on the Duke of Windsor and I thank you for it". To myself, I thought how fortunate the world was to have been spared his reign. The duke's, not the dog's.

When we got back to the hotel I received a call from Rome. It was Italo Gemini. "I will declare a strike next week unless our terms are met within the next 24 hours". Italo was the roly-poly, good natured, always obliging and smiling president of the Italian association of cinema owners. I actually feared sitting across the table from him because he was the sneakiest, lyingest, toughest negotiator I had ever encountered in the film business. Moreover, he had a large dose of this damn Italian charisma, with which I could never successfully cope. It was impossible to get angry with him. When he won a point, he looked anxious to apologize. When he lost one, he seemed ready to burst into tears. His phone call was not welcome. Italo knew it would be bothersome for me to leave Venice before the festival was over. More importantly, he was perfectly aware that our companies had already geared up for the new, autumn release season so that the closing of cinemas at this juncture would prove very disrupting and costly to both sides. Apparently Italo was prepared to take the gamble that we would yield to his demands. I wanted to call his bluff but could not do so without first consulting with all ten members of my film board in Rome.

Italo had phoned me at 2 o'clock in the morning, still relatively early by the festival standards. I found Bud and Gwen Onstein in the Excelsior bar listening to the great jazz pianist, Charlie Beal. I loved Charlie. In Paris, he introduced me to Sugar Ray Robinson, the finest boxer the world had ever known. The Champ took me riding in his fantastic purple Cadillac convertible, clockwise against the traffic, round and round the Étoile, causing a monumental traffic jam. Once they recognized Sugar, the tough Paris cops waived his fine. After our Paris adventure, I always got special treatment at Sugar's Velvet Club in Harlem.

Bud, Gwen and I reached a fast decision right there at the bar. Without going to our rooms to change or pack, black tie and evening gown complete, we took the hotel motor boat to where my car was garaged near the Venice railway station.

Bud did the driving. As we approached the city of Rimini, he turned to me saying: "wouldn't it be a gas to conquer San Marino?" This tiny enclave, a Republic of some 25 square miles, was only a brief detour away. Before we finished climbing the twisting road to the summit, Bud already had a "battle plan". We would inform the mayor of this one thousand population walled capital that only a few hours ago the authority over San Marino had passed to the Duca di Borgo Maggiore. "Would the mayor and councilmen have their resignations ready, per favore?" Bud's plan did not surprise me. He always had an incredibly inventive imagination and made all things sound simple.

It was just daybreak. The town hall empty. Bud settled for the uniformed guard, shaking him awake and instructing him to inform the mayor "immediatamente" that the troops of Il Duca di Borgo Maggiore were on their way and the most significant event in the history of San Marino would take place within a few hours. We could see that at first Bud's atrocious Italian accent confused the poor man, but when he exclaimed: "Dio mio, la guerra", we knew he would deliver our message.

On the way down the mountain we encountered a donkey cart blocking the road. Bingo, I said. For years I had been hoping for the chance to tell someone, anyone, anywhere in the world "get your ass out of my way", without actually being vulgar. Now I got my wish.

I shouted the command with great relish. Then, as I looked at the donkey again, it occurred to me that it was more deserving to say: "but for the grace of God, there go I."

There were no harmful consequences to this inane enterprise of ours. Merely a few amusing reverberations. The mayor of San Marino first called the military commander of the neighboring city of Rimini, asking for troop assistance. When Rimini refused, he appealed to Rome. There, the Ministry of Interior tried to identify the Duca di Borgo Maggiore, finding no trace because he existed in Bud's fertile imagination. The special police force, Carabinieri, quickly decided the whole thing was nothing but a hoax. We were told these details some weeks later by our precious friend Belisario de Mattheis when in a moment of weakness we revealed to him our grand "coup d'état". He promised not to betray us to his boss at the Interior Ministry.

In Rome, I sat down with Italo Gemini to argue our differences. For three days we had a knock-down, drag-out fight before the film board, which I chaired, authorized me to amend several provisions pertaining to playing time in cinemas and to make some other minor concessions. Italo hailed this a victory for the cinema owners. Actually we won because he could have squeezed much more out of us. I looked forward to my next tangle, this time with the Italian association of film distributors and producers. They were in for a huge surprise.

Rome

Fay Allport, the Association's manager for the United Kingdom phoned me from London to ask whether I could contact James Stewart on his arrival in Rome and extend the usual courtesies. While we were not as a rule terribly keen in the Motion Picture Association on getting involved with Hollywood personalities, this time I was delighted. Not only was Stewart my favorite actor, but I had heard many complimentary things about him from his professional colleagues and wartime military friends. Also, Fay Allport, an old pro in the film business, spoke so warmly of Stewart, I was nearly more anxious to meet this man they all called so special, than the actor.

I phoned the Excelsior hotel. They knew me there so I had no difficulty getting through to the Stewart apartment. His wife, Gloria, answered with a defensive air. I was prepared for this. Stars were invariably being pestered by fans and the press, sometimes by cranks. She was just being cautious and protective. Deciding I was genuine and respectable, she let Jimmy come on the line. I don't know why I was surprised he sounded exactly like Jimmy Stewart. That breaking intonation, half hesitant manner of speech his fans knew so well, was all there. Had I not known better, I would have thought somebody was putting me on. The Stewarts graciously accepted to dine at my home that same evening, after I assured them there would be no press, no surprises and an early good night.

It is rather easy to put on a big shindig but more complicated organizing a small, warm, smiling and intimate dinner party where guest compatibility is so essential. As always, Paul Baron was first on my list. This handsome, talented, sophisticated American of Sicilian descent invariably charmed all who met him. Luckily for me he had no other engagements. It was one of the evenings he meant to spend at home composing. "For you Van, I shall postpone creating my third movement. To be serious, nothing could make me miss an evening with James Stewart". I had another inspiration and called old man Murphy. Murph was an RAF chap serving as air attaché, with the British embassy. He had only a couple of years on me and we called him "Old Man" only because he addressed everybody that way. A true Irish wit, he told wonderful stories, could get amusingly tipsy but always the perfect gentleman, never drunk. Murph said: "Sorry old man I just can't make it." I shot back: "You'll regret it. Jimmy Stewart is coming to dinner, so pick up your date and be here by eight". I had him hooked. Murph loved to fly and knew that flying was Stewart's second vocation.

I managed to sneak the Stewarts out of the hotel without anyone noticing. Murphy put-putted in to my place with his MG and girl right on time. We had a good match. The evening turned out even nicer than I expected. Altogether, we were five couples. I had included Baron Belisario de Mattheis de Rocca Cinque Miglia and his current paramour. Belisario, Sario for short, proud of his Neapolitan heritage, had nobility in his soul though not always in his actions. I liked him. For reasons I could not quite fathom, Sario was devoted to me, always ready to do anything I asked him, no questions asked. He had attended Princeton. I never found out exactly what he did at the ministry of interior, but his services to me were invaluable.

We had drinks, a slow dinner, then speculated about the totally inexplicable spells Rome had cast on several of our Hollywood friends. Some heart-rending, others forbidding. Jimmy wanted to know what was it about the eternal city that caused many people who were normally rational suddenly to become unglued. Paul and I were privy to more than one secret and Sario, with his influence and ability to act swiftly, had saved many a reputation by preventing a potential scandal from erupting. I decided it would not do to talk about it and for a while there was an embarrassing break in the conversation. Wisely, Paul sat down at the piano and in moments his soft sentimental music carried us off to a dreamier, less complicated world. Earlier I had activated the automatic modulator which gently, unnoticeably changed lighting in the apartment creating different moods. Now we were all relaxed, drinking coffee and Cognac, arguing no purpose, facing no conflict.

Murph and Jimmy, sitting on the floor, were obviously talking aerobatics because we could see their hands executing complex manoeuvers. Both had earned their wings and served in the war. Now they were flying through their experiences again. We dared not interrupt them but watched fascinated and somehow touched because there was something particularly gentle about these warriors who were more like little boys with new toys, so locked in imaginary combat they didn't even know we were there.

I felt it a great pity but had to keep my promise, so at 11:30 I took the Stewarts back to their hotel. They thanked me for a "wonderful evening". Always polite, always gracious, the "wonderful evening" was their merit, not mine. When professional excellence is graced by nobility of character, as in the case of the Stewarts, it becomes a thrilling and stimulating experience.

For Rome it was still early. Paul and the baron were wide awake. We decided to visit Bud and Gwen Ornstein. Murph begged off. We crossed the river on to the Lungotevere and stopped in front of their residence called Palazzo Fiametta. The architect who designed it must have had a bad case of piles. From the outside this ancient, convoluted structure appeared to have only four stories. Inside, the several winding staircases took one to eight floors. Full of surprise chambers, it was a house straight out of Charles Addams. Standing within a few meters from the Tiber river, where the city sewers met, it combined rich brocade on its walls with rats in the basement. A deluxe nightmare. It wasn't, of course, but could well have been a 17th century cathouse.

Bud Ornstein, who went through his million dollar inheritance even before graduating from college, really did not belong in the 20th century. More likely at the court of Lorenzo de Medici, busy commissioning works of art or plotting romantic escapades to bedevil the Doges of Venice. His Beau Brummell taste for fashionable clothes, his exquisite manners, ritzy imagination and Oscar Wilde sense of irony made him Rome's favorite host. Bud would not be caught dead in a modern, deluxe, marble filled "ordinary" Rome house or apartment. That was for the moujiks, not for his majesty "Bud the Good" as I called him from the time the two of us had "conquered" San Marino.

Laughter drifted down from the upper floor. We swung open the iron gate and followed the noise. It was not the kind of party we expected. We had crashed a poker session. Prince Alessandro Torlogna was leering eyeball to eyeball at Bud who apparently just out-bluffed him, winning a major pot. Alessandro loved to gamble, could well afford it, but it infuriated him to lose.

Bud asked "out" from the game and came over to greet us. "The man is cheating again" he said, meaning Alessandro. He was just joking and smiled at Alessandro's wife, Infanta Beatrix. This exquisite lady, daughter of King Alfonso XIII of Spain, had her own brand of humor and called out to her husband: "Chi vive sperando, muore cacando" (he who lives with hope, dies making kaka). Bravo, I thought, here is one case where noblesse does not oblige dullness of spirit. "When were you last in Spain", she asked me. Actually, I had thought of her while in Toledo and for a very good reason. It was there that I was introduced to professor Gregorio Marañon, the eminent physician, world-famous hematologist; scientist on the one hand, writer, philosopher-educator on the other, called by many the father-trustee of Republican Spain, which replaced the monarchy. At our previous encounter Beatrix told me she knew a lot about professor Marañon from her father. They were not exactly on the same side but as far as Beatrix was concerned the great man's wisdom and unquestioned patriotism transcended all differences the two may have had in the political life of their country.

When I started talking she reacted like a delighted child, laughing, following my every word. She wanted to know more and more about the professor's son Gregorio Marañon Moya (became Spain's Justice Minister), the gay blade of Madrid and Paris and our association's attorney for Spain. From our frequent meetings, professional and as friends, I knew some of young Gregorito's personal secrets but these were not for telling. Not to Beatrix anyway.

I told her, instead, how Gregorito took me to Toledo, the city surrounded by Visigothic-Moorish-Spanish walls, where his father had converted an ancient monastery into his private residence. I talked about the Alcazar and the medieval bridges in this historic capital of New Castile where one had the feeling the clock stopped centuries ago. I told her about the Goya hanging in professor Marañon's private chapel, the Velázquez in the austere dining room where we lunched in awe of the great man, surrounded by many other of his treasures, all of which would go to the Prado museum on his death. I also told Beatrix, whom I knew to be well versed in contemporary European literature, how I attempted to extract from professor Marañon his views on Miguel de Unamuno. The two were intellectual antagonists exchanging many personal letters.

"That would take all day", he told me. "Let me just say this: I am above all a physician. Therefore, para mi el problema es la vida. Para Unamuno la vida más allá de la vida: la supervivencia. To me life is of all importance. Unamuno was not concerned with life but only with the beyond, the hereafter."

Beatrix sighed. "Thank you. Your words were like a magician's holographs. In my personal credo la realidad no importa. Lo que importa es nuestro ensueño. We must meet again soon". Reality doesn't matter. Only our dreams count, she had said.

Morning crept up on us. I had only three hours to rest before going to the office to chair a film board meeting. As the boss of United Artists, Bud would have to be there too.

As always, Eric Johnston was immaculate in dress, conservative in tie and, this time, wearing a brand new face lift. His mirror-practiced smile number 7 seemed nearly natural. We were on our way to see Claire Boothe Luce, the American ambassador to Italy. It was customary for any American VIP arriving in Rome to pay his or her respects to the official representative of our country. Eric Johnston, president of the Motion Picture Association of America, himself a special ambassador in the past for two American presidents, was a stickler for protocol. As soon as I heard he would be arriving, I phoned Mrs.Luce's secretary for an appointment. It was set for 11 am. By 11:15 Eric was obviously straining to keep his composure. At 11:40 we were still sitting in the embassy reception. I knew that my boss was boiling inside. But, this was Eric Johnston, the man of iron discipline who would bleed to death rather than show negative emotion or be upstaged. Mr.Iceberg took over. When Mrs.Luce at last emerged from her study, Eric's smile number 3, reserved for the powerful only, illuminated his face. One would never have suspected he did not like the lady. I was not privy to their conversation, but she invited us both to a reception at Villa Taverna, the ambassadorial residence, for the same evening.

When we arrived, the residence was already swimming in purple, with a sufficient number of cardinals there to hold a conclave. "Mrs Luce, I said, are you running for Pope? I immediately realized it was a feeble-minded, hairbrained quip. She winked at me. A convert to Catholicism, Mrs.Luce was an ardent believer. So much so that according to Rome's waggish tongues, she tried, during her first audience with the Pope to convert him as well until he convinced her he was already a Catholic. This was said not in mockery but with fondness. Everybody in Italy liked Mrs.Luce, except the communists and weak-kneed political compromisers whom she gave no reprieve.

As I had access to many sources I knew how much influence our ambassador wielded in Italy and how well she used it. To those who knew anything about her, and very few in the international world of diplomacy did not, it came as no surprise.

Her brilliant, penetrating mind, granite will, superb sense of timing and the ability to analyze and act on intelligence information made her the most effective American ambassador our country had in postwar Europe. Along the way, she gave Washington many a lesson on the difference between static and persuasive diplomacy. And, when impatient with congressional irresoluteness, she could deal harshly with legislators. Was she not the lady who felt no qualms saying in the U.S. Congress that "Senator Morse had been kicked in the head by a horse", and make both sides of the aisle love it?

At Villa Taverna the curtain rose, the actors were on the stage and the director did not seat Eric at the ambassador's table. My, my, I thought. At ours, we had the distinguished Italian writer, Alberto Moravia, of pronounced leftist leanings, whose novel *"La Romana"* and short stories *Racconti Romani* about the bourgeois Roman society and the spiritual apathy of modern Rome had brought him international recognition. Then, the celebrated conductor, Leopold Stokowski, and, finally, two skull-capped members of the high clergy. The combination was bizarre and I began to wonder if it was accidental or deliberate. Was a time bomb being set? Eric's grasp of foreign languages stopped at two words of Spanish. He could say "nada mas" very convincingly. Would Moravia settle for that? The clergymen handled English with studied finesse, but did Eric have an appropriate joke or story for them in his vast and carefully rehearsed repertoire? He used to tell one about Moses climbing the mountain to take some tablets which started the biggest movement the world had ever seen. I could not imagine what would have been the reaction had he ventured to use it now. That left Stokowski and here again Eric was on shaky ground. As far as I knew, his music appreciation ended with "Home on the Range".

I was sweating the proverbial blood trying to promote some cordial interaction, to get everyone involved. It proved quite impossible. The simple fact was that Eric Johnston always had to be the unrivalled center of attraction, surrounded by an acolyte audience. At this table no one was paying him particular attention so he could not give a shining performance. It was killing him.

Maestro Stokowski spoke good Italian,charming the clergymen. While not wishing to provoke the ire of my boss, I could hardly just sit there saying nothing to my neighbors. Speaking Italian, I turned to Moravia. We were friends of sorts, bumping into each other from time to time in a bar on the Lungotevere Flaminio and bantering over an espresso. He lived nearby and would wander over slowly with his stiff leg, assisted by a cane. He was anything but an extrovert, far happier when left alone. I never gushed over him or asked personal questions, so in our limited way, we got on very well. Now in the Villa Taverna garden he observed that our ambassador was to be envied because she represented a nation of political ideals devoted to the solving of international difficulties, whereas Italian politicians were so totally involved with inter-party struggles that it was less a question for them of solving problems than silencing those who raised them. We agreed to meet very early next morning at our favorite espresso bar.

With ill-concealed irritation, Eric motioned we should go. We did so without saying good-night to our hostess. This left me with a dose of confusion and considerable malaise. I felt sorry for Eric. The poor man was so obsessed with himself he could never enjoy anything. I remembered how one day in Venice I asked count Marzotto to put his luxury yacht at Eric's disposal. Paolo had his captain sail in from Genoa. An evening cruise on the waters of the Mediterranean reflecting the lights of St.Mark' s square are things dreams are made of. After less than an hour Eric had us return to port; there was no one on board to admire him. Then, just like tonight, he was in a hurry to leave but here were no further flights that day out of Venice. Without his knowledge I phoned the Italian Foreign Office. A special flight was put on for ambassador Johnston.

Now on returning to my apartment, after dropping Eric off at the Excelsior, I wondered how I would explain our rude behavior to Mrs Luce.

The Golden Years

Life can be so beautiful when it wants to be. This was one of those golden, subdued Sunday afternoons in Rome when one felt like defiantly punching the air.

The night before we had a party, a real blow out. We were still hungover, with that feeling of being somewhere between lucidity and opaqueness, when all appears to be in plausible perspective yet remains intriguingly indistinct. It was too early to begin boozing again, so when an extra group of friends turned up at my apartment, some of us decided to stroll over to the Parioli Tennis Club round the corner, just to watch.

We found Anthony Quinn on the court in his strictly-for-hackers effort to beat Prince Philipo Orsini. Quinn had a frightful tennis temper but he took it out only on his rackets. He was bashing one now, giving rise to much hilarity among the spectators.

One of our party, Bob Amon, had the instinctive reflexes of a karate black belt when struck with a real-life scene that would make a good movie. Here, right in front of him, was one of Hollywood's finest actors. Bob already cast him as Cesare Borgia, the consummate 15th century criminal politician. Blue-eyed, blond and handsome, Philipo would play himself, a few centuries back in history, when the Orsini family had gained the high appointment of lay acolytes to the Pope, an honor passed on for generations to the oldest son.

I felt uncomfortable revealing the recent unfortunate occurrence involving the Orsini family, but had to hobble Bob's imagination before he did something rash like approaching Anthony Quinn or, even worse, Philipo, causing him further embarrassment. Orsini's papal privilege had just been withdrawn. Philipo's unbridled passion for a pretty English actress was his undoing. Not that the Vatican disavowed sex, it just condemned his lack of discretion. Poor Philipo. His future was no longer what it used to be. More publicity was the last thing he needed. When I revealed his hapless tale, Gloria gave me an accusatory look as if I had committed some kind of barbarous act. Bob, her son-in-law, remarked: "that's what you get when you separate Rimsky from Korsakov". None of us had any idea what he meant by this profound observation. It must have been the sun.

We walked back to my apartment. Bill Holden was already at the bar mixing his definitely-not-the first drink of the afternoon. Friends were beginning to worry about "the golden boy" as his peers in Hollywood called him. He drank too much, too often.

Sleeping Dogs and Popsicles

Paul Baron, the pianist and composer, Rome's arbiter of elegance, the modern Petronius, was on the terrace flirting as usual with a delicious new Italian starlet. Frank Loesser was gently playing arpeggios on the piano and muttering something under his breath. I felt sure he was composing. He never seemed to stop creating, even in his sleep. I had seen him go into something like a trance, whether it be under the spitball-filled ceiling of the bar in his Hollywood home, or at the Algonquin in New York where he kept a suite, or walking down the Champs Élysées. Then one had to leave him be and simply wait till he "got back". It could be a new tune. Perhaps slangy, jargonistic lyrics. Sometimes both together, a perilous trap for less accomplished music-masters but a natural wedlock of song and words for Loesser. As a pianist, Frank was not quite Arthur Rubinstein but then Rubinstein never wrote "Guys and Dolls".

When I first met him in Paris, he was looking for Jacques Ibert. "You should hear his *Sinfonia Concertante* for Oboe and particularly his opera, *Le Roi d'Yvetot*, with its comic vein", he said to me. I confess to having been surprised discovering a musicologist in the man who started his career in New York as a singing waiter.

Why was Frank so keenly interested in a classical composer? Jacques Ibert was not then in France, but somewhere abroad, so I never really found out. He may have wanted to hire him. When I asked, he said "what me? The lesser composer hiring a major one?" I never forgave him this awful pun on his name. My question was not facetious. Frank was always trying to hire talent. He nearly got Tito Gobbi, La Scala's famous first baritone for his new musical until the shocked governors of the Milan Opera threatened to ban Gobbi for life if he dared appear on Broadway. This stuffed shirt attitude cost Tito a fortune.

Walking down the Champs Elysées one evening, in the kind of drizzle that reflects light from the pavements, Frank suddenly stopped and said: "I must get back to the hotel". He spoke no more, merely vanished into the lobby of the Lancaster.

The next day his wife, Lynn, told me Frank worked all night. By morning he had a new song to deliver to his publishers. Later, recalling that Paris episode, I wondered whether the lyrics went: "Standing on the corner, watching all the girls go by".

Now in my Rome apartment Paul joined Frank at the piano and asked "Whom are you plagiarizing from this time?" Paul had said it in jest. Frank took it very seriously, responding: "Every composer plagiarizes, either consciously or by musical osmosis. It is inevitable". Smetana got his inspiration from Slavonic folk music, Chopin stole from Liszt and Liszt from Chopin. Both borrowed from Mozart and others. The examples could go on forever."

"Frank, you're absolutely right. Let me demonstrate". Maestro Baron took over the keyboard. "We all know that boogie-woogie style of piano playing springs from the Blues, don't we? Now listen. "He played Chopin's Polonaise in A Flat Major. "Did you hear some boogie-woogie there? How about this?" Parts of Mozart's piano concerto in D Minor actually sounded real boogie-woogie. "And to confound you even further, I shall play for you the syncopated section of a Beethoven piano sonata where piano jazz really began". I couldn't tell a dominant from the tonic musical form but our ears did not lie. Paul had it right. It was all there. "Well, Frank remarked, remember what Duke Ellington says: it don't mean a thing if you ain't got that swing." Frank could switch from the scurvy of the vernacular to classical elegance and back again without the benefit of harmony. Crashing a cacophonic cord on my Bechstein, he turned to us and said: "Listen you pompous bums. Once upon a time, four hundred years before Christ to be exact, there was a guy called Plato. According to him a change to a new type of music is something to beware of because the modes of music are never disturbed without unsettling of the most fundamental political and social conventions. And, in my new music I'm saying balls to convention. Got it?"

Then, as if apologizing for his outburst, Frank began to play and sing. He bewitched us through the afternoon and evening, stopping only to sip scotch. We listened enthralled to the sorcerous music and lyrics from his musical *Guys and Dolls*, and the yet unpublished *Hans Christian Anderson* melodies. Gloria saw me watching her. She looked away but not before I caught the sadness of her eyes. I knew from her daughter, Michelle, that she had moments of precognition, of clairvoyancy. Was this one of them?

A precariously placed cognac snifter on the green marble bar fell and shattered, startling her. Pretending to swoon she slowly slumped to the floor under the piano. "Sic transit Gloria", Bill muttered.

"That's a real crock so stay silent" she countered, then adding: "Yond' Cassius has a lean and hungry look. He thinks too much; such men are dangerous". Not to be outdone, Bill came back with: "Come, woo me, woo me; for now I am in a holiday humour, and like enough to consent".

They were off. Shakespeare and Milton, Tennyson, then Shakespeare again. I recognized some T.S. Eliot, too.

They re-enacted several scenes from their memorable film *Sunset Boulevard*, sometimes forgetting the original lines, improvising without hesitation, thrilling us with their trained, marvelously resonant voices.

William Holden, Gloria Swanson, Frank Loesser and Paul Baron blending their talents gave us a night worthy of Caesar.

Bill had been drinking all the way through. Frank popped pills as was his habit for years. Downers laced with liquor to sleep, uppers to wake up. Booze and drugs. So I cried inside and I cursed their urge to selfdestruct because they were my friends.

Did Edna St. Vincent Millay have them in mind when she wrote:

> "My candle burns at both ends;
> It will not last the night;
> But ah, my foes, and oh my friends-
> It gives a lovely light"

I felt humbled in the presence of so much talent. I saw myself in that famous *New Yorker* cartoon that depicted a miserable twirp looking at his reflection in a full length mirror and a voice saying: "you don't have an inferiority complex, you ARE inferior".

It was four in the morning. Holden fell asleep on the couch and even the piano must have felt exhausted. Not Gloria. This notorious night owl had to see a Roman sunrise. I took her to the Giannicolo, the hill above Saint Peter's Basilica and Vatican City. We waited till the air shimmered in the sunlight of early dawn, reflecting the orange hue of the travertino stone buildings below. It was magic surrounded by stillness. I told her about the current gossip that the Pope had taken a nun for his mistress. "Thou has committed fornication? But that was in another country: besides, the wench is dead". With that quote from Christopher Marlowe, Gloria fell asleep on my shoulder.

Before leaving Rome she sent me a present. It was a beautiful Siamese kitten. Her daughter Michelle brought it to me.

Venice

Our French press reviewer at the MPAA Paris office sent me a clipping which read something like this: "With its usual boorish lack of finesse and perspicacity, the American Congress has approved the nomination of Mrs. Perle Mesta as ambassador to Luxembourg. Mrs. Mesta has superb credentials for membership in the American diplomatic corps, acquired patiently, one might even say expensively, at America's finest academy -cocktail parties in Washington-, where she is known as the hostess with the mostest.

Why the President of the United States so munificently honors Luxembourg is difficult to guess unless he hoped the gesture would serve as an apology to Grand Duchess Charlotte for General Eisenhower's gaucherie when he declared that he had never believed in immaculate conception until he met Luxembourg women.

At the time I paid scant attention to this product of the scurrilous leftist journal. Hardly did I imagine that during the next Venice film festival I would be sitting tête-à-tête with ambassador Mesta in the deserted bar of the hotel Excelsior, desperately trying to hide my deep embarrassement and wishing I were somewhere else instead. Like Peking perhaps.

It was the night of the most publicized social event of the decade, the Charles de Bestegui costume ball at Palazzo Labia. The jeunesse dorée, the rich fané, the beau monde trend-setters of every nationality had talked of nothing else for months. To be among those honored was the question. The Bestegui public relations team played it well: very limited secret guest list, invitations strictly personal, delivered by special messenger, names top drawer only. The film festival was eclipsed by the Bestegui fever. For the date of his reception all movie activities were cancelled.

The John McCarthys, who brought along Hollywood' s Irene Dunne as well as their personal friend, the piquante copper heiress Barbara Wilkens, were on the Bestegui list; their enthusiasm boundless. For them it would be a memorable night of conspicuousness. To me an evening of palpitating awkwardness, not easily forgotten. I had taken it for granted Perle Mesta would be going to the ball. Only when I saw John and his friends leave without her did I realize that we had committed an outrageous blunder. Unbelievably, of all people, MPAA's honored guest, our ambassador, the hostess with the mostest had not received an invitation to Bestegui's bal masqué. That's why I was slowly dying in the Lido bar, feeling worse by the minute as I listened to this charming, versatile, politically sophisticated lady speak of America's commitments and global responsibilities. Cocktail circuit graduate indeed. Perle Mesta could have given lessons on diplomatic skulduggery to Cardinal

Richelieu. Our ambassador retired to her suite at midnight, thanking me for my company, too subtle to even mention the grand social event we had made her miss.

Knowing I would not be able to sleep, I phoned the chief of Venice police. Guido had already gone home but had left instructions with his staff to provide me with an official police motorboat and crew if I asked. Thirty minutes later we pulled up to Palazzo Labia. Guido's lieutenant had brought me a bersagliere cape, feathered hat and a mask. The guards saluted, letting me through.

I could not find McCarthy or his friends in the kaleidoscope of costumed crowds. Then suddenly, in a candle-lit arcade, I saw Tiepolo's Cleopatra step out of the famed painting that graces the walls of Palazzo Labia. It was the delectable Diana Cooper. From behind my mask I said: "Salve Divina". "Ciao Amore", she replied.

Mrs.Mesta left Venice early the next morning, before I was up. Another gaffe committed. I resolved not to mention our gross ineptitude to anyone. Regretfully, I had completely forgotten about hawkeye-the-sleuth Johnny Perdicari. The omnipresent defender of the faith, Sir Galahad, unabashed nosy newshound, somehow ferreted out the story, putting it on the wire, finger pointed.

Eric attempted an apology sending Perle Mesta flowers when we all happened to be in Paris some weeks later. I caught his card just in time. He had addressed it: Mrs *Pearl* Mesta.

Rome

It was easy to understand why she would always be remembered as "America's Sweetheart". Lovely to look at, fun to be with. A doll just unwrapped, blue eyes gazing at the world in surprise. That was Mary Pickford. Romans followed her. Buddy Rogers, her husband, watched over her. We adored her. Time ignored her. She was fabulous.

She loved to dance. I was her favorite partner. When tipsy, she would press one of her precious jewels into my hand. A diamond ring, a Cartier brooch. Once she even slipped a string of pearls into my pocket. To avoid offending her I pretended to accept the gifts. Only when Buddy put the exhausted Fairy Princess to bed would I return the jewels to her niece, Gwen Ornstein. By morning, Mary had no recollection of her largesse.

Charlie Chaplin was there too. He kept to himself, rarely addressing a word to any of us. Mary warned us to give him space. He wandered into

Mary's hotel suite during that uninspiring afternoon's mental haze when we had just about recovered from the previous night's hangover but were not quite ready to start working on a new one. He picked up a light straight-back chair, wrapping himself round it in the center of the room. We hushed. For the next hour he dizzied us. It was Nero's burning Rome, braggadocio Mussolini, a half dressed timid maiden, Churchill chewing his crapulent cigar. He teased, mocked, threatened and tossed us round from mood to mood. When we could hardly breathe, Charlie stood up, face contorted, lips irate. Draped in table-cloth, the long stem of a flower cutting across his forehead, he berated the Roman Senate. He was Cicero denouncing Catiline's conspiracy. His Latin pure, the cadence perfect. It took me a while to realize that apart from Catiline's name, none of it was Latin but a pastiche of Chaplin-invented meaningless phrases. Charlie joined us in our laughter.

Mary was astonished. "I have known this man nearly all my life and only twice before did I hear him put a voice to his act. Do not assume, that this afternoon Charlie just happened to wander into my drawing room to amaze us all with his spontaneous improvisations. I can tell you that every word and gesture were carefully rehearsed. Talent is a God-given gift. Nurturing it takes patience and sacrifice. Charlie is the ultimate perfectionist. During my long career I have had an inside look at the lives of many accomplished individuals and I know that not one of them got to be famous on talent alone".

Later that evening Mary told us about a reception she and Douglas Fairbanks once gave for movieland notables at Pickfair, their Hollywood home. They had just returned from a trip to the Orient with their newly hired Japanese butler. Charlie, their friend, partner and neighbor was among the guests. He arrived late, creating a good deal of fuss. A group formed round him. When Mary approached she was astonished to hear Charlie speaking fluent Japanese with her new butler. "Whenever Charlie stopped speaking, the butler would bow twice, laugh and carry on the conversation. Then Charlie would bow and talk. It went back and forth so mesmerizing my guests that they all started laughing and bowing to each other. When Doug came in and saw them bobbing up and down, believe me, he thought our butler had served some spellbinding oriental potion that drove them all mad. And Charlie? When I accused him of holding out on us with his extraordinary language abilities, Charlie assumed the air of hurt innocence as if to say: don't all Californians bow when they speak Japanese? Later he confessed to me that the day before the party he had secretly paid our butler twenty dollars to answer him in rapid Japanese when he made a fist, no matter what gibberish he heard".

I had read this story somewhere before, not quite trusting it. Now, after Charlie's Roman Senate Latin parody I could believe it, even without Mary's eyewitness account.

Late evening, Mary took us all to dinner at Alfredo's. No one could be a more appropriate hostess at this famous fettucine restaurant than Mary because it owed much of its fame to her and Douglas Fairbanks. Years before, they had presented the owner with solid gold spoons in appreciation of his culinary art and hospitality. Old Alfredo was still there, now bowing deeply to Mary, showing off his precious spoons, shedding tears of pride and joy. It was a late, late party.

Several days later Bud Ornstein was advised that on the following Monday the Italian government wished to honor Miss Pickford with a special decoration. Naturally Mary was delighted. "But Monday? Why, I am spending a long weekend with dear friends in Paris" she cried. And that was that. Nothing could change her mind. After Bud's many frantic phone calls to the Italian Foreign Ministry it was arranged for Mary to receive the decoration from the Italian Ambassador to France. For me the timing was most opportune as I had to be in Paris the following week to host a luncheon for Walt Disney.

The decoration ceremony was held in the magnificent gardens of the Italian embassy, on a beautiful sunny morning, attended by distinguished members of the diplomatic corps. Mary was exquisite and ecstatic. Buddy kept a careful watch on her champagne glass, not letting it be filled too often. Bud and I could hear her laughter as we ducked out of the embassy for the Disney lunch at the Ritz.

It was against his rules to call him Mister Disney. He was Walt to everyone. Extremely shy, Walt avoided personal appearances. Fans, applause, praise embarrassed him. We had difficulty persuading him to attend the luncheon offered in his honor by the French film industry. He accepted only because its purpose was to promote contributions to a fund for the underprivileged children of Paris. There was no limit to Walt's generosity where children were concerned. Every year, he would instruct his French releasing company to hire, at his expense, the Paris Circus for a special grand benefit performance followed by a Disney movie. All of Paris waited for this event and the French too knew how to be generous.

Poor Walt cringed through the eulogy-filled luncheon. His own speech was brief, ending with "whatever task you undertake, give it your best effort."

Venice

Most of them were very, very nice. A few were uncooperative or plain horrid. In planning American participation at the Cannes or Venice film festival I would ask Hollywood studio bosses to cooperate by sending us a star or two. Quite naturally, they would try for an actor or actress featured in the film being presented in competition. The battle between the festival governing bodies and the companies over the selection of titles went on year after year. Cannes and Venice wanted films they thought would best appeal to the critics, thereby, presumably, enhancing the prestige of the organizers and juries. The companies favored those with the best box-office potential since a title accepted in competition was automatically accorded an above quota free import license, and exempted from high dubbing fees. Protectionist import and screen quotas were a source of never ending friction between the American film industry and foreign governments. Roughly speaking only one third of each company's productions were seen by European audiences. Despite such onerous restrictions, American movies commanded a very major share of the total box office receipts due to their popular appeal, also thanks to our highly persuasive distribution methods which included block booking, the bane of cinema owners.

This particular year in Venice, Metro-Goldwyn-Mayer was presenting *Ivanhoe* starring Joan Fontaine and Robert Taylor. The movie, though an expensive spectacular, was not likely to impress the blasé, hypercritical jury. Dr.Antonio Petrucci, president of the organizing committee, accepted it only when appeased by my promise that Joan Fontaine would be present at the festival. As soon as he gave out the news, the press, producers and even members of the jury phoned me with congratulations. It was a matter of national prestige for Venice to outshine France's Cannes film festival. Competition between the two countries was always fierce so I understood their excitability. I too felt pleased and relieved because this year, more than ever, the American side needed all the help it could get to compete with the new brilliant talents of Italian and French cineastes who were dazzling the world with their phantasmagoric creations.

The morning following Miss Fontaine's arrival at the Lido, I organized an on-the-air press conference. A well known Italian journalist threw her the first curve, maliciously asking how she liked her role in the "horse opera" *Ivanhoe*. Without hesitation she answered: "it gave me great pleasure to be reunited with Sir Walter Scott". A wonderfully diplomatic answer if I ever heard one. Clearly, the press boys needed to sharpen their wits in a hurry, or be eaten alive by this sophisticated lady.

To get away from the stereotype, commonplace champagne-cum-caviar receptions that every participating nation spent big money on year after year, entertaining hundreds of official delegates and journalists from all over the world, not to mention high numbers of gate-crashers, we decided this year to do something different.

A full three months before the festival's opening date we formed a committee of the publicity heads of 20th Century Fox, Metro-Goldwyn-Mayer, Paramount, Columbia and Warner Brothers, with the overall supervision going to Fox's European publicity manager in Paris, Giulio Ascarelli.

The barren end of the Lido island, far from the hotels and the festival palace, was selected as the site for a "Wild West" party. Our experts went to work, first pulling six kilometers of electric cables, then connecting them to several thousand multicolored lights placed in newly planted trees and bushes. Carloads of potted plants and flowers created miniature gardens. Three and a half tons of lumber were used for corrals and bunkers. Western covered wagons built to order were shipped in from Verona. Hundreds of stuffed toy animals, for after-the-party souvenir gifts, came from Florence. Thirty four magnificent horses were transported to the Lido from stables in Bologna. Rome shops supplied cowboy hats, scarves and toy pistols. As the centerpiece, an enormously tall flagpole was erected from which the American flag would fly.

The Venice authorities thought us totally insane. "Sono matti da legare" -straight-jacket nuts- they called us. But, at the same time they allowed us to circumvent safety regulations, city ordinances, and all other official rules that might have impeded our project. Italians, forever dedicated to imaginative innovation regardless where it comes from, shared our enthusiasm. Without their co-conspiracy our party-reception would have never materialized. After twelve weeks of intense and often frustrating effort, the Wild West set was finally ready. We hired a troupe of dancers and an orchestra. I had gone so far over budget it made me shudder to think what the film companies would say when I presented them with the bill.

As news of the special American party got round, the company publicity men and I were besieged day and night by knowns and unknowns of every nationality seeking invitations. Phone calls were coming in from as far as Melbourne and Mexico City.

It was dark and hot. We arranged for our guests to be transported from their hotels in darkness, the guides using only flashlights. When all four hundred were seated, the sound of bugle pierced the night. Simultaneously, powerful search-lights spotted our high flying flag and the American ambassador, Ellsworth Bunker. As he finished his brief welcoming address, thousands of multicolored lights switched on, revealing fantasy-land. One could hear the gasps of delight.

Just as the waiters, dressed as cowboys, started serving and the show was about to begin, thunder rumbled. Then lightning scarred the sky. Torrential rain came down on us without warning, dousing candles. Electric wires fused, horses panicked and bolted, tables overturned. It was sudden, total pandemonium. I felt like crying. First for myself and my publicity team, then for the five chefs whose magnificent culinary creations were now being drowned.

A familiar cheery voice coming from under one table called my name. I dropped to my knees. There, sitting on the muddy ground, laughing, nose to nose with the Italian undersecretary of State, wet evening gown clinging, was the incredible Joan Fontaine. Her sense of humor, her reaction so courageous and amusing, spread like magic. In minutes all our guests were sheltering under tables, wine bottles in hand.

A glance round instantly cured me of all self pity. This was a photographer's dream. We had invited thirty of the very best internationally known professionals. They were at work crawling under tables, taking shots of dignitaries in undignified positions, of beautiful ladies with mascara streaking down their faces. I never thought I would hear any woman, whose Shubert exclusive evening gown was being totally ruined, shriek with delight. Hollywood's gorgeous French import, Corinne Calvet, was doing just that. True, we were rained out. Yes, all our work of months destroyed in minutes. But the Gods favor show people, for we wound up with the most hilarious, unforgettable party Venice had seen in a very long time. The photos proved it. They appeared across the world. The publicity was stupendous. Giulio Ascarelli phoned from Paris a week later to thank and congratulate us.

I was happy for other reasons as well. None of the four hundred guests sued us for ruining their evening clothes and the film company managers overlooked the size of the bill. The "Wild West" party turned "Rain Dance" party got me off the hook.

The same night, after two in the morning, a new group of English, German and Spanish photo-reporters arrived on the Lido, requesting a photo session with Miss Fontaine. I hated to do this but after identifying myself to the switchboard I phoned: "Would Milady mind very much talking with journalists again this late?" She had been asleep, I could tell, but her answer came quickly:"that's what I'm here for". Thirty minutes later, smiling and perfectly groomed, she faced the admiring gentlemen of the press. Had she not been quite so beautiful, I would have had the courage to kiss this gracious and disciplined star. "Isn't she just marvellous "I said to no one in particular. "Breeding, chum, breeding", muttered an English photographer standing next to me.

Next morning I was up early. So was Italy's foremost publisher Angelo Rizzoli. He caught me at the espresso bar. Would I arrange for Miss Fontaine to meet with him and Federico Fellini within the next hour or so to discuss a film project? It would not have been politic to turn down Rizzoli whose millions financed major film productions. And Fellini? He was the wonder boy of Italian cinema who always had intriguing ideas.

At first Federico talked calmly, explaining the story, carefully watching Joan Fontaine's reaction. There did not appear to be any. He switched to a louder tone, now prancing about the room, gesticulating, acting out the parts. Rizzoli loved it. I thought he was a convincing performance. But the plot called for two equally important female roles. Joan demurred. Fellini looked crushed.

The year following Joan Fontaine's unforgettable success, Hollywood sent us another famous actress, Claudette Colbert. Would she too become the Queen of Venice? It didn't turn out that way. The festival had temporarily lost its sparkle. The weather turned nasty. The films selected for presentation to the international jury were not of the highest caliber. Miss Colbert showed no enthusiasm for meeting the press, keeping very much to herself.

Claudio Vila, the winner of many song festivals, called "Italy's Bing Crosby" by his fans, arrived in Venice at the invitation of the festival organizers. He was young, he was famous and really quite humble. He asked me to offer Miss Colbert several of his most successful recordings as a token of his admiration. If it were possible to pay his respects in person, he told me, he would be "truly overwhelmed with joy".

I thought this was a very nice gesture on Claudio's part and a good photo opportunity. My idea's legs were promptly broken when Miss Colbert declared that she was not about to provide publicity for "some Italian singer" and would I please return his records to him. I was too embarrassed to face him. What could I possibly say to lessen the insult?

He must have guessed the truth when I failed to get back to him. Mutual friends later reported Claudio was deeply hurt. I never saw him again. His voice, constantly on Italian radio, kept my embarrassment alive for a very long time.

Then there were the crazies. The troglodytes, the insensitive, the vulgar, the spoilers. Arthur Koestler had a more polite word for them. He called them "mimophants", -a hybrid species, a cross between a mimosa and an elephant. A member of this species is sensitive like a mimosa when his own feelings are concerned and thick skinned like an elephant trampling over the feelings of others.

Two actors, Rex Harrison and his then current wife, Lili Palmer earned not only the double mimophant award but a few other, far more pungent titles, at their first and last Venice Film Festival.

Columbia Pictures was presenting *The Four-Poster* with justified high hopes of capturing a top prize. The film, starring Rex and Lili, was of the calibre even the most discerning critics would have had to acclaim. My colleagues from Columbia felt really smug that year. A Venice prize, or even a favorable mention by the renowned international jury automatically translated into vastly enhanced box office receipts round the world.

I traced Harrison and wife Palmer in Rapallo, Italy, a month before the opening date of the festival, inviting them to attend the official showing of their film. We agreed on the specific date and time of their arrival at Lido-Venice, so that the press could be advised, cocktail parties arranged and, last but not least, rooms made available at the Excelsior hotel which, if not secured from block-bookers far in advance, could not be had for anyone or at any price.

Rather pleased with the arrangement I had made for Columbia Pictures, because the presence of featured stars at a gala performance would bring more publicity and add to the glamor of the occasion, I certainly did not foresee any complications or problems lurking round the corner, even though I had been warned the couple was notorious for vile tempers and abominable manners. What could possibly go wrong in the fairytale setting of Lido-Venice? Something did, and with a bang.

I was hosting a black tie dinner in honor of the new Argentine ambassador to Rome. Other guests included the Undersecretary of State, the Director General of the Italian Foreign Office, the Inspector General of the Italian film industry and the Chargé d'affaires of the French embassy. All accompanied by their wives.

As the ambassador rose to return my toast, an infernal racket could be heard from the lobby. The hotel's manager appeared at my elbow to whisper that my festival guests had arrived and would I please go to the lobby immediately. Managers of famous luxury hotels are not easily ruffled but this one seemed close to panic. I apologized to my dinner guests and rushed downstairs.

To my horror, I saw Rex Harrison holding the reservations manager by his jacket lapels, already ripped in half, screaming insults at the poor man. I quickly approached to intervene. A desk clerk called out my name. "Aaa" growled Harrison leaping at me. He seemed to have a special grudge against lapels. In one instant mine were gone. Fine beginning, I thought. What next? One had to see the "next" to believe it, for now came the charge of the light brigade in the form of gentle Lilli Palmer. Her series of barnyard invectives outclassed anything I had ever heard. The flashing long red fingernails looked menacing. I retreated behind the manager. Lapels were one thing, a bloodied face something else. The volume of their combined shouting carried not only throughout the vast hotel but down to the motorboat moorings beneath the lobby from where burly attendants appeared to investigate the commotion. We now had a large audience, including a dozen or more bulb flashing photo reporters of every nationality to whom, when they recognized Harrison and Palmer, the fracas came as a real front page bonus. For me it was an unmitigated embarrassment, all the more so because also my dinner guests came down to find out what was happening.

The Italian general manager of Columbia Pictures and I tried reminding the wild couple they were guests as well as representatives of the American motion picture industry at Italy's prestigious film festival; the world press watching.

The return volley was so loud it could have bounced off St. Mark's Basilica miles away: "F... the American movie industry, F... the Italians, F... the press, the festival and F... you".

The burly boys from the landing dock, my friends from previous festivals, moved closer to Rex and Lilli signaling to me they were about to throw the two into the canal. I was sorely tempted to let them do it, knowing they would not be allowed to drown. But what if they got pneumonia? Reluctantly, I waived my friends off.

A most extraordinary thing then occurred. Turning backs on the actors, all photographers present exposed their films, ostentatiously yanking them out of their cameras. The crowd fell silent.

In all my experience, never had I seen the working press so totally, unanimously and spontaneously protest vulgarity. The reporters destroying their sensational photographs made it clear they would not submit a single photo, a single line of text about the stars or their movie for publication. By so crassly insulting the festival, the host country and the press, Harrison and Palmer had not only willfully thrown away priceless personal international publicity but caused enormous financial damage to a fine film for which Columbia Pictures had paid them very handsomely.

Why the megalomaniac fury? Their rooms were not ready because they had arrived a full day ahead of schedule.

I wondered how I could ever explain away the events of that evening to my diplomatic friends. I need not have worried. One week later, in Rome, the Argentine ambassador sent me a gift of pearl cuff-links with a note:

> Muy Querido Amigo,
> Estupendo! The most exciting floor show we ever saw. Gracias. You must join us for cocktails next Thursday. OP

Rome

I was now beginning to put together the operating mechanism which would allow me to implement the plan I had formulated in my mind before leaving Paris, concerning the fundamental revisions in our agreement with the Italians. I needed leverage. A lot of it.

I had two natural allies: the Vatican and Professor Max Hussman. Both were money avid. Max needed to support his many student scholarships. The Vatican, to emulate Vespasian, the Roman emperor who's motto "pecunia non olet" -money has no odor- helped restore the economic stability of the Empire after the civil wars.

The bona fide of our companies had already been validated with St. Peter by their substantial Lira "donations" to the Holy See. Heavenly bookkeepers must have been thoroughly puzzled why gentlemen with names like Cohen, Loew and Balaban were being so generous with Mother Church. No one had told them that our company presidents had placed their trust in the wondrous ability of the Vatican Bank for Religious Works to instantly convert Catholic Italian lire into kosher American dollars and, after receiving His Eminence Francis Cardinal Spellman's costly blessings, deposit them to film accounts in New York. A most admirable practice until these frequent charitable contributions began to strain the credulity of even the most faithful and had to be discontinued. Fortunately, without depriving us of St. Peter's saintly flow of information and advice.

Professor Max Hussman, founder of the world famous Swiss school for boys at Montana was Merlin incarnate. During a many-hour secret train journey through the Swiss Alps,arranged by British intelligence agents near the close of the military campaign in Italy, he single-handedly persuaded general Wolf, the commanding German officer in Northern Italy, to surrender his troops to Allied forces. Max described it all in his book called *The Broken Axis*.

On retiring, Max chose Rome as his permanent residence. Here, wisdom and character were not his sole instruments of persuasion. The multiple drawers of his wall safe contained the most extensive confidential dossier on Italian personalities ever assembled by a private individual. It all began when Max, in a private interview so impresssed Mussolini with his personality and vision of Italy's future that Il Duce authorized Italians to send their sons to Montana, the only foreign educational institution accorded such privilege during the Fascist regime. After the war "Max's boys", now grown men, became key players in Italian politics and business. They were dedicated to maestro Hussman from whom they would have no secrets. What started as a hobby became Max's second nature. By the time I met him the files on Italians of prominence and influence had reached truly impressive proportions. Thanks to the peephole he had into the outhouses of their conscience, compliance with his suggestions was axiomatic. Max used his powers with discretion. He gave me limited access to the files and only on a need to know basis.

My first priority was to ascertain, through my own connections, which sector of Italian industry would be most readily approved by the political and other powers to benefit from the premiums American companies were willing to pay for government-authorized transfers to the United States of very substantial and constantly accumulating motion picture funds blocked in Italian bank accounts. The Director General of the Ministry of Finance, having been assured by mutual acquaintances of my grateful discretion, confidentially advised me to explore the matter with his intimate friend, head of Finmeccanica, Italy's largest government holding that controlled 67 major companies in almost every branch of the engineering industry.

Italy is much more peculiar than it appears. It is particularly dangerous to people who think they know it well. To virtually any imaginable situation Italians are capable of adding some last minute rococo feature of their own, -an originality that can inflict sudden incontinence on the unwary. I had to be extremely cautious, tread gently between the different spheres of economic influence held monopolistically by specific political parties.

After four months of mutual feinting, dodging, dickering trade-offs and dissembling, Finmeccanica's chief executive agreed to accept a formula which, while formally respecting government regulations, would unofficially provide for a flow of hidden funds needed to assure frictionless cooperation of the Foreign Exchange Office, the Presidency of the Council of Ministers, the Bank of Italy & America, of the film trade associations and a number of other assorted components of the Italian bureaucracy, which if not appropriately muted, would surely obstruct or even defeat our design.

After exhaustive and at times heated discussions about ethics, principles and final objectives, I persuaded Max to become chief of staff and financial administrator of the hidden funds. He agreed with the understanding he alone would have direct and total responsibility for administering of what was known in Italy as "la bustarella" -the bribe envelope. It was just what I hoped for and would not have had it any other way. "I shall be most careful to effect no casualties, no victims, among our chosen friends, he said. I shall reward many, punish none. They will all be sworn to secrecy and not know of each other".

Incomparable Max. One day, when our system was in full operation, I discovered, entirely by chance, that some of his "rewards" were advance tuition fees paid to American and English colleges. The Italian parents of the lucky students would, I knew, be forever indebted to him.

The part of my Paris promise to Eric Johnston concerning the remitting of company frozen funds was now a reality. Though it took longer than I expected, no one really believed it could be done at all, so I felt reasonably pleased with myself. One big question continued to bother me. The professed premise of lending financial support to Italian industries was, in fact, pure fiction, a sham. While the bulk of the monies released from blocked accounts was being officially transferred direct to film companies in the United States, the remainder, the so-called premiums, were disappearing into the personal wallets of various officials instead of helping finance Finmeccanica projects. Cui bono? We had agreed with Max that the payoffs would be his exclusive domain. Still, I had to ask.

Max seemed exasperated. "Cosi fan tutti" he bristled. "And was not this the whole idea? I now have two major institutions and nine key officials on my direct payroll. Add to that the secondary distributions and you will see where the money goes to buy us support and obedience. Denaro, always the all important denaro, he grumbled. Se mio sedere avesse soldi, se chiamarebbe Don Sedere (even my ass would be called "Sir", if it had money). And, do remember that when you were in New York with the Italian delegation and I phoned suggesting we amend the allocation formula, you strongly objected because it would have meant taking a bite out of St. Peter's share as well, something you did not wish to allow". "Yes Max, you are right". I recalled that visit to New York very well because John McCarthy, the only person I trusted to understand the complexities of the Italian situation had already been forced to resign. I had no one to confide in. Eric had replaced McCarthy with some sophomoric mistletoes bowing on command, whose only mission was to feed his ego. Surreptitiously, they listened in on Max's call to me. A friendly secretary tipped me off. I pretended not to know and teased the eavesdroppers with double talk phrases in French and Italian, hoping it would all be recorded and later translated. In any language it was still gobbledygook. Max had chuckled then. Now in Rome he said: "Damn money, damn the whole corrupt world". For most of his life Max preached honesty, loyalty and morality. To now find himself the chief executioner of these principles mortified and disgusted him. I felt pretty sick myself. "Cosi fan tutti" was no excuse for either of us. Still, we had very skillfully put together a system which would lead to the fundamental revising in our favour of MPAA's film accord with the Italian government and film industry. I would have to be patient. The Italians say "chi va piano, va lontano" -Who moves slowly gets farther." I meant to observe this maxim, waiting until the joyous elixir of our regular monetary injections became addictive, a habit hard to kick, a necessity. Only when representatives of the other party to our negotiations were no longer able to distinguish between being customized, canonized or sodomized, would I present my terms for the new film pact: my coup de grâce. I just hoped that in the meantime there would be no leaks. The MPAA and its member companies had approved of the premiums being paid to Finmeccanica but were not made fully aware of the details of the "bustarella" system.

They might have felt constrained to make me desist. On the other hand, I felt quite sure that Max had not withheld the truth from Skouras. They were good personal friends, playing golf together at sunrise whenever the president of 20th Century-Fox came to Rome, which was often. These two white haired Titans had much in common. Only that one of them was more righteous.

Max's corrosive financial choreography at the highest level of authority brought quick results. In less than six months those who would have opposed me at the negotiating table were like stripped away prawns. Naked, vulnerable, ready to be barbecued. I did not like being hard on the Italians even though they had been taking unfair advantage of our companies for years. Albert Cornfield, European head of 20th Century Fox used to say: "they spit in our face and we say it rains". The new, long term deal contained all the improvements I had promised Eric Johnston. I asked him to come to Rome for the signing ceremony. He came, but insisted the signature should be mine. To celebrate the new contract, I held a reception at my home in Eric's honor. All the stars and all the striped trousers of Rome were there to congratulate him and to make merry. We danced till morning to the South American rhythms of the famous band, "Bruno's Boys", which I brought for the occasion from Venice.

The next day Eric's secretary told me he was provoked by the opulence of my lifestyle. "Van, she said, Eric is a multi-millionaire and doesn't live half as well as you do". That was not a good omen.

I waited for him to say something about his Goldwynesque promise made in Paris that he would "triple my salary ad infinitum". He left Rome without mentioning it.

I had much work to do. In a few weeks the Venice film festival began. This year we would have a particularly important and marvelous guest, my favorite lady, ambassador Clare Boothe Luce.

Venice

Mrs. Luce telephoned asking me to come to her hotel suite. Though it was late morning she was still in her dressing gown. Issuing instructions left and right to members of her staff, she motioned me to the breakfast table. "You better sit down. I want you to do something for me. Will you pull *Blackboard Jungle* from the festival? I hate doing this, especially since the director, Richard Brooks, is a personal friend of mine and a great talent, but I feel very strongly we would be doing a disservice to our country by showing this film in Venice. Movies are like flashes of lightning. They illuminate a scene, then blind you. The scene keeps reappearing on the background of darkness until your vision clears, but the initial impression always remains. The audiences believe what they see and you know what the communist press will do to us. It will say: "look, this is America".

Blackboard Jungle was entered in competition at the Venice festival by Metro-Goldwyn-Mayer. It painted an uncompromising picture of an American school which resembled a prison, with teachers and students as the inmates. The nerve-jangling performances of Vic Morrow, Sidney Poitier and Glenn Ford increased the impact of the already powerful story. It was a good movie. The New York Times critic, Bosley Crowther, called it "a vivid and hair-raising film ... as hard and penetrating as a nail".

It would have been nothing short of foolhardy to disagree with one's ambassador. Particularly if the ambassador happened to be Clare Boothe Luce. In all honesty I had to admit agreeing with her judgement. "Ambassador", I said, "what you want me to do is fraught with all sorts of dangers. I could ask the festival president to withdraw the picture from competition and he would undoubtedly adhere to my request. Then all hell will break loose. MGM will be after my hide as I have not the authority to so arbitrarily interfere with its choice. Why don't you say something to the festival committee?" "You should know better than that. For an ambassador, such action would be totally inappropriate. But I will say this: either the picture is out or I leave Venice". Sweet Charlie Brown. What do I do now, I asked myself.

I got on the phone to Eric Johnston in Washington. "Clare Luce is unhappy about MGM's *Blackboard Jungle* being entered in competition. I agree with her. It would be wise to replace it". All Eric had to do was tell

MGM's international president, Arthur Loew, that in the interests of the industry, the Association would like him to select a substitute entry in Venice. It was not such a big deal. An experienced, sophisticated man like Arthur would have complied without hesitation. Except that it did not happen that way. A vicious spin was deliberately put on the ambassador's request. Arthur Loew reacted angrily. "I certainly agree that this kind of unwarranted interfering with our business cannot be tolerated", he told Eric, as was quickly referred to me by MGM's Italian manager. Eric did not call me back. I phoned Dave Lewis, Metro's man in Paris. I said "Dave, this whole situation is getting out of hand. The ambassador is right, you know. Is there anything you can do? After all, you are MGM's top boss in Europe and I know you are also Arthur's close friend". "I just finished talking with him, Dave said. He is sore as hell and has already chewed out your boss for letting a meddling female dictate to him. If you think I'm going to tell Arthur he is wrong, you're out of your mind." Mrs. Luce had her own information network. She did not like what she heard. One of her staff members let it slip: "What is Johnston trying to do? Put her on the spot?"

Not surprisingly, the Italian film selection committee took *Blackboard Jungle* off the list. Its president told me: "the Prime Minister made it very clear he would be mortified if the American ambassador decided to leave Venice before the end of the festival". I rushed to see Mrs. Luce. "Ambassador, everything is just fine", I said. She already knew. "That is not a very accurate assessment of what occurred", she answered me. Obviously, Mrs. Luce was not amused.

Two days later, as I was playing tennis with the hotel pro, Griff Johnson materialized on the court bench. Nobody had told me he would be flying in from Washington. And for a good reason. He had a message for me: "Your impropriety, your lack of loyalty shocked and embarrassed Eric. You are fired. Except that officially you are not fired. You will resign of your own accord sixty days from now. If you don't, or you make noise, he will bury you". I double-faulted on my next serve. Not too clever, I thought. The two months was "distancing", a device to cleave connection between the *Blackboard Jungle* affair and my firing. His reasoning was flawed. If concerned with static, he should have waited till I got back to Rome. To send Griff so urgently from Washington revealed how overwhelming was the compulsion to instantly find someone to blame, to punish, in protestation of the humiliation he believed he had suffered from the hands of Mrs. Luce, with me as her acquiescent accomplice. Eric could have found more plausible, perhaps even some valid excuses to fire me. I was not exactly Caesar's wife, either personally or professionally. Why not accuse me of too liberal a life-style, moral turpitude in corrupting government officials, of ignoring of what I described to him as obsolete company guidelines. Or, of my often expressed belief that to do a job well one had to sometimes act with a bit of arrogant anger and that who uncritically pursued organizational aims, with little regard for the human element wound up either a frustrated drunk on welfare or a cabbage with a pension. These were but a few of my obvious shortcomings. The only thing I was sure no one could accuse me of was torturing iguanas in my basement. But, as an expert at assembling spurious circumstantial evidence, so well demonstrated in the McCarthy case, he would have even found some iguana dreck. In fact, he later did, and it was not exactly in my basement either. More like in my bedroom.

Until Griff arrived I never once thought I could become one of Eric's victims. It was a crushing experience. Not so much the firing in itself. I would feel the full impact of that later. Now I could only think of how many times I told Eric, jokingly but thankfully, that he had saved me from "lying in State". Many years had gone by since I acted as his interpreter when he came to Warsaw on a special mission for President Truman; later to have me hired away from the State Department to join the Motion Picture Export Association. It is so nice to be beholden to a person one admires and it is very difficult to let go of the illusion even after a Dorian Gray complex corrodes it. To my profound sorrow Eric proved he was what I always wanted to believe he was not. As Jorge Luis Borges put it: "El original era infiel a la traducción" -the original was unfaithful to the translation.

Mrs. Luce was incensed. I could tell by the tone of her voice. We were both back in Rome now. She wanted to see me immediately. I knew why. I also knew that once I found myself face to face with her she would get the whole truth out of me. I liked and admired her too well to allow any implication she was a kind of unindicted co-conspirator, responsible for my being fired. That was unthinkable. I invented the excuse of a badly twisted ankle not to visit with her. "You're hiding, she said. I am sending my special assistant, Arthur, to see you this afternoon". His humor and soft manner relaxed me. He was very adept at asking questions. "Mrs. Luce is very concerned and would appreciate your telling me exactly why Mr. Johnston fired you". Her solicitude touched me. My answers were evasive, admitting no linkage. Not now, I kept repeating to myself. Later perhaps. Yes, I would write her a letter someday. There were other reasons as well for my stubborn reticence. Quite conceivably, Mrs. Luce might have thought it right to offer me a job somewhere within the Luce empire. The very idea trampled my ego. A further motive to keep silent could be traced to the Russian professor in Warsaw, my friend, my "starets". "If someone unjustly and deliberately hurts you and Nemesis is to be your goddess, he told me, remember that to make sure retribution is exacted, you must resist all temptation to take advantage of the wrong committed against you by shifting the burden of responsibilty for your wounds to the innocent. Should you falter, all chances of the garotte slitting the throat of the culpable will be automatically forfeited. Say nothing, wait patiently, but be careful not to make a religion out of it. People might think you weird".

I was ending a very exciting period of my life. I would miss it because anybody can tell you "there is no business like show bizness".

Arrivederci Roma? Only someone who lived in Rome during that period of metamorphosis from Fascist to Partigiano, of pride and of prejudice, of love and hatred, of passion and dolce vita, the time of guilt, shame, desire for cleansing, pessimism, despair, fear, longing, ambition and creativity, the quasi schizophrenic split between reason and emotion and when Italians needed to be forced to their knees and elevated, aroused, frightened, shocked, sent wailing, amused and delighted, could possibly understand what it was like.

I threw my coins into the Trevi fountain but knew I would not find Rome the same ever again. Oscar Wilde wrote: ....."when good Americans die they go to Paris".... This good American was not dead yet and he was going to his favorite London. Caveat British Museum.

London - Rome - Madrid - Paris - New York

I was having lunch in London at Les Ambassadeurs club with a few acquaintances. At the next table some film people were arguing rather loudly about the merits of a new English movie queen. John Mills, the club's manager and friend since the very lean days immediately after the war when I managed to smuggle yards of brocade from Paris for his club, came over: "You must meet Ken Harper", he said. "He's making a new movie and wants Sophia Loren. Can you get her?" "I may be able to", I said. Ken and I agreed on the terms. The next morning I flew off to Rome to see my close friend, the prominent motion picture attorney, Massimo Ferrara de Santamaria,who gave Sophia her first introduction to movie-land. She was just a Neapolitan urchin when she parked herself in his reception room telling him him she was bent on a career in movies and would become famous. Massimo told me he was so taken by the determination of this scrawny, long legged, big eyed rather plain looking creature who had the nerve to refuse to leave his office until he promised to help her realize her dream that he gave her introductions to his movie friends and became her trusted friend.

Massimo took me to Carlo Ponti's villa in via Appia Antica. Carlo, a successful Italian producer, partner in the Ponti-De Laurentis film studios, was Sophia's sponsor-manager. I had met Ponti at various film parties, but only casually. He had the reputation of a very tough businessman. Massimo warned me that since Sophia was very much in demand, Ponti would be hard to sell. I found him all charm, especially after I told him that Ken Harper had already signed the fine English director, Terence Young. For some peculiar reason, Ponti did not wish to read the screenplay or even an outline. He could not take a decision for Sophia, he said. We should talk to her directly. She was in Madrid at the Hilton. Did we wish him to call her to set up a meeting? Massimo consulted his secretary finding that for the next twenty four hours he was free of major appointments. We flew to Spain the same evening.

Sophia had a dinner engagement. We settled for late cocktails rather than wait an extra day. Massimo and I wanted to leave Madrid the following morning. All we needed was for her to agree to take the part. Carlo Ponti would do the contract negotiating with me in Rome.

While I described the plot of the movie we spoke Italian. At one point Sophia interrupted me to say in fluent and virtually accentless English "I have seen the script before under a different name and really did not think much of it". Her statement came as a very unwelcome surprise to me. Massimo was astounded for another reason. "How did you do this" he asked, obviously referring to her new language skill. "Caro Massimo, you know me. I work at it". "Forgive me, Sophia, but I must tell Van that when you first came to Rome you could not speak decent Italian, just a miserable Neapolitan dialect even I had difficulty understanding. I am really impressed". Sophia was pleased. More power to Carlo, I thought. This producer, turned magic sculptor, must have had the ear of Aphrodite to bring the urchin to life. I was angry no one had had the decency to tell me the script had been shopped under a different title. Now the damage was done. There was no point in even mentioning the high salary we were willing to pay her. Sophia was gracious enough to blame a conflict of schedules for her refusal. She had already agreed, she told us, to make several pictures for the American producer Ray Stark. I was angry that my immediate fee of some sixty five grand flew out the window but couldn't blame her. On the scale of 1 to 10, as far as producers went, Stark rated about an 8. Stretching it, 3 was probably the best I could reach. Anyway, I consoled myself, she didn't like the story.

It was the first time I had the opportunity to observe Sophia up close. Analyzed separately, her features were anything but perfect. The ensemble, however, was pure seductive beauty. Did she have innate talent? No question. But, so did half of the female population of Italy. Sophia had much more: an insatiable hunger for success, the drive, the appreciation of excellence, the naughtiness and haughtiness that would later bring her world acclaim as an actress and, as a woman, to so dangerously intoxicate Cary Grant.

I flew to Paris to visit with Bob and Michelle Amon. Bob was promoting new talents with enormous success. He and Ray Ventura had been instrumental in launching the career of Audrey Hepburn. I told him about my fiasco with Loren. "Don't worry, I'll fix it", he promised.

A few days later Bob phoned me in New York. "I have an option on a sensational new actress. You can have her and for little money. Trust me and act quickly because she will not be available for very long". "Thanks Bob, please send me an urgent cable about her."

Cable in hand I went to see the powers at Metro-Goldwyn-Mayer, the company from which most of Harper's financing was coming against distribution rights. "Who is this new discovery of yours", they asked. I showed them Bob's cable. The big chief burped: "who in the hell is Brigitte Bardot?" He pronounced her name brigit barr dot. "We can't use her".

Ken Harper hired Martine Carol, a French actress. I had fond memories of Martine. The French director Christian-Jacque discovered her, made her famous and married her. I first met Martine in Athens, just before a French-sponsored gala performance of one of her "spectaculars". As she walked down the stairs of the hotel Grande Bretagne I said: "Martine you look very beautiful". "Non, non, mon ami" she replied. "I don't *look* beautiful, I *am* beautiful. Touché, Martine. She had given me a lesson in savoir-dire.

"It rained all over our plain on location in Spain as Harper growled in pain" is how the assistant producer described the filming ordeals. That was only a part of it. Lovely Martine, like a spoiled child, now discovered she did not like the part. It really didn't suit her, she said, and sulked. From the time Ken signed her, some of us feared the outbreak of her tantrums. Others had doubts regarding her box office attraction in America. Van Johnson, the male lead, got a bad case of flu. Terence Young tried shooting "round" him but there was just so much he could do. On top of it all, some equipment got lost, the accommodations were a disaster, the Spanish crew called strikes. With all this plaguing him, Terry Young nearly went berserk. Just the location costs in Spain put the picture over time, over budget. The production was jinxed from the start. MGM released it in second run theaters only. It bombed and was quickly pulled from distribution. Without looking at the figures, I knew the receipts didn't cover even the cost of prints.

Some time later, the movie called *And God Created Woman* was released in New York to ecstatic reviews. It was also a huge box-office success. Overnight, Brigitte Bardot became the "sex kitten", the most sought after actress on either side of the Atlantic. Her fees astronomical. I could nearly see some guys at MGM contemplating suicide, and Bob Amon laughing all the way to the bank.

New York

New Yorkers intimidated me. Everybody was chasing about, either getting divorced or psychoanalyzed, or both. Forwards, backwards, one day peacocks on elevated shoes, next Cartesians in reverse. When being shaken from their trees, the acrophobic arrivists bowed before any throne, no matter whose buttocks it cradled, anxious to clinch a lateral move, like from NBC to Time, or perhaps Wall Street, even if the prospective patron and his favorites were but mutually supportive parvenus. Others crossed fingers that "it would all even out in the end", which it never did. At half time they went to the theater or paroxized over the wicked self-righteousness of the media they worked for. There was also ingenuity, wit, curiosity, creativity, sensitivity, and Pavlov's laughter. I tried absorbing it all, under the gentle, patient tutelage of Howard and Shirley Katzander, the only truly altruistic, life's emancipated sophisticates I ever knew. They petitioned their hearts to succor Humpty Dumpty. They might have succeeded even though my head went missing and it was all far too clever for me, had I not gone to see their physician for a thorough medical. Tests revealed I suffered from Chronic Lymphocytic Leukemia."The average lifespan after diagnosis of CCL is three to four years, he told me. "I'll prescribe some cytotoxic anticancer drugs". "Doctor", I said, this reminds me of W.C. Fields who on hearing the results of his medical tests told his friends: "the nefarious quack found urine in my whisky". You are certainly no quack but I don't want the medication. Your candy is dandy but my liquor is quicker and I'm going on a vodka cure. Wish me luck". I told no one. An Italian saying goes "Non c'è due senza tre", meaning that adversity always strikes thrice. My quota was now complete.

A very bright and attractive young lady, Shirley Potash, who had a daughter-mother relationship with Clare Luce invited me to lunch. I knew her from Rome but Shirley "Pot", as her friends affectionately called her, could not have had the slightest personal interest in me. I surmized that the luncheon invitation was suggested by Mrs. Luce. Considerable time had elapsed since we both left Rome so I was deeply moved that she had not forgotten the *Blackboard Jungle* incident and continued to show her concern. I wanted very much to express my gratitude but when one tries to put real emotion into words it becomes too maudlin. I told Shirley "Pot" nothing new. There was no purpose in trying to fix the past. Like my jeweller friend, Julius of Warsaw, I chose to continue being superstitious. Would the bullet fired through the crooked barrel of his high-powered rifle really double ricochet and inflict a mortal wound on the inquisitor, just as Yuri Sergeievich Orlov made me believe, or would it instead lie spent somewhere? It didn't much matter now. I only wished "Pot" hadn't embarrassed me by paying for the lunch.

I was close to a "basket case" and still Shirley Katzander refused to give up on me. She had connections and introduced me to someone with whom I would share some notable adventures. It was the remarkable Jack Beane, president and founder of Foreign Research and Management, Inc. Nearly immediately, the company commissioned me to open offices in Rome. "There is nothing wrong with reality that a little artifice could not fix", I said to Jack, thinking of Italy. He knew a lot about me from Mary Smith who, before marrying Jack, had been Eric Johnston's confidential secretary for many years. Eric deeply resented losing her.

Rome - Costa Brava - Madrid

A pre-glimpse of Bob Ruark's remarkable career could be gleaned from his books *The Honey Badger* and *Poor no More*. He also wrote *Uhuru, Use Enough Gun* and, his most important novel, *Something of Value*. I first met him in Rome where he was a frequent visitor. Actually, my dear friend, Sario De Mattheis introduced us at the bar of the Residence Palace hotel. Over the next couple of years we wore out the bar stools there. Now that I was back in Rome, I had to drop in on Amadeo, the bartender, for the latest news. Amadeo knew everything about everybody. He had several messages from Bob inviting me to visit with him at his home on the Costa Brava. I postponed some business appointments and flew to Barcelona. Bob picked me up in his Rolls Royce. On the way to his villa he joked that the RR on the car grille really stood for Robert Ruark. To me and to many other friends Bob was indeed a Rolls.

I had read his books. I knew quite a lot about his character. How many times do you need to get drunk with a man before you figure out what lies behind the façade? I liked him a lot. He had a big heart. He thought no evil. His one big weakness, complex nearly, was the consuming ambition to surpass Ernest Hemingway. As a writer and in daring life-style. I wondered if that was behind Bob's obsession with Spain, the reason for his large collection of trophies, the tiger skins, the cabinets full of the best English hunting guns, and the big game safaris in Africa, when killing of animals was in fact abhorrent to him. That part I never did figure out. Possibly he was striking out in anger at his shortcomings.

At his home in Spain one entire library wall, from floor to ceiling, consisted of chronologically filed newspaper clippings covering virtually everything he had ever written. From his beginnings as a police reporter, to essays, short stories, gossip columns, social commentary. I spent many hours skimming, then reading more carefully. It was hard to believe that a single writer could embrace so much human travail. It represented a prodigious literary output.

The unusual as well as amusing background to his prolific, syndicated "eyewitness" society gossip column was that it continued to be published uninterruptedly all during Bob's long residence in Spain. He wrote it based on cable and telephone reports supplied by his stringers and agents in America. His readers were never suspecting Ruark was not in New York. How else would he have known that Miss Victoria Dongola of East

Hampton had drifted horizontally into cafe society only to wake up pregnant one Sunday morning?

"This kind of crap", Bob commented, referring to the column, "is bread and butter money. When you sit down to real writing, first you must open your vein". "You just quoted Hemingway", I said. "Screw Papa. If it's good, use it. It's only a back-handed compliment anyway because nothing original has been said since Aristotle". Bob was annoyed. To change the subject I asked: "Why do so many gifted people drink heavily?" "Because it gives one perception with perspective" he replied. "Do you remember the scene in Hemingway's novel *Across the River and into the Trees*, where two people on a hotel terrace in Venice are talking and getting plastered? No I didn't say that right. Make it, getting plastered and talking. It is one of the best sequences he ever wrote. I guarantee you he could have never done it sober. You see, as Ernest was writing he was actually getting drunk, right with his characters. That is perceptive perspective or whatever you want to call it, but it was real. I myself write better when I'm loaded". I was not prepared to really believe this but I got a suggestion of what he meant that same night when after dinner, and so many drinks he could barely sit up straight, Bob got to his typewriter and dashed off, non stop, a 1500 word story. I read it. No corrections were required.

He returned to the subject later. "What one must not do is to drink out of desperation or anger". As one drunk to another, I told Bill: "the way you are doing it, drink will drown your soul first, then physically kill you dead." Bob was referring to Bill Holden, then in Kenya, pouring money into his private game preserve and liquor down his throat. He had turned his back on Hollywood, on the world really. A broken marriage, an unhappy love affair with a French actress, demanding and selfish friends had, as Bob said, already drowned his soul."Yes Van, drink will kill him dead and I shall cry because he is one of the finest human beings I have ever known".

Bob had his own giant demon. He was haunted by the thought that one day, no longer able to write, he would find himself penniless. I had a pretty good idea that with all the royalties coming in from his stories, articles, books and the very substantial amount of money he had been paid for the film rights of "Something of Value", his dollar bank account never sank below seven figures.

"You probably don't know what it is like to be poor. Dirt poor. I'd rather be dead than poor" he'd say. I heard this kind of Greek sob story from Bob very often. It seemed to me there was a gross inconsistency between his scrooge tone and his actions. He worried about money, yet kept spending it with a light hand. He was a soft touch, never turned down a pal or fellow writer. He was running through small fortunes for travel, guns, Savile Row suits, expensive presents for friends round the world.

I knew I might be treading on sensitive ground but said "It's all in one's head" and related my encounter with Mike Todd who had come to my Rome office asking whether I knew of anyone who would help finance the production of his motion picture. He had been trying to find money for many months without success. Mike was hurting. I had no way to solve his problem. In trying to express my sympathy I said to him: "cheer up Mike, you won't be poor forever." It was a dumb choice of words and Mike, chewing on his ever present wet cigar, turned to me with what was something between a smile and a snarl. "Van, he said, to be broke is a temporary state of one's affairs. To be poor is a state of mind. Don't ever forget that". Indeed. The movie he finally got to make: *Around the World in Eighty Days* netted him fame, fortune and a beautiful star, Elizabeth Taylor, for a wife. Bob pretended he liked the story. He knew all about Mike Todd, of course. His face told me I was wasting my time.

I had noticed a change coming over Bob since he parted with his wife, Ginny. Clearly unhappy, he was losing his zest for life and adventure, retreating behind increasing cynicism. He had company. Sad company: Bill Holden and Ardis, Frank Loesser and Lynn, Paul Baron and Heather and so many more of our friends, their lives split and troubled. I asked Bob: "how do you explain that in nearly all cases that we know of, the man proved to be the more vulnerable, less resilient than the woman?" "I shall write a novel about it, casting action into the future, he said. It will predict that in a few years from now the world will see a new race of female warriors, like the legendary Amazons. But, instead of cutting off their own right breasts so as to draw the bow more easily, they will shoot invisible rays between man's neocortex and the hypothalamus, instantly reducing him to a state of helpless schizophrenia. With no one sane left to stop them, women will then forever reign over the world with pitiless cruelty.

"That's a perfectly reasonable scenario, Bob, but it sounds like today's reality, not tomorrow's fancy. Can't man defend himself ?" "Not a chance. Remember that behind every successful man there stands a woman, stiletto in hand and .....". Bob's face went red before he could finish the sentence. He "looked" me an apology.

There was a row of real wooden dog houses in the garden behind Bob's villa. When a guest went beyond acceptable drunken decorum, swore too loudly, chased the maids, or otherwise rudely trespassed on Bob's hospitality, he or she would get inducted in the Robert Ruark Dog Hall of Shame. Name prominently displayed, life membership, no further invitation. There were no vacancies. I regretted having missed all these wild Ruark parties.

We left for Madrid ahead of schedule because of a a midnight call which seemed to greatly upset my host. We went to the Jockey Club to lunch with Ava Gardner, Bob's life-long friend. They were both Southerners-Carolinians, and knew each other when neither had shoes to wear. "Dirt poor" as Bob called it. She brought along a famous bullfighter. The atmosphere was strained, uncomfortable. We had too much wine. As I got out of the taxi in front of my hotel, someone rushing out of the revolving door nearly knocked me over. He didn't apologize, didn't even turn his head. It was Frank Sinatra. I didn't really mind too much. All of us music lovers owed him. Besides, I knew he had come to Spain to see his great love, Ava. She seemed to prefer the bullfighter. That could make anyone mad.

The following afternoon my lady companion insisted on dragging me to a corrida. I was not exactly an enthusiast of bullfights and could not quite understand why this frail, sensitive Marchesa enjoyed them so well. I didn't dare tell her. In Spain, this would border on blasphemy. The great matador, Antonio Benvenides, killed four bulls that afternoon for charity. I didn't count the ears and tails they awarded him. Aficionados carried him from the Plaza de Toros on their shoulders. It was a tremendously bold and exhausting performance, so I was pleasantly surprised when Antonio and his American girl friend joined us later for drinks at the Castellana Hilton. He looked fresh and rested. She appeared drained.

Bob never told me who had phoned him at his Costa Brava home the previous midnight, but I guessed it must have been Ava. "Would you like to come with me to Turkey?", I asked. "Do they have Turkish bullfights"?

Ankara

"There are times when the unfairness of life must make the creative imagination roll up its bloody eyes and yearn for an early lobotomy". I couldn't remember who said that but it was exactly how I felt. They also say that the opera isn't over until the fat lady sings. This very fat lady had been at it for nearly four hours and it was far from over. One might survive *Rigoletto* or *Traviata* but *Aïda* in Turkish was carrying it too far. Lee Dayton was sitting a few seats away grinning, purposely avoiding my eye. I knew why. As the American ambassador to Turkey he had to act with proper decorum,especially as we were guests of the President of the Republic at this gala night of the Ankara Opera. We could be certain he and his entourage were watching us, anxious for signs of approval. Thanks to Lee's able diplomatic manoeuvering, some rather serious differences between our two countries had been smoothed over. He had a lot to say also about American military aid to Turkey and that was going reasonably well. At this point everybody was being very nice to everybody. We applauded the singers with enthusiasm.

Politics apart, it was really friend Ali's fault we got invited to the opera. I could also blame the Neapolitans. I tried to shut my ears and think back a few years to a very noisy night in the streets of Naples, when I stopped to pick up a young man in uniform who was standing next to a sports car waving frantically. He introduced himself in a slightly formal fashion. "I am lieutenant Ali Enver, Turkish Air Force, on detached service with the North Atlantic Treaty Organization, Southern Command. I am sorry to bother you but my car is disabled". All this in passable Italian. In English, I said, "Lieutenant, this is your lucky night. Obviously you were unaware of the mad Neapolitan custom of throwing crockery, dishes, pots and everything else considered ready for replacement out of the window into the streets at midnight to greet the New Year. You got caught right in the middle. A broken chamber pot slashed your tires but you will forget this slight misfortune if you join me. I am on my way to a party at the home of a friend, Baron de Mattheis". Ali was all smiles. The party lasted until breakfast. We went to find Ali's car. It had disappeared. A trio of small, innocent-looking boys offered to locate it for a fee. As soon as we paid, they told us the truth. Having moved the car to a concealed garage just two blocks away, they cannibalized it during the night, down to the frame. The youthful entrepreneurs had been waiting for us to collect the bonus for finding it, knowing the police would not arrest them. It was all so cleverly done and their joy of hoodwinking us so evident, we could'nt even get angry. Ali actually started laughing: "that, my friends, he exclaimed in his best Italian, is an example of superb Neapolitan initiative".

The incident was really a stroke of luck for me. Ali had a sense of humor, charm and boundless energy; all basic prerequisites for joining our exclusive "Club of Rome". I introduced him to our other members. Their approval was immediate. We "drafted" Ali. He was a crack pilot, very serious about his NATO job. Rome was a different world for him. Soon it became his favorite playground, where he could enjoy the kind of special filmland perks he never even dreamed of.

I had arrived in Ankara, heading a group of Italian industrialists from Turin, introduced to me by an extraordinary femme d'affaires prominent in the armaments business. Lee Dayton, my old friend of Warsaw days, with whom I was now staying, threw a party for us inviting key members of the government as well as prominent businessmen. Among them Ali, who literally lifted me off my feet in a bear hug. He insisted I come to his home later that evening so that he could introduce me to his mother. There was something very formal in the way he made that invitation. It should have tipped me off. Round midnight, in one of the most sumptuous homes I had ever seen, I entered Ali's inner circle. I bowed deeply to an imperious-looking lady, who greeted me with: "thank you for being such a good friend to my son". Her elegant entourage softly applauded. Ali smiled, offering me a glass of champagne. "Come, he said, I wish to show you the portrait of my father". Only then did I discover that Ali was the son of Enver Pasha, general and onetime Minister of War during the turbulent era prior to the Turkish Republic's first presidency under the great reformer Mustafa Kemal Atatürk. Ali had neglected to tell us of his family history when he shared our company in Italy. Now he had arranged for the presidential invitation to *Aïda* and was behind the scenes when my Italian associates and I negotiated an important contract to deliver rolling stock to the Turkish railways. Seeing Ali again was a very special bonus. I had grown very fond of him. As we parted, I said: "Ali, there is always something mysterious about the workings of this world. But for a slashed tire, I might have never met you. "My friend, he replied, have you not heard of kismet?"

Before returning to Italy, my Italian associates and I stopped in Holland, taking an option there on an industrial plant to augment Turin's capacity for producing railway cars.

In a week, Jack Beane would be arriving in Rome. We had a dynamite deal in the making, up North.

Turin - Vatican - Reims

Our company had an important business involvement with the Angelo Viberti Works in Turin which produced virtually all of the heavy automotive trailers in Italy. We grew very fond of Angelo, the blue-eyed, fire-ball industrialist, gentleman and sports enthusiast.

I used to half tease Jack Beane, our company's president, calling him "Joachim von Beanovitch" because he too, like the German military genius von Clausewitz, was a master strategist. Jack's bold ideas and brilliant presentations persuaded Angelo to take the extraordinary gamble of producing in Italy Studebaker's first American compact car. Confidential negotiations, held on both sides of the Atlantic, were progressing well when Angelo was injured in an automobile accident. I immediately left Rome for Turin. Jack joined me a day later from New York. We were relieved to find Angelo in one piece and good spirits, but neither Jack nor I could shake off the suspicion of foul play because the accident occurred under strange circumstances. Angelo was a qualifed racing driver, superb at the wheel. Yet, he was forced off the road he travelled daily by a lorry and would have gone over a cliff had he not first smashed into an unattended tractor. The police could not trace the lorry.

We spent the day at the "Eagle's Nest", Angelo's splendid villa on top of the hill, discussing the forthcoming business meetings and playing tennis. Angelo beat us easily until a headache forced him off the court. "It must be that bump I got in the accident", he said. The next day he seemed fine, so Jack flew back to New York. I returned to Rome.

About a month earlier in Rome, an executive of Finmeccanica phoned me insisting I meet him urgently at an out of the way bar in via Cassia Antica. I was to tell no one. In the past, when I represented the American film industry in Europe, we had channelled millions of dollars of motion picture monies through this holding company. Gianni, my caller, was then on Max's secret payroll. I could not imagine what he wished to tell me that required so much secrecy.

After gulping down two stiff drinks he warned me that my discussions with the Viberti industry of Turin made some important people very unhappy and could lead to "disastrous conseqeunces". Gianni was extremely nervous. "You must give it up,get out of it", he insisted. What he said angered me, but I was not too surprised word had gotten round about our project. Jack and I knew that no matter what precautions we took, it could not be kept secret. Top executives of Swiss, British,

American and French high caliber banking like Gutzwiller, Schroder, Bowmaker, were constantly flying into Turin for meetings with Viberti. The frequent presence of Norbert Bogdan, onetime president of the Rockefeller American Overseas Finance Corporation, whom we had hired as financial coordinator, could also not pass unnoticed.

I refused to believe Gianni's "disastrous consequences" but thought it better to mention the warning to Sario. The baron nodded wisely, sighed: "povero me, ci penso io.- Me again. I'll look into it." A few days later he came to see me bearing a strange message, declining to reveal its source. "I am to tell you that your good friends are watching over you but you must be very careful." Hiding his sources from me was not like Sario. Normally he would tell me direct or at least give me an important clue to let me guess. I knew exactly whom Gianni meant by "some important people" but the statement that I was being watched over by some mysterious good friends irked me. I questioned Sario again. "I can say no more, just trust me." That was all I needed to really set my nerves on edge.

Chapter 4

The Vatican and Soviet Intelligence Services

Santa Cittá

The small desk clock in his Vatican office showed 2 am. His eyes were red from hours of scrutinizing the voluminous report personally compiled, over several months, by His Eminence Egidio Cardinal Vagnozzi, head of the Prefecture of Economic Affairs of the Holy See. His Excellency had seen many important documents. Few matched the astonishing revelations of the one in front of him.

Under normal circumstances even His Excellency's high position of authority would not have given him access to these particular records. They came into his possession after having been stolen from the safe of Cardinal Vagnozzi by members of the Pontifical Institute of Oriental Studies which was created in Rome to prepare priests for undercover missions in communist countries. Regretfully, the Institute had recruited some seminarians from Eastern Europe who gathered intelligence information for the KGB. His Excellency's friend and fellow officer from the days when he was still a General in the Soviet intelligence apparatus tipped him off to the whereabouts of the stolen Vagnozzi Report. His subordinates, members of the religious order *Opus Dei*, managed to retrieve it before it reached Moscow. The original went back to the cardinal's safe. Unofficially, he made and retained a copy. The red leather cover said nothing.
The first page:
> TOP SECRET
> *General Digest of Vatican Holdings and Participations in the Italian Economy & Related.*

The loose-leaf pages contained detailed information on banks, industrial concerns, financial, commercial and holding companies, owned or controlled by the Vatican. It listed shares, bonds, as well as cash balances in banks round the world. It showed that Vatican-controlled banks held 28 percent of all deposits in Italy, financed over 50 percent of all foreign trade transactions, placed 69 percent of the new shares and bond issues on the stock market, directly owning nearly 50 percent of the total number of shares quoted on the exchange, valued at $ 7 billion. That the largest banks under its ownership and/or control: Banco di Santo Spirito, Banca Commerciale Italiana, Credito Italiano and Banco di Roma kept time deposits and current client accounts of over $ 9 billion. Seven additional banks were owned outright. The Vatican had heavy participation in 14 banks and lesser possession in a further 62. The Banque de Rome in Swizerland was 100 percent owned. In addition to money and banking, there was not a single sector of the Italian economy in which the Vatican did not have either majority or important interests. These were in textiles, shipping, chemicals, hotels, insurance, electronics, engineering, armaments and other. 53 Vatican companies were engaged in construction alone. Abroad, Vatican holdings in major enterprises spread to all five continents. From The Watergate Improvement Corporation in Washington D.C. and the Novamont Corporation in Virginia, to the Madras Aluminium Company of India, the Redbrook Estates in Montreal, Lomas Verdes of Mexico City, Heliogas in Brazil, and endless other companies in Spain, France, Luxembourg, Tunis, Chile, Greece, Holland, Panama. The extent of the Vatican's reach and wealth challenged imagination. The report consisted of three hundred and twenty eight printed pages.

Despite hours of close study, His Excellency still failed to find the leverage he needed to prevent the clique of rogue managers in Italy's most important family owned concern from implementing their plan to financially cripple the Viberti industry by coercing suppliers and labor unions. Then it came to him. Through the Institute of Industrial Reconstruction -IRI-, the Vatican held authority over the holding company, Finmeccanica, which coordinated and financed IRI's activities in almost every branch of the engineering industry from automotive to precision instruments. He would turn tables on them, have his people warn the anti Viberti managers to desist or face immediate and serious supply problems. They could not afford to take such a risk. His Excellency found the thought eminently pleasing. Since the end of the

Second World War various agencies of the Vatican had used every conceivable manoeuver to gain a measure of control over this private industrial complex. They got nowhere. It was galling. Time to teach them a lesson. Tomorrow he would begin issuing instructions. Now His Excellency was in need of rest.

Before he could leave the room, a small pale blue light started flashing on his desk, emitting a barely audible buzz. He had banned all shrill ringing telephones from his Vatican chambers. They interfered with his concentration. He picked up the receiver of his personal line, used by his closest collaborators in emergencies only. "Pronto?" He listened for a few moments. In a hoarse voice he exclaimed "sukin syny"! He never expected them to go to such lengths. Then he commanded: "blanket the whole zone, the entire city if necessary. Immediately. Now! No harm must come to him. Report to me at least every thirty minutes. Understood?" "Si, Eccelenza, Si".

Franco Ficodoro, chief executive of the Viberti finance corporation, Finauto, formed in Rome with Italian and foreign capital by Norbert Bogdan, telephoned me from Turin that Angelo Viberti had an emergency operation to remove a hematoma resulting from his earlier automobile accident. "Nothing to worry about really, he said. Angelo is fine and will be back in his office in a few days."

Not only were our fortunes linked, but I liked and admired Angelo. Wasting no time, I got to Turin on the first available flight, taking along Angelo's good friend Marie. She had introduced me to Angelo when we made our trip to Ankara to negotiate the Turkish railway deal. We were unable to reach any of our usual Turin contacts. The office numbers just rang, without answer. We got no reply at Angelo's residence. Dr. Sala, his personal secretary, could not be found. Was Angelo in one of the hospitals or in a clinic? I had neglected to ask Franco when he telephoned me in Rome. Marie got on the phone once again. No results. I rushed over to Franco's hotel. He was very surprised, indeed obviously unhappy to see me. I dragged him to my hotel bar. I couldn't understand why Franco was so terribly nervous. He mumbled about Angelo being in good care. Laughing, then on the verge of tears, he seemed to be suffering an emotional crisis, downing neat scotch, one after the other. This was very odd because Franco rarely touched hard liquor. Something was awfully wrong. Half drunk, he finally gave me the name of Angelo's clinic. I whispered to Marie to keep him drinking. I went out to investigate.

A taxi took me within a block of the clinic. It was now nearly two in the morning. The streets empty. A lone figure of a nurse was dozing at the reception desk. Lights were low. I got past her. The place seemed "deserted". It was eerie to find a clinic with no doctors round, no apparent activity. On the ground floor here were only offices. Quietly I crept upstairs trying door after door. All empty. No patients. At the end of one long corridor I found a person on a respirator, the machine that regularly pumps air in and out of the lungs to compensate for the loss of natural breathing. No nurse in attendance. I approached the bed and recognized Angelo. His face was blue. I lifted the covers. The body was horribly bloated. Angelo must have been dead for many hours, perhaps even days. My feeling of nausea was overwhelming.

There was movement in the corridor. Instinctively I fell to the floor and rolled under the high hospital bed. Two figures in white entered the room. In the dim light they did not notice me. From their quick exchange I understood they were looking for an intruder. Did Franco guess where I had gone? Had he alerted the clinic? "You had better lock the door, Giulio", one said. As they turned their backs to leave the room, I burst through them, running. They yelled after me. I reached the street, kept running. After several blocks my lungs were wheezing. I had to stop. I was leaning against a wall panting when a calm voice behind me said: "put this on and follow me". It was a young priest. He wrapped a cloak with hood round me. I was too startled to protest or ask questions. Just minutes later we were in a sacristy. "It would not be wise for you to return to your hotel at this point. Have some rest. I'll call you when things are under control". "May I use the phone", I asked. "Yes, as long as you don't say where you are". I was quaking but not enough to stop me from being very angry. I had to think fast. I called my hotel. Franco was still in the bar, now hardly coherent from drink. I told him I had gotten in touch with the famous Swedish brain surgeon, professor Oliver Cruna, who would be arriving from Stockholm on the earliest available flight to examine Angelo. I thought I heard Franco choke. I hung up before he could say anything. He would sober up in a hurry, I thought.

My friendly priest shook me two hours later. "You certainly stuck a hot poker in a hornet's nest. The whole town is awake. Lots of people have been looking for you. There is quiet now. The press has been told about the clinic. Drink this Catholic espresso and go back to your hotel".

Franco and Angelo's brother-in-law, professor Ravera, were in the lobby waiting for me to show up. Marie was still perfectly alert. I told them I had to take a shower and would be right back. From my room I called Stockholm. Professor Cruna was an old friend. Years before he had operated on my mother. He didn't mind my waking him. I told him about Angelo's sudden operation and the cover-up of his death. He suggested I try to get the Italian surgeons to phone him to describe the procedures they used. He would be available at his Stockholm clinic later that morning.

The two visitors in my hotel lobby, now quite aware I had discovered the body, went to great pains to convince me Angelo's death had to be temporarily kept secret because when a prominent millionaire industrialist unexpectedly dies, the law requires that his business and even personal papers be immediately sealed to prevent their manipulation.

"You see, they said, Angelo was very neglectful. He made no provisions to protect the interests of his wife and children. Something had to be done". Why were they lying? Angelo had disclosed all his assets and liabilities to the financial institutions involved in the Studebaker deal. Various properties were in his wife's name. We knew she was also the beneficiary of a two million dollar life insurance policy. In view of the fact that we had gone over Angelo's financial statements together, it astonished and puzzled me that Franco should be party to this transparent lie. Franco was a coward but no fool. He was trying to tell me something. It was entirely possible that someone needed time to either remove documents or forge Angelo's signatures or both, but I felt sure it had little connection with purely family interests. "I don't believe this cover-up has anything to do with cheating the exchequer, I shouted. I want to know how a young, strong, healthy individual could die as result of a simple hematoma operation. Explain that to me and if you can't, the doctors better tell professor Cruna of Stockholm with whom I have scheduled a conference call from the clinic for this morning at 11". Franco and Ravera rushed out.

I arranged for the Stockholm telephone call to be made from the clinic, on speaker, making sure a dozen independent witnesses and a magistrate were present. The two specialists responsible for Viberti's surgery stared at me with unconcealed animosity. Although obviously nervous and hostile, they could not refuse to speak with the world's most famous brain surgeon. But, in talking with the professor they were also far too clever to provide any evidence of error let alone wrongdoing. I knew, of course, it would be impossible to find any proof against them then and there. The purpose of the phone call was to make them and the witnesses clearly understand I strongly suspected the doctors not merely of professional negligence but of foul play. Trusting the law would take care of the rest, I didn't think they had much of a future.

Jack Beane came for the funeral. So did our good friend and treasurer, Jack McMillin, a decent, dependable, reliable, usefully obtuse, intellectually unthreatening man, incapable of any creative inspiration, to whom everything was, by his own definition, "impossible". Just the kind of fellow we needed to keep us from going overboard.

After the heartaches of Turin, we decided to take some time off in Capri to review options for our company's future operations. No conclusions were forthcoming. A few days later in Rome we had the good fortune to run into Prince Guy de Polignac. Guy was a dear friend ever since he began instructing me in the ways of the French when I came to Paris for the movie industry. His and my time permitting, we would meet at the grill of Fouquet's, or at his apartment-office round the corner in Avenue George V. A wonderful raconteur, connoisseur of art, historian, critic, I listened to him for hours, invariably fascinated by his extraordinary erudition and talents. Guy's enthusiasm for America was boundless. It was inspired, he said, by his ancestor, Prince Jules Armand de Polignac, who in 1823 issued the Polignac Memorandum in support of the Monroe Doctrine.

I told him we felt responsible for Viberti's death. Guy exclaimed: "Zut pour les scrupules, come with me to Reims". We drank a lot of his best Pommery at the château, carefully listening to his advice. Guy thought our business philosophy was ahead of the times. "Europe, he said, was not yet ready for large scale joint ventures with Americans. Go home and come back after a few years when, with luck, your countrymen will better understand that the business part of human affairs is not the whole of them". That stung because what he said about us was largely true.

With Viberti's death, the automobile project automatically died too. Our other ventures business was running into snags, becoming increasingly difficult to control. The long arm of Eric Johnston, with a hook at its end, was being wrapped round our neck, choking off sources of outside financing. It was not only because of me. Jack had committed the ultimate lèse-majesté by marrying Eric's longtime personal assistant, Mary. He resented losing her. She told us how Eric enjoyed sticking poison pins in our careers. He could now kill two pigeons with a single blow. Really there were three because also Mary was made to pay a price.

We were losing all enthusiasm for new challenges. Our zest was gone. Jack wisely decided to heed Guy's advice and liquidate our company. He instructed our man in Beirut, Jack Brady, the intrepid Irishman whose go-aheadability brought us and our Italian partner-the construction giant Cidonio - a lucrative housing contract in Iran, to sell our interests there. Cidonio was intimately linked with Giovanni Gronchi, then president of Italy. The president, in turn, had close ties to the powerful Turin industrialists. We knew that after the Viberti affair "Turin" would not allow us to conduct any further business in or with Italy. Fortunately, the deliveries to the Turkish railways had already been completed. In Kuwait we would sell our shares in two companies to our partner Sultan Ajeel. Inevitably, this meant closing our offices in Rome, Zurich, Beirut and New York. Not without tears. After all, they had served us rather well.

Beane, McMillin and I had our last grand super bender together in Monte Carlo. Angelo's ghost would haunt us forever. We resolved not to see each other again. They went home to America. I retreated to the base of the Matterhorn. Since childhood mountains had been my best friends. It was there I heard from contacts in Rome that the two Turin magistrates charged with investigating Viberti's death and eventually bringing his doctors to trial were no longer pursuing the matter. One had taken early retirement, to settle in France. No one knew what happened to the other.

Rome - Vatican City

For two months I'd been hiking in the Pennine Alps, never less than 15 miles each day, trying to get my mind back on rails and my legs in shape. My friend Theo Rudzin, in whose chalet I was staying, had a message for me one evening to urgently phone Paul Baron in Rome. "Sario is dying, Paul said. He misses you. Come quickly". Next morning Theo drove me to Geneva. Paul met me at the Rome airport. We went direct to the clinic. "It's cancer. He has no more than a few days, perhaps only hours", the head doctor told us. An elderly priest, with assistant, were leaving the room. Sario smiled at us and said: "God's cop just read me my rights. It seems I don't have many left". Then, lifting his head off the pillow he addressed me, this time with tears in his eyes: "Caro Van, there were so many things I still needed to do for you and I've run out of time. You must forgive me. Take this envelope. Open it when I'm gone and do what I tell you. Now leave, both of you, for I need to cry".

Our precious friend, the incomparable little baron, wonderful Sario died that evening. We went to Paul's apartment. We drank all night.

When I opened the envelope, it had the name of a Monsignore and a telephone number. "Call him" was Sario's message. When I gave my name, a voice said in English: "We were hoping to hear from you. Would you find it convenient to come in tomorrow at ten?" " Yes, I replied, but where and whom am I to see?" "Vatican City. Use the Museum entrance. The guards will accompany you to an office near the Borgia Apartments".

I could admire the gardens and Villa Pia as we walked the long colonnade toward the Raphael rooms. The brogue of the young priest who greeted me at the door reminded me of that fearful night in Turin. He kept watching me with undisguised curiosity. He stood up at the sound of a buzzer. "His Excellency will see you now".

The white-haired man sitting behind a huge desk strongly resembled my "starets", my dear professor from St. Petersburg and Warsaw, Yuri Sergeievich Orlov. There was a strong fragrance of lavender cologne. "Evgenii, he said, I am very happy to see you again. Sit down please. I have much to tell you".

"Da, Grigori. Da".

Vatican Chambers

Could it really be Grigori? Mon Colonel, my friend, my guardian angel Grigori? I knew it was him, of course. Pivotal events in man's life are preordained. One must learn to expect them. Even so, I was not quite prepared for such an amazing turn of events. It startled me. I held my breath and on to my chair, silent, afraid my voice would break with emotion. In physical appearance he had changed little, except that his once dark hair was now all white, his face more furrowed. He was still slim, trim and compact, radiating a sense of dynamic energy. When he got up, I noticed he had a rather bad limp and supported his weight with a cane. The biggest difference though was in his eyes, now more deeply set, a shadow tired, melancholic rather than penetrating, but comfortable and friendly, with the familiar half whimsical, half insolent glint that made me trust him when we first met at the outbreak of war.

"A thinking man is just another dupa z mózgiem - an asshole with a brain". Grigori was addressing his young assistant, half in English, half in Polish while motioning him to leave the chambers. "He's an *Opus Dei* colleague of mine", he said to me. I had to laugh. Grigori was a study in incongruity. A Soviet military officer embracing *Opus Dei*, the Catholic movement whose stated goal is to promote the Gospel through exemplary behavior, both socially and in one's work. A highly cultured Russian resorting to coarse mahorka humor. A Monsignore who employs colorful merrymetaphors. I had many questions to ask of him but would have to wait for a more opportune time. Grigori's authoritarian temperament, I remembered only too well, was not to be taken lightly. He growled when interrupted...

Warsaw, London, Rome, Turin flashed through my mind. Then Lodz and Olomouc and Paris. What was his role in all these extraordinary events? He sensed my unspoken questions. "We have both travelled a long way. You still have far to go. For me night is near. "Starosc nie radosc". Old age holds few joys, he had said in Polish.

His mood changed. "Evgenii, I am pleased with you. You did not forget my advice to always keep a poker face. Good. Now listen.

Inasmuch as each of us has come back from the dead more than once, let us pretend we don't exist. That we are merely the ideality of our respective absurdities."

"Forgive me, Grigori, for saying so but you lost me. You sound incomprehensible. Another thing. How should I address you? Excellency? Grigori? Colonel?" "You are right. I am not always easy to follow. At times I confuse even myself and must command my brain back to order from that deceptive irrelevance. What I meant is that for the outside world much of our past should remain secret. Now I will revert to straight talk. I would not like you calling me Excellency. Frankly, I don't feel *trop catholique* in this fancy costume I acquired under somewhat sophistic circumstances. Praise the wisdom of the Church that permits it under Canon Law 372 to make special arrangements for special needs. It is a most convenient expedient. Just imagine. The General vanishes. Prestissimo, before you can say Amen, a Monsignore materializes. Quite providential, don't you think? And, you tell me you don't believe in miracles. It does not change the fact that in this frock I feel awkward, like a chicken readying to sit on her eggs. I much prefer my hard earned military rank but my personal history is to be treated with a high degree of discretion. Call me Grigori when we are alone, Monsignore in front of others. Confound unfriendly ears, I'd say. Puzzle the curious."

I still felt perplexed. What did Grigori mean by the curious and unfriendly ears? Was he unable to escape from what the French call the idiosyncracies of one's profession? He probably realized my bewilderment for after walking to the window and lighting one of those horrible Russian mahorka cigarettes he said to me: "you ought to know from our literature that we Russians enjoy riddles, all forms of enigma and the art of useful concealment. That is why I liked the mystery play written by your favorite author, Don Miguel de Unamuno. He called it "El Otro" - The Other One- It was about identical twins. One killed the other but no one could tell who was the assassin, who the victim."

"I never spoke to you about Unamuno. How on earth did you know he had made such an impression on me?" "True. You never said anything to me about him, but long ago in Warsaw you did tell my father, along, I might add, with some childhood secrets which included the hurtful experience involving your dog called Shadow. You must have really liked my father, for you confided in him and revealed a lot about yourself then. Let me tell you something else. My father talked with Miguel de Unamuno more than once in Paris when he and his friends frequented the Café de la Rotonde in Montparnasse, a place also favored by celebrated exile Spaniards such as the novelist Blasco Ibañez. Unamuno was always the most admired of them all, the center of attraction. My father envied his patriotism. Politically he thought him a liberal socialist. By that he meant a socialist who denied Marxism. So you see, all three of us were influenced by this patriot philosopher. Quite a coincidence, isn't it?

From the moment you, my prisoner-guest, spoke with such affection of professor Orlov, calling him your friend and mentor, though having no inkling I was his son, I made it a point of honor to do everything in my power to watch over you through the services at my disposal. I could not help liking that maverick rebel in you even when, with unmitigated insolence, you denounced Russian imperialism, saying we were repeating the crimes of previous centuries by raping Poland once again.

Imperialism, you said, born of malignant historical xenophobia that wags in Russian blood, in her literature and even in her music. I was angered by your reckless gall. Did it not occur to you I could have had you shot? You did not seem to care. I knew that at least part of your bravado, of your protest was caused by the continuing nightmare of the flowing blood of Warsaw. I confess you intrigued me. I had met other Americans before. You were somehow different, so I encouraged you to talk. Your mutiny soon changed to eccentric short-circuited reasoning you called neoteric philosophy. I could nearly smell the smoldering of your misconceptions. They echoed anti-Jesuitism, so I listened even more attentively, curious how and what you had been taught, dimly suspecting we might be sharing a similar heterodox theology. I soon realized, however, you really had no tested creed at all, Catholic, Jesuit or other. Just synthetic tutoring, accepting what you wanted to believe, rejecting with your green untried intellect all positions that did not suit you, calling them narcissistic and just plain gavno -shit in your language-, a term you used far too often as if shaking off the inhibitions of a conformist selfrighteous youth. Evgenii, you were a self-serving dilettante on the one hand, and a wizard of the tendentious paraphrase on the other; bold enough to twist and labor the thoughts of sage authors in attempting to validate your own defiant prejudices and your seething animosities."

Grigori was lecturing me. In the past tense, but lecturing nonetheless. I didn't like this too well. It hurt and I always hated to dwell on anything connected with the past. My past, that is.

But Grigori, this unaffected, still complex man, had fallen into some kind of fervor which I began to suspect was now caused by subconscious desire to air his own beliefs, and his doubts too. Timidly, too timidly, I tried to change the subject. He merely continued his blitz. "You were an exhibitionist as well, Evgenii, loftily quoting Unamuno in Spanish, not realizing my command of that language was far superior to yours. How adamant you were in your young convictions. "One must simplify, always simplify", you would declaim. "There may be mystery to life but not to living." "It hardly surprised me you readily accepted the quasi existentialist premise that man is not a part of some predetermined metaphysical scheme but, to the contrary, is able to shape, indeed to create his own destiny without any interference from the Almighty. I had no time to argue the elementary laws of reasoning, or to confute your paradoxical conclusions but I wanted to ask where the Catholic Church would find itself if our faithful were to accept that the hand of God had no part in their transgressions. That they, they alone were indivisibly responsible for their sins. How could they then possibly confess their profanities to profane beings like themselves and still believe in divine absolution? Why, we should be chased out of our confessionals as fakes and obliged to swap our birettes for yarmulkas. Evgenii, you look more and more befuddled over my religious convictions. You need not be. It is all rather simple. But first, some tea and sandwiches".

I welcomed the break. Grigori was getting to me and I needed to collect my thoughts. Silent clerics served us and we were briefly joined by Monsignore Clemente Grotto of the Pontifical Academy of Science who brought some documents for Grigori, deferrimg to him with extraordinary courtesy. I felt they had some link from the past. Grigori seemed highly annoyed. When Grotto left, Grigori, still munching a sandwich, turned to me saying: "these fellows always manage to screw things up. Still, I owe him a lot. For years he acted as my secret liaison with the Vatican, the *Hermitage Coefficient* and the outside world. I see your eyes light up with curiosity again. Never mind. That will come later. Now retournons á nos religieux moutons, if you don't mind.

Over the years I went from a Russian Orthodox non-believer, to a non heretical nonconformist in a long soul-rending process. And now? Now I adhere to the Church of Rome which in my thinking is a preposterous compromise between two mutually destructive forces: the Gospel and the Roman Law-un mostruoso compromesso fra due cose che si distrugono, il diritto Romano e il Vangelo-, he added in Italian. Do you follow?" "I refuse to incriminate myself, ergo cito Emendationem Quintam, I replied in my ersatz Latin version of 'I am taking the Fifth Amendment'. But, do you mean such contradictions as Pontius Pilate putting Jesus on trial which was impossible to do under Roman Law?" Grigori smiled. "All right, no more parabola. Considering your atrophied mind, I shall make it all elementary from now on.

Thanks to my Communist masters who despatched me at the age of 20 to France as an immigrant student, out of uniform, a sub rosa civilian, I started out receiving a conventional Western World religious education. I myself and my equivalents from other Soviet intelligence services were selected for assignments at universities in Paris, Poitiers, Grenoble and Caen. I was determined to get to Paris to enroll at the Institut Catholique de Paris, one of the schools targeted by my bosses. I asked my uncle Alex to help. The same wonderful uncle Alexander who had seen to my teenage tutoring, and later, found political sponsors for my officer training. Now he pulled strings in Moscow once again. Some said his influence was well earned by secretly aborting wives of Party bigwigs of their bastard embryos at his Lake Ladoga cottage. Whatever it was, he got me to Paris. Under superb teachers I studied Ecclesiastical as well as French Civil Law. By sharpening my capacity for sophistry in argument they were actually helping me attract sensitive youngsters of the future French governing classes to Lenin's political religion - the Communist Party's insidious long term objective."

"Don't tell them to become Communists. Just give them a whiff, a soupçon of the intoxicating excitement that derives from one's ability to manipulate man's mind and his emotions", the Party man told me.

"Sons of affluent Catholic families had a Pavlovian response to what they liked to call "intellectualized dialectics of materialist philosophy", without having any idea of its meaning. They were the easiest of preys. I would have been far less effective among the instinctive logicians of the factory workers or among farmers where Catholic priests in coveralls were particularly active. As I listened to them, to these diguised pastors, I began to understand that the forces of control and inquisition already imposed on my Russia were now being midwifed by the Communists in France.

In my spare time I read voraciously. Instead of Maxim Gorky whom my bosses recommended because of his enthusiasm for bolshevism, I secretly devoured several component novels of Balzac's *Comédie humaine*, works of the incomparable Victor Hugo and of Alfred de Musset. Flaubert's *L'Éducation Sentimentale* gave me insight on French society of the mid 19th century. And Zola, of course. His novel *Germinal* evoked the brutal surpression of strikes in Russian coal mines".

"Grigori, I must interrupt to ask an important question. You mocked my non-philosophy but without really telling me why. Now you say that while in Paris you read voraciously which I can believe because all young men at the age of 25 passionately devour the writings of famous authors. However, you seem to have concentrated on French Romantic writers, completely ignoring works of philosophic enquiry. I must be wrong. Tell me, did that come at a later time?" "Of course you are wrong. In different periods of my life I not only read but took great pains to analyze the postulations of many philosophers and schools, from ascetism to transcendentalism, from ethics to metaphysics. The deeper I interrogated, the better I realized that among these exalted minds I could find none capable of making me understand myself better, of contributing to my spiritual well-being or to my intellectual fulfilment. So, just as you advocate, Evgenii, I began to simplify and to follow the rule that unless the argument can prove immediately useful or the subject is highly beguiling one should not waste time on it. You can call this shallow thinking,the vagaries of an empty mind if you wish, but it reduces the chances of getting ensnared in contradictory results from parallel tracks of reasoning. I found that most heavy thinkers make many plausible observations but fail to arrive at any provable conclusions. They are not unlike the heroine in a Proust novel who needs many elaborately structured metaphors to feel that she feels nothing. Often I wanted to say to them: "If only you could convince me you are right, it would be so happy to agree with you". Is that simplified enough for you, Evgenii? Or evasive enough?"

The most important, the happiest part of my life in Paris was seeing my father. I knew where to find him but my every move was monitored. My obligatory weekly reports were supposed to list all persons I saw and what we talked about. My mission control spot checked. Still, it was not too difficult to arrange our secret meetings. My father's trusted friend, onetime member of the Diaghilev troupe *Ballet Russes*, would leave messages for me with one of the university's employees, a circumcized Russian from Kiev.

The first time I embraced this sensitive gentle man who was my father he wept. For me seeing him was like finding myself, like coming home from war - a delirious vertigo. "I can never forgive myself, he would tell me, for abandoning you and your mother. For running". I tried but could find nothing to console his inconsolable Russian soul.

In Petrograd, renamed Leningrad by the Bolsheviks, we regularly received news of him. Paris was home to many Russians. Igor Stravinsky and Prokofiev and Rachmaninoff were there. So was father's special friend, the great impresario Sergei Diaghilev.

After Stalin seized power thousands of Russians poured into France. Not one admitted being bourgeois. All claimed princely titles. The French joked that the Czar must have had an incredibly large family. Sadly, all of them believed they would be going home soon.

The Bolshevik nightmare would not last, they said. I knew my father shared their hopes and even from far away I could hear his cries of anguish, for he loved my mother desperately and there was no life for him without her. I wanted my mother to join him. Uncle Alex had the means to arrange it. He was angered by my pleadings, calling me a fool. Her inexplicable absence would put us all in danger, he explained.

I too had chosen to escape the Communist entrapment and though this might not have been evident to anti-Bolsheviks in Russia who no longer called me their friend, I was not guilty of betrayal. Nor did I feel remorse deceiving the young French collegians. I got to know them well enough to be convinced they would soon forget my conspiratorial tuition. After all, they were incorrigibly French and stubbornly Catholic. I did hope they would retain in their sentimental memory the beauty of our Russian music and ballet to which I often introduced them. While following my chartered course I had to play the game. There would be no wavering in my resolve. To the end of my life I would seek the destruction of

Communist rule in my country and remain a Russian patriot. My father understood me and knew that in different ways we were both prisoners of fate. This brought me solace. Still, Evgenii, I was not made of steel. There were moments of paralyzing doubt and of fear. In the loneliness of my Paris room I could not always hold back my sobs". Grigori stopped. It was not too hard for me to imagine Grigori as a young man torn by conflicting emotions and I wanted to tell him so. It would not do. He would accuse me again of sentimentalism. Instead I asked him to continue his story.

"Like a well trained dog, I had performed so efficiently during two and a half years in France that on my return to Russia my superiors had me transferred to Military Intelligence with the rank of Major. I would be relatively safe now. Not a Party member, still a trusted tovarish no longer subject to constant surveillance.

I went through several more years of political drill, of Spanish studies, then more indoctrination. It was their way of training young minds so as to make them deceivingly polished. But like manicured French lawns they were fed with manure. After a brief teaching spell at the Krupskaya Institute of Culture, the devoted mechanical device they thought they had in me was ready for a new assignment.

In 1937 the great tacticians of the world-wide Communist movement, these absurdly powerful men sent me to Spain. I spent a year reporting to Moscow on the war, hiding my own feelings. The atrocities committed in the Civil War by both sides but especially by the anti-clerical Popular Front of Republicans, Socialists, Communists and Syndicalists sickened me. As an escape from reality once again I began reading everything I could put my hands on. By force of circumstances the choice of authors was desultory: Ortega y Gasset's *Revolt of the Masses*, the anti-clerical writings of Pio Baroja, Federico Garcia Lorca's *Romancero Gitano*. Secretly I travelled to the University of Salamanca where until a year before my arrival in Spain Miguel de Unamuno had been rector. There I permanently borrowed several of his books including *La Agonia del Cristianismo*. His judgment that philosophy could not bring one closer to God because philosophy is not unlike mathematics, whereas religion is intuitive, that God did not exist and that man was God because he created God, pained and tormented me. A Catholic *sui generis*, he was forever attempting to separate orthodox dogmatic catholicism from popular sentimental catholicism, refusing to accept the authority and the teachings of the Church of Rome. He disapproved of the clergy. In a letter to his friend Maurice Legendre he called clergy 'une ordure avec une admirable politesse' -admirably well bred garbage. He detested monasticism. He held that Jesuitism preaches and teaches implicit faith,a passive submission. I suspect, Evgenii, that his view of the clergy was among the reasons you liked him so well. And, I must admit that whether I agreed with him or not he made a deeper impression on me than any French writer. Generally, I found Spanish authors less capricious, more sanguine.

I had been thinking too hard,too long. Spain made me drive myself too hard, too long. A kind of neurosis was taking me over. I had to get liberated from too many convulsive influences, the split between rational thinking and irrational beliefs. From the depths of my soul I was crying out: Allah give me back my eyes, free me of philosophers.

Allah may have been listening. Just at that time I chanced to meet a young Spaniard, Alvaro de Portillo, who brought me into the religious society *Opus Dei*, founded in Spain in 1928 by Monsignor Maria Escriva de Balaguer. Alvaro, of whom I became very fond, told me that liberal Catholics considered *Opus Dei* secretive and elitist. This appealed to me. Yes, Evgenii, Don Miguel de Unamuno influenced your thinking. The *Opus Dei* near mystical concept of moral laws crystallized mine. "Simplify, always simplify. There may be mystery to life but not to living". Those were the words you shouted at me out of your rebellious mind when we first met in no-man's land. I had heard the same words before. Da, from these remarkable men in Spain who inspired but imposed no constraints on me.

Do you remember the words of Fevronia in Rimsky-Korsakov's opera *Kitezh*? She sings: "God does not bless the tears of sorrow, God blesses the tears of celestial joy". Thanks to my new apostles I found spiritual serenity. I was no longer a barefooted crusader without a cross.

They told me I was welcome to stay with them. They would arrange my asylum. I could not accept. I had to go back to Russia where I would wait, hiding the crucifix under the pillow while pretending to read Lenin in the library. Leaving my friends caused me doubt and anguish. To tear myself away from my love Maria Dolores, whom I called Kiriki, was excruciating torture. What is it, Evgenii, that makes man run away from happiness to embrace pain instead? I would return soon. To a new Spain, I said. My friends knew I hoped for a Franco victory".

Grigori was locked in reminiscences, so I refrained from telling him that in a different period, years later, I too had made friends with a prominent member of *Opus Dei*. I met Alberto Ullastres through a high Spanish government official and distinguished playwright José Antonio Jimenez Arnau, with whom I had concluded several agreements on behalf of the American film industry. He told me about Alberto's dedication to *Opus Dei* and that this Catholic group was winning much political influence in Spain. I immediately liked Ullastres. He reminded me of my old friend Lee Dayton, the man of silent combat in postwar Poland, who some years later was appointed American ambassador to Turkey. Lee and Alberto were spiritual twins, exceptional men of iron wills, purity in character and of ascetic bearing who radiated tranquil self-confidence.

When Alberto told me he would be visiting the United States, I immediately cabled the New York office of the Motion Picture Association strongly recommending he be extended every courtesy. The Association's vice president to whom I had sent my cable somehow managed to forget all about it and when Ullastres appeared at our New York office, no one troubled to receive him. Fortunately, he was not a man to hold a grudge. Still, New York's gaucherie put me at a considerable psychological disadvantage in my subsequent talks with the Spanish authorities, because shortly after his return from America Alberto was appointed Spain's Minister of Commerce, and *Opus Dei* became a political powerhouse.

Within approximately the same time frame Stanton Griffis, the stretch-limousine-high decibel landlord, the American diplomatic casse-pieds of Warsaw fame was again appointed ambassador. This time to Spain, promptly shocking the conservative, straight-laced old fashioned, prudish and superbly elegant Madrid society by breathing down the décolleté cleavages of beautiful women at diplomatic receptions while rudely pinching their bottoms. One day he invited me to join him for lunch at his favorite Madrid country club. There he was, sitting next to the pool sipping a drink. In the background I could see Xavier Cugat rehearsing his famous rhumba band. Stanton was noticeably edgy. He had a gun on him. "Stanton, I said, what gives with the artillery?" "I guess you don't know. Basque terrorists are trying to kill me. I keep bodyguards and a Beretta in my belt". "You can't be serious", I said laughing. Then I remembered what the famous actor Antonio Vilar had told me about Spanish husbands vowing to kill Griffis for his insulting behavior toward their wives. I did not for a moment believe there was any real danger to his life. But, knowing Spaniards I had to admit that all considered this was not a laughing matter. Stanton, to save face, invented the Basque threat.

I could not help sympathizing with Stanton's predicament provoked by his vigorous pursuit of beautiful women, as I myself had just recently barely escaped a catastophe of my own making that brought me close to hysterical trauma. My new personal secretary in Rome, instead of taking messages, unwittingly informed all callers I was vacationing in Spain and could be found at the Madrid Hilton.

At the time I had several lady friends, three of particular attraction. One was Spanish and lived in Madrid, the other Parisian, the third a New Yorker. I was eminently successful in keeping them separated and unaware of each other. Then, one incredible day in Madrid, as my Spanish companion and I walked into the Hilton bar, I saw my New York paramour surrounded by a coterie of admirers. I should have been on my guard when the concierge told me an American lady had been inquiring about me. I paid no attention because in the film business one tends to become blasé and immune to the attentions of aspiring actresses. However this time it was no stage struck novice hoping for a part but an accomplished actress about to star in a new Broadway play. I backed out of the bar as if stung by a bee, dragging my precious Madrileña to the lobby and out of the hotel. She thought I had suddenly gone bonkers. Normally, after a drink and lunch, we retired to my suite until cocktail time. Somehow I managed to pacify her and send her home.

My knees buckled when on returning to the hotel lobby I saw my Paris love checking in at the reception desk. She saw me too and discretely awaited my move. "Chérie, I gushed, you are ravishing. How I missed you". "You can make up for it tonight", she said. As my luck would have it, I was spotted by New York while attempting to duck into the elevator. "Dahling, I've gone nearly mad trying to find you. The flight from New Yohk was positively ghastly. After I've made such sacrifices to join you here you must console me. Aren't you simply thrilled?" "How wonderful of you to surprise me, I said, but forgive me I must run to an important appointment with a Spanish minister". "Never mind dahling, she chirped. Pick me up in my room for dinner tonight". So now there were three, two in the same hotel.

During the next forty hours, lying, frenetically dashing from tryst to tryst, I staggered through four tête-à-tête luncheons, three dinners, several breakfasts, a lake of drinks, all with strenuous excercises in between. They never met. I remembered having heard that if you lift a guinea pig by its tail his eyes fall out. I feared that if I got discovered this would happen to me. I bribed the chief concierge, Angel, to smuggle me out of the hotel before dawn amd drive me to the airport. There was only one early morning flight. I went to Casablanca. From there I sent three telegrams.

Chapter 5

Grigori's Story

Castel Gandolfo Gardens

Grigori was spreading some documents on the table in the gazebo. "Yes, I know, he said to me. You first want to hear more about my father. Very well. Let us forget intelligence matters for a while and drive down to the local village for a glass of Frascati wine. We can relax and I shall give you a glimpse of my family history".

"James! William!" He called out to two young men who were leaning against a nearby tree: "Come along. Quickly." I had not really paid much attention to them but now hearing their names I got curious and apparently showed it. "Evgenii, meet my trusted companions. They are American, like you. Both played football, or what YOU call football, for the University of Notre Dame. They are bulky and strong as bulls". Bulky? Why yes. Now that they came close I could see that. But not only the way Grigori meant it. They were wearing civvies. The large bulges under their jackets were obvious. I guessed they were either priests or lay members of *Opus Dei*. Probably the latter, considering Grigori's affiliation. Noticing my surprise William smiled at me, sat down and pulled up his trouser leg exposing what looked like a long thin sheath with a little knob on top fastened flat above his ankle. He had to be joking, I thought. Churchmen wouldn't be running round with guns and knives, at Castel Gandolfo of all places, -the summer residence of the Pope-, would they? "Get off it, I said. You're not fooling me". "His Excellency tends to drop his guard and you have forgotten your bible. Be sober, be vigilant, it says, because your adversary the devil as a roaring lion walketh about seeking whom to devour. And Sir, if we didn't know our jobs we wouldn't be worth a fart in the dark, would we?" "Isn't this rather colorful language for Notre Dame, let alone men of God", I asked. "Nothing to do with our university or with the Almighty. The expression is strictly Chicago". This came from James. I could not help wondering if they were all having fun at my expense.

James did the driving. We went downhill a few miles, stopping at a small nondescript trattoria with only four uncovered and dusty tables. "Let us have some good Frascati wine", Grigori said. I didn't want to protest that there is no such thing as a good Frascati. It was always young, raw, only slightly aromatic and invariably left one with a monumental hangover. "Cameriere, bring us some apples too", Grigori commanded. Then to my astonishment he began to slice pieces of apple with a penknife that appeared from his pocket, dropping the cuttings into his wine before sipping it with gusto. I had never seen Grigori like this before. Today we was not the stiff military, the lecturer, the stern philosopher. He was just Grigori, the friend. Relaxed. Smiling. He seemed younger, too. It was wonderful to find him that way.

"Let us begin, he said, by telling you about our beloved St. Petersburg in 1917 and before. Once it was the city of light. A city of opulence, of splendor, of exaggerated richness and born of a dream. The dream of Czar Peter the Great who during his wide European travels became enamored of Paris, its fine public buildings, its open boulevards, its parks. The royal and princely magnificence of the Versailles Palace built for King Louis XIV intoxicated him. Czar Peter was known as "The Great" not only for his territorial conquests but also for his vision,imaginative concepts, love of beauty and his devotion to the virtues of perfection. He resolved to turn his dream into reality and in 1703 founded the city of St. Petersburg. For many years afterward the most accomplished of French and Italian architects, city planners, civil engineers, painters, sculptors, draftsmen, furniture makers, gardners, artisans and all manner of craftsmen were bought, coerced, blackmailed, bribed or otherwise transacted to contribute their talents and labors to the creation of the Czar's wonder city, while his agents purchased or purloined from the world's museums, art galleries and private collections the finest masterpieces to enrich St. Petersburg which became Russia's capital. For generations to come it continued to thrive, to glitter, to amuse, impress and often shock Europe's dissipated rich and noble with its intemperate lavishness. A single bejeweled gown of a debutante presented at the Imperial Court would have bought a serf's freedom. Rich noblemen amused themselves by deliberately having their mounts lose solid gold horseshoes as they galloped through throngs of peasants, just for the thrill of watching the poverty stricken fight for possession of the prize, then cheering when Cossack silver-tipped cat-o'nine tails tore flesh off the bloodied backs of the moujiks in an obscene obedience lesson.

But, and much to the envy of other capitals, St. Petersburg was also the center of music, grand opera and ballet. Here Rimsky-Korsakov held the baton of the City Symphony. Mussorgsky presented his opera *Boris Godunov* with Fyodor Chaliapin, the greatest basso voice of all time. Alexander Borodin composed the opera *Prince Igor* and audiences thrilled to the dancing of the prima of all ballerinas, the divine Anna Pavlova.

The first major social tremors began in St. Petersburg with a short-lived and quite unheeded revolution of the proletariat in 1905. Few Russians imagined that this butterfly's wingbeat would eventually lead to a hurricane. Matters were getting progressively worse in all of Russia. The country was at war since 1914. Russia's attack on East Prussia was crushed by the Germans at Tannenberg. By the end of 1915 the Germans forced the Russians out of Poland, Repeated defeats, costing Russia two million dead, sapped her morale. The government ran out of money, unable to borrow abroad because previous loans were in default. At the beginning of 1917 the Vestnik Pravitelstva -Government Messenger- newspaper announced the collapse of the Ruble due to uncontrollable inflation. The government tried launching Liberty Bonds and found no buyers. There was no money to pay striking workers. Labor minister Skobolov desperately tried to get them back to the factories. Their reply was: "we need bread, not work", but grain stocks for the capital were estimated to last not more than ten days. For lack of locomotive parts rail transport broke down. Farmers refused to bring produce into the city, hoarding it instead. The threat of famine was ever present. Social unrest increased by the moment. Amidst enormous confusion no one knew what was exactly happening or where the numerous political factions stood. There were the Bolsheviks, the Mensheviks, the officer organizations, the Cadets, the workers and their unions, the Communist Party, the so-called Spontaneous Political Delegations, the Councils elected by workers, peasants and soldiers known as The Soviets, the many military garrisons inside and near the city, each with commanders of a different political color, not to mention the ever shouting anarchists who were against everything and everybody crying "destroy them all", or the agitators, the rabble rousers, the thugs and gangs of thieves, the German spies, agents-provocateurs and the milling mass of ordinary but very angry citizens unable to find food for their families.

Now listen carefully, Evgenii, for this is how it was. In the *petit salon* of our home my parents, trying desperately to ignore the implications of the turmoil around them, were having a lively discussion. "Dushka, my father was saying, I think we shall have to forego Nikolai's concert tonight. It is getting too dangerous out there in the streets". "But Yuri, my mother interrupted, Tcherepnin is such a good friend. He wanted Grigori to meet his son whom, they say, is superbly talented. We promised Grigori we would take him. You always say one should not disappoint 13 year olds. Besides, we are only ten minutes from the conservatory. Mikhail will watch the carriage. Also Glazunov will be there and you were anxious to talk with him about his latest symphonic poem you thought so emotional, so very romantic."

My mother knew very well that when my father called her "Dushka" it meant he was leaving it up to her to decide. Nervous and irritable for weeks now, coming home late at night after meetings at the Conservatory, he looked pale and drawn. We could not understand the reasons for these midnight gatherings. What was a voice instructor doing there anyway, we wondered. Also, he was visiting the Lunacharsky Library more and more often. He brought home a Russian -English dictionary. Among the borrowed books on his library desk was *The Great French Revolution* by Prince Piotr Alexeievich Kropotkin -the social philosopher and anarchist-, a collection of Charles Péguy's *Cahiers de la Quinzaine*, a volume by the Englishman Chesterfield. My mother told me she knew nothing of Péguy even though she had taken compulsory French at school, but she had heard that Chesterton was a dangerous propagandist for Catholicism. She was mystified why anyone would say "dangerous", as if Catholicism was some kind of infectious desease. A Catholic priest had baptized her in Oranienbaum where she was born, even though my grandparents were of the Orthodox faith, or at least we were so told. The priest gave her the name Christiana. Her parents called he Natasha. This was a mystery in her life. Her mother mentioned it only once just before she married without, however, explaining the circumstances under which it all occurred.

"You must tell Yuri. There are to be no secrets between man and his wife" she said. Yuri kept it quiet. In conservative Petrograd any deviation from the conventional was bound to cause gossip. Sometimes she wondered if Stravinsky, born in Oranienbaum like herself and whose father was of Polish extraction, could also be a Catholic. She knew this was just silly curiosity. Yuri admired Stravinsky but confessed he could not fully understand why Igor was beginning to stray from the grandiloquence of Romanticism to an academic kind of Neo-Classicism, the brusque unsympathetic style of discord.

Observing Yuri she could see he was deeply troubled. He seemed different, changed, his behavior erratic. It frightened her. So did the anger of the streets. Well, tonight was tonight. She would insist they go to the concert. She needed to get out of the house and Yuri enjoyed music above all things. Glazunov was among his favorites. Just at breakfast Yuri told her Glazunov's work had the vigor, the majesty of an oak. "Always serene and beautiful. It reflects joy and triumph", he said.

"Concert tonight?", she asked Yuri adored his petite, blonde, blue eyed wife. "All right, let us go but I wish Glazunov would write an opera with a good part for a splendid baritone like me", he said, kissing Natasha's forehead.

The concert was a disappointment. Many seats remained empty, an unheard of insult to the Conservatory. The restless, unresponsive audience whispered, shifted, coughed. The musicians were listless. The program was cut short with an apology from the twitchy conductor.

Mikhail, their coachman, had difficulty manoeuvering the carriage. Groups had collected on corners to unexpectedly rush across streets shouting. Some carried crudely painted signs. Others made threatening gestures. Yuri ordered the coachman to stop. They were at the French embassy on Nevsky Prospect. "Funny we should find ourselves here". Their old friend, Georgi Vassilevich, was pointing to the other side of the Neva river. "Look, he said. Over there stretches the Vyborg quarter, the vast industrial zone of our city.

Can you see the bonfires at the end of Sampsonievsky Prospect? The workers of the giant Poutilov industry are preparing to march on city center. There are thirty six thousand of them and I am told they may be joined by the ten thousand machine-gunners from neighboring military barracks. We also hear rumors that anarchist sailors at the naval port of Kronstadt are close to mutiny and they are but fifty kilometers from here."

Yuri could feel Natasha pulling hard on his arm."Please, let us go, she said. The smell of this rotting river sickens me. Why don't they clean it up?" Yuri thought there was no point in frightening poor Natasha further by telling her that all public services had stopped functioning long ago. He just tightly held her tiny hand.

By the time they got home, bringing with them Georgi Vassilevich, they were longing for a stiff drink. Georgi Vassilevich had connections close to General Kornilov. They hoped he might tell them what was really going on. His words staggered them. Russia would be torn, he said, by a revolution that was heir to the vast tsarist empire of all the Russias. The entire nation was so far behind other countries in social development that it was too late for a bourgeois revolution. It was being preempted instead by a bloody insurrection of the proletariat.

"You understand, Evgenii, I was too young to take part in the conversations of my elders but I did have my father's tacit permission to sit in the library adjoining the petit salon, just behind the half closed door and to listen.

I heard my mother sob. My father protested: "I must do something. We must all do something to avert this calamity." But history moved fast in 1917. In March the Russian parliament, the Duma, forced the Czar to abdicate. A provisional government was then organized under the leadership of Kerensky, a naturalized American citizen, a social revolutionary without the socialist doctrine, a totally useless flamboyant idealist. His government was soon overthrown by the Bolsheviks and he fled abroad.

Let me tell you, Evgenii, that to those artists and writers who looked forward to a new social order it seemed that their hopes had been fulfilled. In its first years the revolutionary state was indeed a sponsor of social reform and also of artistic discovery. But after the first period of relative creative freedom writers, painters and even composers were instructed to help build socialism, to choose heroic worthy themes, abandoning free-ranging experimentation. The Soviet realist line held that a work should fulfill the criteria of party spirit, form commitment to prescribed ideology and give true portrayal of the life of the common people.

The pervasive reverberations of these slogans infuriated my father. When bolsheviks distributed their leaflets at the Conservatory he would tear them up. Increasingly disillusioned and bitter witnessing the social strife and political betrayal, he joined anti-Communist forces. The movement failed. Its leaders were arrested or went into hiding. Though my father remained free, Georgi Vassilevich warned us that police investigations would continue.

My uncle Alexander Romodanov was a well known surgeon at the largest hospital of St. Petersburg, now called Petrograd. I liked my mother's older brother. He would come to supper at least once a month. During the warm weather we often visited with him at his country cottage on Lake Ladoga.

One late autumn night my parents were awakened by knocking on their bedroom window. It was uncle Alex, breathless and in a state of considerable agitation. He herded us into le petit salon. "Don't bother with tea, Natasha, he rasped. We don't have the time. Yuri, Natasha and you too, young Grigori, listen carefully for I must give you very bad news. This evening I had an emergency conference at the hospital to discuss our finances. As you know, the place is practically broke. Doctor Dobrovolsky, our head administrator, reported that during the afternoon he had gone to see the authorities who told him to stop sending petitions because the treasury had other more important priorities and could not spare any addtional funds. When he protested, they threw him out of the office.

"Imagine, he said to us. They had the audacity to treat me like a beggar. Me, a distinguished doctor, known to all of St. Petersburg". As other board members prepared to leave, Dobrovolsky asked me to join him in the maternity ward at the end of the building. There he told me that an old friend, high in the Bolshevik hierarchy, who had witnessed his humiliation at the hands of government officials, caught up with him in the street to quickly whisper: "I'll wait for you at my home, but hurry now". Making sure he was not being followed, Dobrovolsky obeyed the summons. "Don't ever betray me, his friend pleaded, but I must tell you that I participated in today's meeting of the Party's Executive Committee where it was decided to immediately arrest thirty enemies of the Revolution. Romadonov's brother-in-law is on the list. I saw it. You and Romadonov are close friends so I had to alert you. Now do what you must do and do it without delay."

Red in face, sputtering with anger, uncle Alex continued. "Yuri, pack only a small case. Better still, just a knapsack. Leave after dawn when the streets get busy. Go to my cottage at Lake Ladoga without attracting attention. Wait there until someone you know arrives with my instructions." We were stunned. No one had the courage to speak. We all knew that to hesitate, to postpone would mean arrest, a hasty military tribunal, no defence, a death sentence or, at best, a Siberian labor camp. Uncle Alex returned three days later. "Everything has been taken care of, he said. Yuri is on his way to France.I gave him the address of professor Morin. You do remember Philippe Morin? He was always correcting our French when he came on vacation here. Now brace yourself for a shock. To make sure you, Natasha and Yuri are not subjected to police persecution, I contrived also a second scheme. Tomorrow you will have to attend Yuri's funeral. You see, he died in the hospital under the surgeon's knife. I personally operated and signed the death certificate. Of course it was not Yuri but another man. I gave his papers to your father who is now Yuri Sergeievich Orlov. Don't despair, Natasha. Lenin is a very sick man. He will go soon. The whole Bolshevik hell will disappear with him. Yuri will be home sooner than you think". "Evgenii, it did not happen that way. Trotsky and Stalin fought for power. Stalin won and created OGPU, the vicious State Police. Then, from the darkest depths of man's schizophrenic nature the most violent reign of hatred and terror would convulse the life and spirit of Russian people for many years to come." Grigori said nothing further. It was the silence of his remembrance. James drove us back to Castel Gandolfo.

Vatican Chambers II

I sent several messages to Grigori through his Irish secretary asking to see him when I knew he had returned to Rome from Castel Gandolfo. After some weeks which I spent amidst the craggy slopes of the Abruzzi mountains from where Hitler's man Skorzeny rescued Benito Mussolini, following his capture by Italian partisans, word finally came through I could use my Vatican pass. By then I had pretty well sorted out my notes, though I had to admit in all honesty that Grigori's s discourses on religion still had me baffled.

Grigori greeted me with warmth but I sensed some annoyance as well and wondered over the cause. Then I saw his face twitching as if reflecting pain. I realized he was a sick man. I knew better than to say anything and soon he reverted to his lightly patronizing didactic mode.

"Why you should wish to delve into all these matters I cannot imagine, for you can put them to no practical use. I will restrict your research to the files headed Summaries and Comments and shall have to approve any notes you take. The folders marked Case Documents must remain secret.You can see some but not all of them. You will not mention any names. As you well know, one of the cardinal rules of intelligence services is that under no circumstances can names of double agents be revealed by the service that turned them. This rule is never broken. Any claims to the contrary are nothing but deliberate, calculated lies.

The contents of the files in front of you have all been translated from Russian and other languages on a highly confidential basis at the Pontificia Universitas Gregoriana where, by the way, I often lecture on Marxist philosophy and on the phenomenology of religion.

Being an unwavering anglophile, Evgenii, you wanted to know if the British intelligence services were really as good as you found them to be in postwar Poland. I think that in many respects you will be disillusioned. Schedule "C" in front of you contains summaries of communications received by the First Chief Directorate of the KGB responsible for all foreign activities. Also those received by my own military intelligence organization, the GRU and by the Joint KGB-GRU Committee on Technical and Scientific Intelligence, the GKNIIR. I will let you read the English translation of one particular report submitted to the Central Committee by the KGB just after the Second World War.

"British intelligence and in fact the British Civil Service in general is plagued by budgetary cramps that cause enormous problems. Chronic shortage of qualified personnel results in function overload. This touches off protracted inter-service frictions. The frequent shifting of department and section heads jeopardizes continuity of essential actions which, in any event, are often ill defined. British inability to clearly determine priorities, to prepare relative blueprints and to assign follow-through responsibilities makes for constant chaos and frustration. One of our American friends described the British intelligence modus operandi with great sarcasm but truthfully. He said that when confronted with the new and imponderable, the normally phlegmatic Englishmen become high-strung neurasthenics, behaving like ants in heat. The team of Oglethorpe and Pettigrew rush east, while their associates, Ipswich and Frobisher, scramble north with the other half of the secret file, never managing to have their paths converge. They just stumble from one departmental cock-up to another. Obsessive fear of political fallout among top leadership filters down only to increase the overall stress. In this climate of unstableness Englishmen complain a lot and, inevitably, talk too much. The flow of informers is constant. We find it extraordinary that the British Services employ such a conspicuous number of sexual deviates whom we find easy to exploit. Graduates of England's famous universities appear to be the chief examples of this decadence in British society."

After reading the report I said: "Grigori, this is so much moonshine, invention, balderdash and, if his Excellency will pardon my French, just plain *merde*". Grigori grimaced.

"Well, perhaps not entirely. Would you like to hear my own assessment of the British? "Definitely, but only if it is less one-sided, less prejudiced and not so obviously loaded with envy", I exploded. Then realizing how offensive I had become I said "please accept my apologies. You know I value your views".

Grigori looked at me sharply. "I'll try to be totally impartial. First let me say that British Intelligence had a number of traitors at the highest level of their services to whom the English themselves, in their infinite arrogance, attributed aptitudes the turncoats did not in fact possess. Compared to our professionals the British were inept bunglers, many of whom found themselves in important positions and privy to secret information solely due to their family or school connections. Even traitors like Burgess, Maclean, Philby, or the man we called Casey, whom the British considered real top-notchers in the intelligence game, actually had very little to add to what we already knew about the structure and methodology of the MI5, MI6 and our only real nemesis, the Government Communications Headquarters-GCHQ or their respective derivatives.

I don't mean to say that these Englishmen were of no value to us. The remarkable skills in dissimulation, manipulation, prevarication and techniques of disinformation they had acquired during their fruitful academic years brought us both immediate and long term dividends. They were able to perfidiously deceive and misdirect their own people with regard to Soviet-intended moves while at the same time providing us with details of British planning. This inside information permitted us to anticipate British actions, neutralize them or even turn them to our advantage. Still, their contributions were dwarfed by the only really important, determinative type of intelligence that was provided us by our most valuable sources namely British scientists and technicians.

Very early in the game we were able to discover that in the counter intelligence sector neither the British nor the Americans had any qualified knowledge of KGB's First Chief Directorate or its Department "S" which controlled so-called illegals, our agents entering countries under deep cover for secret missions with forged documents and not protected by diplomatic immunity."

"Moreover, Grigori continued, the British MI5 was particularly ill-equipped to discover illegals because, believe it or not, its Registry had no fingerprint records, an important element in counter-espionage work. Also, the MI5 could not do voice analysis directly as it had no forensic facilities of its own and had to make arrangements with Scotland Yard through Special Branch.

Even with their significant scientific breakthroughs in the intercepting of electronic signals by use of sophisticated probe microphones which allowed the British to record encrypted Russian communications, their cryptoanalysis H Division of GCHQ never succeeded in deciphering our cryptonyms. Consequently, at any one time we were able to maintain high numbers of undetected active Russian agents in the United Kingdom.

On the nuisance side we had the warped British intellectuals, the frustrated government employees, the crackpot idealists interested only, they would say, in saving the world from destruction, the cashiered ex-military and a host of others constantly volunteering to work for us as spies. Never totally discounting the potential value of such offers, we were, nevertheless, extremely careful to avoid entrapment by the A Branch of MI5 or by the FBI. Sometimes we enjoyed setting up the more obvious liars with the Double Cross Committee of MI5 which believed itself expert in turning our agents. When it worked, it amused us to later find proofs of the confusion these phonies caused their new masters. When our ploy failed, the British made sure to let us know they weren't fooled. In violation of accepted intelligence operating procedures, but often enough, agents on opposing teams would exchange information as a kind of "you owe me one" insurance. From our side nothing ever of a critical nature.

In the psychological warfare area we injected into the wellsprings of British thoughts and emotions a virus of American origin called I.P.P. - Intelligence Penetration Paranoia. We nurtured its widespread effects through our carefully documented and well briefed presumed defectors who under GRU or KGB control generously furnished the British with clues implying the existence of an informer at the highest level of their Security Services. For instance, one of our spurious defectors from Russian Intelligence in Tokyo, Rostvorov, refused to go to England because he said he knew that British Intelligence had been infiltrated by the KGB. He insisted on being taken to Australia instead. Once more MI6 bought the story and London got super nervous again. Just what we had in mind.

The British and the Americans wasted precious time, manpower, and huge sums of money tracking the phony leads round the world. The super mole was never discovered, not because he did not exist but because our experts in the double cross planted clues that pointed in the wrong direction, followed at a later stage by further signals which were just sufficiently transparent prevarications to make the British wonder if they were being hoaxed. But as the predictable British by nature always remain faithful to doubt, they created for themselves that psychological monster Americans called omnidirectional suspicion. This spy phantom continued to haunt the corridors of Whitehall, sow fear of political fall-out among the members of the Joint Intelligence Committee and paralyze the actions of even the most sharp-witted British administrators. We never let them off the hook, constantly adding new elements to bedevil them.

The list of British Intelligence foul-ups and incompetence was staggering. Where they did excel was in their unbelievable willingness and ability to cover up major blunders for which men in our own services would have been shot. A classic example is that of the espionage activities in England of a German woman, Ursula Beurton, and her English husband Leon, both Soviet agents. They were denounced to MI5 by an English member of another Soviet spy group in Switzerland coded The Lucy Ring. However, the Director General of MI5, Roger Hollis, buried the information, permitting the Beurtons to continue their unmolested espionage activities in England, primarily in the field of atomic secrets, for a long time, until they suddenly disappeared in East Germany. MI5 later discovered that Ursula's father, René Kuczynski, who taught at Oxford University, also spied for us supplying political information secured in talks he had with a member of the British War Cabinet, Sir Stafford Cripps. Poor Sir Stafford remained totally unaware of the professor's treachery. Again MI5 did nothing. At first our baffled analysts believed the British had some spectacular coup against us in mind, but in fact it was just their willful dereliction of duty. Suffice to say that in the mid-sixties their own so-called Fluency Committee formed by the D Branch of MI5 and the Counter- intelligence Division of MI6 to research the problem admitted to some 200 cases of Soviet penetration of British Intelligence Services. Actually, Evgenii, this figure applied to the examples the British believed they had post factum information about. They actually missed another 70 percent.

In contrast, we disposed of the world's finest intelligence networks, with collaborators virtually everywhere. A constant flow of information reached our central system day and night from our Directorates, our missions abroad and their agents. Take it from me, Evgenii, the scope, the precision and the sophistication of our organization defied imagination. We were invariably way ahead of the British, scoring success after success. In 1964 we contrived a plan to embarrass the British Conservative Government. It succeeded beyond our expectations. And how did this occur? The KGB had a very handsome operative parading as assistant naval attaché of our London embassy. His sexual prowess was much talked about among the wives of diplomats. It was not difficult for him to become the lover of a beautiful young woman called Keeler whom we knew to be the secret mistress of Britain's War Minister, Profumo. When, at KGB instructions, Ivanov publicly exposed the Profumo-Keeler liaison, admitting his own involvement with the lady, and it was leaked to the press that our naval attaché Evgenii Ivanov was in fact a KGB agent, it caused a political earthquake. The Conservative government fell, and after General Elections the Labour Party's Harold Wilson became Prime Minister. Reportedly Winston Churchill snorted: "Poor Harold. He needed genital erections to win the General Elections". This Churchillian quip, true or false, echoed all the way to the Kremlin. For us it was political victory of much consequence.

Now I must ask you to leave, Evgenii". "Hasta cuando Grigori"? "Until I call you".

Vatican Chambers (a month later)

Grigori did not look well. He was pale. His hands shook as he greeted me. I had hoped we could just exchange friendly reminiscences without tiring him. Also I was just a little bored with all the spook stories. Most of them were off the record anyway and what he authorized me to write about would have to wait, he said, till after he died. In any event, I was firmly convinced I would never put anything in writing because I was too personally involved with most of the happenings he described. I would prefer to hide, rather than open wounds of the past. Secondly, because I would not know how to do it even if I tried. When I told him of my doubts, he impatiently pointed to the papers on his desk as if to remind me time was running out.

"Do you remember, Evgenii, during the war when you were in the War Department and flew from London to Washington enraged by the activities of Communists and Communist sympathizers in the

Department of State? Ironically, I was responsible for your mission, having sent you papers documenting the murder of Polish officers in the Katyn forest. My sole intent was to conserve documentary proof of Stalin's madness, for it was at his directives that this mass murder was carried out. You thought you had failed your Washington task. In fact, though, your Congressman friend from Minnesota and some others did not ignore your warnings. Silently they kept digging and digging. A few years later the Republican senator Joseph McCarthy began an anti-Commmunist campaign. He temporarily succeeded in changing American insouciance to alertness. We had to sidetrack McCarthy's homosexual lieutenants Cohn and Shine while feeding McCarthy's fervour. By spreading wild rumors that resulted in false accusations against many prominent but innocent people, including Hollywood actors and directors, we aroused public indignation and protest. We provoked McCarthy into going too far and, as we expected, your system of democracy eventually caused his ruin. He was discredited and censored by the Senate. In any event, Soviet Intelligence was too well entrenched and too sophisticated in the United States for a McCarthy to make any real difference. In fact, the Senate's outrage over his rantings probably helped us.

Now look here. This series of documents labelled "Merry Widow" is of special interest to you because in the most part it deals with your compatriots. I know you experienced similar situations yourself. You will not like what you see. It sounds more like "Alice's Adventures in Wonderland" than reports about working intelligence people.

Very revealing are these excerpts from the diary of one of the KGB's most talented graduates of our American school in Russia. He paid with his life for these indiscretions. Agents are not supposed to keep diaries".

I opened the file to read: "equipped with first rate passport forgeries, our men travel back and forth to America at will. In their luggage they carry letters from pretended relatives, who are in fact KGB agents sent to the United States many years earlier and who became American citizens. They are teachers, doctors, restaurant owners, civil servants, truck drivers and politicians, together constituting a truly formidable espionage network, with high sabotage potential. Among ourselves we like to speculate what extraordinary havoc our resident agents could create by merely inciting racial riots across this wide open, vulnerable country called America.

Our electronic surveillance operations are facilitated by the renegade British officials in Washington who identify for us the prime sources in America of U.S. government and military electronic transmissions. We can monitor them very successfully thanks to British scientists who unwittingly provided us with their most sophisticated listening probes when MI6 installed them in our Paris embassy, and friends within the French *Deuxième Bureau* alerted us to this fact. We found the bugs and replaced them after study by our experts. The British never caught on and kept monitoring the disinformation our Paris embassy fed them. We had the device duplicated for our dummy American corporation by a legitimate electronics company in Ohio and we use it widely in America. It is a real marvel. Last but not least, British officials in Washington give us access to every important communication passing between the British and American governments.

The National Security Agency, the FBI, the CIA are all penetrated. Most importantly, we have several top level informers inside the Atomic Energy Commission. Routinely we enter government offices to interview top executives, or we invite them to three-martini lunches at expensive restaurants. They always pick up the bill. Americans are peculiar that way. Never are they well prepared for their jobs. Undisciplined and naive, unwittingly giving out fragmentary but important clues to their current directives. It is hard for me to believe that these pompous, conceited, inept graduates of Harvard or Yale, Princeton or MIT, could have such uncorked, porous brains, hopelessly void of any understanding of history, of geopolitics or even elementary psychology. How, we wonder, can these people occupy posts of critical importance to American national security?

Natural allies proliferate. Americans publish everything. Their books, magazines, newspapers, government documents provide us with invaluable intelligence data. The Library of Congress, public and university libraries are delighted to do free research for anyone who asks. We do ask and then they thank us for using their services. We also take advantage of the ever obliging American editors who, eager to boost circulation, will publish virtually any story we plant, however bizarre, as long as a foreign source can be cited. I could not resist asking a prominent Washington editor whether he knew what the French slang word for rumor was. "Sure, he said, a canard, which means a duck, particularly when applied to the press." "We have the same expression in Russian, I told him. And you know what, Fred? Even if one of our Russian ducks had an ass full of lead, it could still fly round Washington crapping on the Capitol Dome without any danger of being shot down". I don't think Fred got it, but he laughed anyway.

Inasmuch as Americans had no idea we had infiltrated their prize institutions long before the outbreak of the Second World War, what would normally be a precise and dangerous business of espionage is more like a Franz Lehar operetta. In fact our code name for the director of the CIA is "The Merry Widow". We are well positioned in this organization with little fear of being discovered. My journalist friend, Fred, once bitterly remarked to me that a CIA man wouldn't be able to find his own shadow on a sunny afternoon.

"Are you sure, Evgenii, you can stand more? If so, I shall offer some additional personal comment. Don't get angry but it seemed to us that your people practiced a peculiar providentialist philosophy, dismissing hermeneutic inquiry for the interpretation of facts in favor of mere speculation, because in the opinion of some muddled CIA quarters Dumb Ivan did not have the brains to ever catch up with American ingenuity, no matter how he tried. At the same time the CIA high priests of elaborate forms of masked prevarication formulated report-analyses about the Soviet Union that were by design invariably misleading. Soviet military technology and production potentials were grossly overestimated. Economic statistics fabricated and overblown. It was clear that to perpetuate the myth of its indispensability the CIA had given itself a carte blanche on inventiveness, continuously stressing to the American leadership the inferred threat of Soviet aggression while at the same time helping to accommodate the economic requirements of its paymasters, the American military industrial complex. We knew precisely how to read the CIA. In large measure, so did the British and the French, as we could see from their respective evaluation reports on American positions. We found it astounding that American Central Intelligence was allowed to function with such pernicious freedom unchecked. In GRU we used to say that the only people who did not know what the CIA was really doing, were the American President and the Congress.

On the humorous side, we enjoyed shadowing your agents over the frontier. They were walking advertisements our men could immediately identify by their short haircuts, button-down shirt collars, their hats and what we called their three-quarter trousers that always fell a few inches short of the wide-soled American shoes".

Grigori was so amusing in his description of American cloak-and-dagger men that I had to laugh. "You are absolutely right, I said. Both your double-wide trousers and our short ones were a dead giveaway. But let me point out that your English is slipping. We do not call it "over the frontier". We say: in foreign countries or abroad." "Yes, of course, Evgenii. Perhaps I should stick to Italian."

Then, Grigori continued, there were the despicable roll-up deals sought, ever so often, by your agents abroad. Give us information that will sound good to our chiefs, they would propose, and we will tell you something of interest to yours. The insensibility with which some American agents could in cold blood sell out their foreign operatives to Soviet Services revolted us. We despised these swine. Whenever possible we made sure they met with violent death.. Had enough? You may now ask your questions."

"Grigori, you keep me spellbound, you tantalize, you insult and insinuate. Now tell me honestly. Did the KGB have an undiscovered mole within the inner core of British Intelligence? Did one or more exist in the Central Intelligence Agency?" "Of course. It is all revealed here in the blue files marked "Aardvark." How do you say it in America? It will blow your socks off? But Evgenii, I would advise you to resist opening these files. Too much knowledge can be very dangerous. Naturally, the decision is entirely yours. While you ponder, let me say that what I let you see is but an infinitesimal part of one section of our immense and secret Vatican *Trichèco* file, or *Walrus Profile*, if you prefer the English denomination."

"Grigori, please. This is too much for me to handle. What on earth is the *Walrus* profile? How did the Vatican, or should I say the Catholic Church create it? How long did it take?" "Gracious, Evgenii, you ask me several questions in a single breath. They cannot be answered in a brief manner. *Walrus* is a complex subject, nearly impossible to describe. It consists of a series of continuous investigative reports, compiled year after year from widely disparate sources all over the world that comprise national intelligence and police organizations, as well as a plethora of non-state actors such as revolutionary movements, religious groups, the Mafia, multinational corporations and even terrorist networks. They are collated, then analyzed by some of the finest specialists in every branch of human endeavor. I shall add that *Walrus* also enlists the collaboration of dedicated clergymen with trenchant ears who know how to play on man's fear of fiery hell.

Let me explain the fiery hell part. Stalin, it is said, once ironically asked Beria, his chief of the secret police, how many divisions did the

Pope of Rome have under his command. Beria chose not to answer but could have said that the church has countless battalions of exorcists clothed in black soutanes running round the world like ants, poking their noses into everybody's business and capable of ferreting out all secrets at will, while not betraying any. Do you know why the faithful tolerate their inquisitiveness? Because the Church, in its infinite perceptiveness of human weaknesses, receives automatic benefit from its finest invention since the Holy Ghost: the mighty confessional.

Can the sanctimonious ever resist telling their father confessor all about the sins of their brethren? Or muster the audacity to turn down his humble priestly request for a favor? Or not heed the silent command of his ominously raised eyebrow? Lavrenti Beria understood the dangers to Communism of such psychological strangleholds. He insisted it was not sufficient to be just an atheist. In the Communist Party one had to go further: defy God by destroying his churches and his disciples, his popes and all those who pray forgiveness for sins they never committed.

Because I had to return to the United States for personal reasons, our next meeting with Grigori took place three months later. This time his limp was more noticeable. He was never without his cane. "Damn Germans", he said when I asked how he felt.

"Last time we talked you were most curious about the strange events surrounding your Czechoslovak visit, what you referred to as the Olomouc affair. I am really not surprised you failed to decipher that whole situation on your own for it is indeed very involved.

The little black ants I told you about before you left for America played a role in your life as well. The Man in Prague had scores of them running errands for him in Czech intelligence, just as you had in the Polish secret police, though you did not always know they were churchmen. One of them, father Florian, the fellow who planned the escape of Dan Laroche from Poland was among our finest operatives.

Bless them. But for their vigilance I might not have been advised in time to bail you out when you made some serious mistakes. Your timing in the Slowik elimination was all wrong. You nearly got back to Lodz before his accident occurred. This could have had fatal consequences for you and for Daniel. I had a signal sent to my people to intercept and delay you right after you left Green Lake. When you mistakenly turned off the main road they lost you. Then like a madman you ran into a motorcyclist at 120 kilometers an hour, killing him, and getting arrested by the Kriminalka. My agents in Brno and Ostrawa, though closer to Olomouc, did not have sufficient rank to obtain your immediate release. I was fearful that physically weakened by injuries, traumatized by the death of an innocent young man you might, under duress of interrogation, compromise the Archbishop, known to you only as The Man in Prague. Does his identity surprise you?" "He had an aura of authority about him, I admit. Yet, I can usually smell a priest. I took him to be a military man". "That is understandable. He was so important to us that I decided to send Elizabeth all the way from the Czech capital. I am sure you remember the exquisite Elizabeth? I myself never met her but I was told she was very beautiful." "Was she ever. So stunning, Grigori, that I was seriously tempted to find her again. It never happened because one day in Warsaw your little bird, Augustus of Moscow fame, flew into my office window and scared me out of my pants and out of Poland, all the way to London. Grigori laughed. I could see my comment pleased him. "Yes, he said, we all owe a lot to Alexander Sergeievich Pushkin."

Good thing, though, you did not guess then that Lizzy, as we called her, was in reality a British agent. Married to a high level Czech intelligence officer whom the British MI5 turned with Lizzy's help, she had the rank of captain in Czech counter-espionage". "Then why on earth didn't she say a word to me during our car ride together while seducing me with her limpid blue eyes?" "Because she had not been briefed about you. All she knew is that you were probably still in shock and spoke no Czech. She could not risk your asking too many questions on recognizing her unmistakably genuine English accent". "Then why did she get into my car instead of letting me drive off alone?"

Grigori got annoyed. "After the many experiences you had with the Communist secret police, how can you still be so naive? Her taking you to the border was to prevent the Kriminalka from possibly staging an incident, then shooting you for attempted escape. Don't forget you killed a Czech national and had no diplomatic immunity. At the time I was very angry with you for the whole mess you got us all into. While it was important to prevent your being interrogated, I did not like sending Elizabeth on this precarious mission. In an improvised situation like that many a slip-up can occur. She had to take the Czechs by surprise, get you out of the country before anybody decided to ask Brno or Ostrawa superiors for instructions. She hoped that once you crossed the border the matter would be covered up, because the police in Olomouc would not risk self-incrimination by admitting to having released you without clearance from higher authority.

However, escaping immediate danger did not make you permanently safe. I knew that the disciplined Czechs would eventually send signals about you to the Polish secret police, so I instructed my people to closely monitor Prague-Warsaw inter-service communications. I must tell you, Evgenii, that if you had not been released in time and subjected to interrogation, this Olomouc affair could have caused a major operational disaster, endangering my operations and the lives of trusting friends. Only my affection for you induced me to take the gamble involving Elizabeth. Professionally it was a serious error. There was another way to shield The Man in Prague. Uglier perhaps, but with fewer risks." My blood chilled under the impact of Grigori's words."I get your point,I said. You could have had me simply eliminated. Tell me, was the doctor who attended me in the Czech prison one of your men?" "Ah Evgenii. Had you been familiar with the full ramifications of my position, you would have understood. Though Lizzy officially worked for the Czechs, she was in fact the MI6 control in Prague. She and several other British operatives unknowingly depended on my double role to save their skins in case Czech counter-intelligence or the KGB got on to them. As head of GRU for Europe supervising, among other things, the briefs of national communist counter-espionage organizations, including Elizabeth's, I had full current knowledge of all operations. Believing me to be pure Soviet military intelligence, General Bocek kept furnishing me with much important information on Czech communist activities, ironically behind the back of his anti-Soviet boss, the Czech minister of defense, Svoboda. Directing separate networks with diametrically opposed interests is not for the ordinary intelligence officer. There were moments of such mental fatigue that suddenly I would feel despondent and desperate. The knowledge that turncoat informers were active in both the British and American intelligence systems never stopped haunting me. Only faith in the attainability of my ultimate objective kept me going, though I often wondered if I would last long enough to make a difference.

Evgenii, I shall give you more riddles to solve at some future date. Remember that what you saw in the documents, the Americans and the British is just a small part of the story. Both could boast some professional triumphs. But once relative nuclear parity was reached, the rest was only a game of oneupmanship, a charade played by obstinate fools on a grotesque stage."

Castel Gandolfo II

During all the hours of our talks not once did we mention war as if wishing to deny that under the pretense of patriotic duty we participated in the insane, horrifying barbaric acts of inhumanity costing the lives of millions. All I wanted to hear was Grigori's personal story as it developed in the years after I said good-bye to him in no man's land and Germany invaded Russia.

"Do you remember, Grigori, when your soldiers picked me up like a bag of potatoes in Eastern Poland? You instructed me how to get back to Warsaw, obtain a German exit permit, then head for my home in the U.S.A. I did, but soon joined British forces in England. And you?"

Grigori's face turned grim and hard. "Evgenii, he said, that was the beginning of hell. Moscow knew, all Russians knew that the Molotov-Ribbentrop non-aggression pact was a sham, an absurdity because for generations we feared and hated each other. We only hoped Hitler would respect the pact long enough for us to fully mobilize and put our military production lines in order. To provide for additional buffer zones we annexed part of Poland, then all of Estonia, Latvia and Lithuania. Also, after invading Finland, we took Bessarabia and Bukovina. Just look at this map, Evgenii. You can see, it was not Russian imperialism, as you liked calling it, but the creating of extended zones of defense. When Germany overran Belgium, Holland, defeated the French forces, subjected Britain to massive air attacks, we knew her formidable war machine would next move against Russia. Time ran out before we were ready. German armies invaded us, ravaging our country, besieging Leningrad, devastating Stalingrad, nearly taking Moscow. Close to two years went by before we were able to launch a successful counter offensive..

All this is in the history books. Books are not reality. They can't make you feel the horror, smell the blood, or hear the soldiers crying their eyes out into vodka glasses while asking themselves if it was true that when they sang their nostalgic folk songs, while encased in walls of glacial cold, the sound of their voices froze into silence, to be heard only with the Spring thaw. It could not be so, some said, because by Spring most of us would be dead and how can one hear voices from beyond the grave?

And yet one can, Evgenii. We who survived could hear the voices of all twenty million of them in the bloodied, smoldering ruins of Stalingrad, Rostov, Kharkov, Kursk, Orel, Voronesh, Kiev, Sevastopol, Smolensk, Odessa, Novgorod and a thousand other places where German tanks crushed old men, women and children as they pleaded for mercy. This was not war, Evgenii. It was genocide".

Did Grigori not say that one cannot re-live the horrors, smell the blood of war? His face denied it. He was very pale. Suffering, eyes glazed. I had seen him like this before. Each time it took just a little while longer to pull himself together.

"Yes, and our beloved St. Petersburg too. A city cursed ever since the Bolsheviks changed its name to Leningrad. I lost my mother there. She died of pneumonia because secret police thugs, suspecting everybody, would not allow my uncle Alex to take her across military lines to his hospital or to bring her medicines, even though the enemy was still far away. When I came to kneel at her grave many months later, Alex told me she died with my father's name on her lips". "Poor Natasha, he said. She lived alone, in sorrow, waiting for more than twenty years years to be reunited with your father. And you, Grigori, you were not even here for the last embrace." "Uncle Alex, have mercy on me. I loved my mother. I knew nothing of her illness. I was far away, organizing a special project in Kuibishev on the Volga."

Uncle Alex could not stop crying. "I, the great doctor, could not save my own sister. You, beloved nephew, are my only living relative now. Be careful, be wise. Survive. Grigori, I am beginning to feel my age but do not want to die ruled by Communists. Thousands of Russians, perhaps even millions think as I do, as we do. I have my doctor friends. You have knowledge of the inner workings of the Party apparatus. Could we not work together to subvert these swine?" We talked through the night. At dawn Doctor Dobrovolsky joined us. Lights were going on at the Hermitage Museum as we walked past. "That's it, my uncle exclaimed. We shall call our secret organization *The Hermitage Coefficient*". I turned to Doctor Dobrovolsky: "I have the beginning of a plan. It may be useful to know who are the doctors and administrators of hospitals in and near Moscow. And, at the Ministry of Health as well. You could prepare psychological profiles of key individuals. I will complement this with what we already have in our intelligence files". Dobrovolsky visibly shuddered. "Isn't it frightening, he said, that virtually everyone in Russia has a personal, detailed police dossier which can be used against him or her at any time by such monsters as Beria?" "Uncle Alex, could you produce a series of coded messages incorporated into prescriptions of pharmaceutical preparations and think up some especially toxic non-detectable substances?" "Why, of course, Grigori. You are not thinking of....?" He left it unfinished. Then he said: "Just remember there are senior Party men around and above you. All of them have networks of their own and friends in Moscow, in St. Petersburg and as far as Murmansk. Be careful not to cross them". "No need to worry, uncle. At present we shall be merely laying the groundwork for future action. Right now I'll concentrate on developing closer ties with my ecclesiastical friends." Uncle Alex looked baffled. I did not elaborate.

The special project on the Volga I mentioned to uncle Alex involved moving the KGB Intelligence Center to Kuibishev, when Moscow was expected to fall. The KGB Disinformation Department,using codes and elements supplied by GRU, began sending a stream of coded radio messages to the *Abwehr*, Germany's secret services in Berlin, about alleged Russian strategic military plans. The real source was a special Russian transmitter controlled from Kuibishev, but because the *Abwehr* was convinced the messages were coming from the capital of its Bulgarian ally, Sofia, our operation was singularly effective.

What you will not like to hear is that the British, who intercepted and deciphered the radio messages, were equally fooled into believing they originated in Sofia. They fed the false intelligence into their own analysis system while telling us nothing. We learned of their perfidy from our man inside the British Government Communications Services. He also gave us a direct quote from a British war cabinet meeting where Churchill, advised of the interceptions, declared: don't tell the Russians a thing. Let the blighters bleed each other to death."

"The Western allies were lucky we did not bleed to death. They might have lost the war, had we not inflicted mortal wounds on German forces. In critical moments our disinformation tactics and our military victories relieved German pressure on Allied armies. Thanks to our informants inside Eisenhower's Supreme Headquarters we knew of Operation Overlord - the Allied invasion of Europe- already in May of 1944. The accuracy of GRU analysis enabled me to issue very specific intelligence directives so that in June, just a week after your first landings in Normandy, Soviet forces launched a massive offensive on the German Army Center deployed in Byelorussia, to make it appear that Rumania and its oil fields were our objective. German commanders hastened to deploy additional divisional forces there, thus eliminating their availability for the Western Front."

"Grigori, Monsignore, Your Excellency, General, I shouted, boiling inside. You were so smart, so heroic, so unstoppable. Where were you in

August of 1944 when Warsaw erupted in an uprising? I know where you were. You were warming your cowardly Russian asses on the beaches of the Vistula river while watching the Germans massacre Polish combatants, that's where you were". Grigori went deathly pale. It frightened me. Probably no one had talked to him this way since he was a recruit. I was immediately sorry for my explosion.

"This treachery, this infamy will gnaw at our conscience forever, he said. But, there are many things you don't know. It was not the fault of our military commanders. Not only Stalin and all members of the Praesidium, but also Russian intelligence and Marshall Rokossovsky who commanded our armies were aware that before the end of summer the Poles, led by Bor Komorowski, would try to liberate Warsaw from the occupying Germans. That is why during the final days of July on Stalin's personal instructions, Soviet radio stations broadcast continuous appeals to the citizens of Warsaw to strike and destroy the Nazi invader, telling them that the Red Army was quickly advancing toward the Polish capital. In fact, Komorowski could hear Russian guns when on the first of August he ordered his 35,000 men into action. He did not know that two days later Stalin would order the Red Army High Command to halt the advance on Warsaw. Russian commanders were stunned. They could see only strategic disadvantages in choking the momentum of their offensive. Some had an eye on history as well. Warsaw's uprising was being broadcast around the world. They knew Russia would never be pardoned for her complicity in the murder of Polish patriots. On my own authority, I infiltrated our Captain Kalugin into Warsaw to develop a plan for coordinated Polish-Russian action against the Germans. When he returned, I sent the plan to Marshall Rokossovsky. He did not act. We soon learned why. Explicit orders from Moscow forbade him to extend any assistance to the Poles. Hour after hour we could see and hear the raging battle destroying the city and its citizens. We listened to Komorowski's desperate radio appeals to London for airdrops of arms".

"Grigori, this is shaking me to the core. I was on the receiving end of Komorowski's cries for help and know that General Eisenhower asked Stalin's permission for Allied aircraft to land and refuel at airfields under Soviet control. In Moscow, Soviet Foreign Minister Vishinsky read Stalin's reply to the American ambassador. It said that the Soviet Government did not wish to associate itself with the Polish adventure and therefore, it had to object to American or British aircraft landing on Soviet territory after dropping arms for Warsaw. On learning of Stalin's decision, Eisenhower could not contain his anger. "My God, he exclaimed: the Russians are decided to let the Poles die." He ordered drops from airfields in Italy. Two hundred and fifty allied airmen, including ninety-eight Poles, lost their lives in this operation, managing to drop only 100 tons of supplies, a totally insufficient quantity to do any good. The Germans killed twenty thousand of Komorowski's men and six hundred thousand unarmed citizens of Warsaw, while the Red Army sat and watched from across the River. At Supreme Allied Headquarters everyone realized that Stalin had succeeded in his objective to have the Polish Home Army totally annihilated." "Yes, Evgenii, we Russians also knew. As soon as Stalin's secret war against the Poles was closed, our armies continued to roll over German forces in an offensive which would stop only after we reached Saxony. Then we took Berlin. But this is jumping ahead. When we crossed the Vistula and entered devastated Warsaw, I began to look for my father, praying I would find him alive.

I had neither seen him or heard from him since the winter of 1938 when I was returning to Russia from Spain. His Paris friends had informed me then that he had left for Poland at the urging of Grzegorz Fitelberg, the Polish composer, conductor and director of the Warsaw Radio Symphony orchestra. I knew that my father felt great admiration for the group of composers, known as "Young Poland", dominated by Karol Szymanowski who had marked musical affinities with the Russian, Scriabin. So I was not surprised he left Paris,especially since many of his emigré friends had either died or gone on to America.

In Warsaw, I immediately ordered a search for one Yuri Sergeievich Orlov. I told no one he was my father. In any event my rank protected me from inquisitive subordinates. On the third day of the search, NKVD's Major Kovtun reported to me that Orlov had been found. "This man Orlov, Kovtun said, presented himself to my men pretending to have information about some German deserters. He talked bourgeois and stank of capitalism. Obviously, he was an enemy of the people, so I had him shot."

"Evgenii, it was a blow I would never fully recover from, never forget. Time could neither dull the pain or lessen my accumulated hatred". Hardly able to breathe, I wheezed: "misericordia for us, and for them let it be perpetual hell". Grigori's pallor urged me to go on. "That is why I didn't find him when I returned to Warsaw after the war. Another victim of Stalin's paranoia. How many thousands of innocent men did he have killed?" Then, recollecting the fate of Russian soldiers freed by Allied forces from German prisoner of war camps, Grigori's answer did not surprise me."The Vatican *Trichèco* file shows, he told me, that at war's end the NKVD held more than 150,000 people accused of spying in former Nazi concentration camps. Those not immediately executed died of hunger or disease. About 33,000 of them were Soviet nationals.

Eight months after the NKVD killed my father in Warsaw, the Western allies crossed the Rhine and met our forces in Saxony. When we took Berlin, the Soviet Union could celebrate two great victories: the political subduing of the Western Powers at the Yalta Conference and the pulverizing of Nazi Germany.

On the political front we were winning consistently and with relative ease. Think. Did you never wonder why the Western allies voluntarily forfeited easily reachable geopolitical advantages by ordering Eisenhower to hold back when our respective armies met in Saxony? It happened because Allied intelligence and consequently your political and military leaders had no idea we were then close to total exhaustion. With the exception of Winston Churchill and the maverick general, George Patton, they were all afraid to engage the Soviets and push on. Your ignorance handed us both territorial and ideological advantages.

Now put on your Judas cloak and tell me what were the behind-the-scene influences that determined the fate of nations at the conference between Stalin, Churchill and Roosevelt in Yalta. Why did the British and the Americans readily agree to hand over Eastern and Central Europe including Poland to communist control? Do you remember who sat at the conference table at the Livadia Palace in Yalta? Who whispered into the ear of the desperately ill Roosevelt that after early defeats, the Red Army had been completely rebuilt, as demonstrated by its rapid advance through Czechoslovakia, Poland, East Prussia, and East Germany? And, that the Soviets had new secret weapons and could overrun all of Europe if Stalin so decreed? Was it not in the same vein that Sir Archibald Clark Kerr, then British ambassador to Moscow, reported to Britain's Foreign Secretary, Anthony Eden, just before Yalta? Or Charles Bohlen, your assistant Secretary of State, to James Byrnes, the U.S director of War Mobilization? They all said what they were led to believe by our disinformation strategies in various parts of the world and the propaganda in America carried out by the many citizen-agents we had infiltrated into your country over the years and who were to be found at all levels of the State Department, the Intelligence Services and in the media.

What the British and the Americans perceived as important intelligence they cleverly distilled from Soviet papers like Krasnaya Zvezda and our technical journals was, in fact, adroit invention deliberately inserted by our editors. The Americans were especially easy to deceive in Europe, because their intelligence services almost didn't exist. The shoot-from-the hip-cowboy operatives knew more about wine lists and converting currencies than about the Russian army and, what more, they didn't really care. Rebuilt production lines? Secret weapons? Renewed courage and discipline among Russian military? It was all rubbish. We couldn't produce toilet paper to wipe our bleeding asses, let alone cannon.

Of course, at the Yalta conference we also had the "plus one", that crucial factor we always had in reserve to stack the deck. The 'plus one' was actually 'plus two', one British, one American. I invite you to find answers to these apparent enigmas that *Walrus* deciphered but so far has elected not to reveal. Who were they? All I can tell you is that only a single, non-involved member of the Anglo-American delegation knew their identity. Now see this revealing document which the GRU retrieved some years later from CIA files. It is the memorandum Sir Alexander Cadogan, then Britain's Permanent Undersecretary of State for Foreign Affairs, wrote to Winston Churchill, describing the Yalta Agreement as a "monstrous betrayal". It must have secretly pleased Sir Winston that someone else shared his suspicions and his opinion of Yalta. He himself had not been fooled, but his view of British national interests and his geopolitical instinct told him it was not the time to provoke the Russian bear.

In war we paid a bitter price. Do you Americans have any idea what it is like for a nation to lose twenty million of its citizens: soldiers, teachers, writers, painters, farmers, scientists, believers and atheists, good men and bad men, all united by the powerful summons of patriotism?

Evgenii, Americans don't really know very much about war and nothing about fighting the enemy on their own soil. How could you possibly know? In the American Civil War six hundred thousand American lives were lost. That was not a war waged against a foreign aggressor but shameful fratricide. Four hundred thousand Americans died in the Second World War. And Vietnam? Your leaders never admitted how many of your servicemen were sacrificed. All we know is that at the height of your commitment you had five hundred and fifty thousand military there. You continue to cry over those who perished in that far-away jungle, yet refuse to admit that as the invaders of a foreign land you yourselves were the real executioners of your compatriots".

The Vatican

This time Grigori sent a message asking me to meet him at the Pontifical Academy of Science situated in the Vatican gardens. When I joined him there, he told me the Academy was composed of 70 Pontifical Academicians chosen from experts in mathematical and experimental sciences in all countries. "I wanted you to visit the Academy where the *Walrus-Trichèco* file was conceived, then directed, and without which the activities of the *Hermitage Coefficient* would have been seriously handicapped, if not impossible.

The events I shall describe, Evgenii, were often deceitful, perhaps even shameful acts we perpetrated within the Soviet Union. Yet they were crucial to the success of our struggle to rid our country of Communist despotism.

We needed to destroy the main pillars of the regime -the Communist Party, the security forces, the central government. Contributing to economic erosion would be the first phase to begin only after the wounds of war were at least partly healed. For several years my closest collaborators and I travelled throughout Russia and to some Republics of the Soviet Union seeking allies taking note of political infighting within local Party hierarchies, drawing up plans for individual regions, selecting potential group leaders. We accumulated an extraordinary amount of secret information thanks to the complicity of fear, ever present in Soviet citizens when confronted with badges of authority. We kept our growing impatience in check even though *Walrus* repeatedly cautioned that undue delay could nullify our plans. We understood why we were being counselled not to waste time. Soviet leadership suffered shock when America dropped atom bombs on Hiroshima and then on Nagasaki, killing 110,000 Japanese. Our military intelligence discounted any possibility of Americans hitting our cities even though at that point we had little to tender by way of retaliation. However, some top commanders feared, -and Marshal Georgi Zhukov confirmed this to me privately- that as soon as our scientists developed a nuclear arsenal, the "android with creeping paranoia", as he called Stalin, would order a preemptive strike on targets in the United States. Tcherenkov, Landau, Bassov and other Russian physicists were working round the clock. Just four years after

Hiroshima, Russia exploded its first atom bomb. And, we had the world's finest nuclear physicist, Andrei Sakharov, whose part in providing Russia with nuclear weapons earned him a place in history.

Hermitage knew from its own analyses and from *Walrus* studies that the main weakness of the Soviet Union was political. That there were many resentments simmering within the vast Soviet empire of diverse nationalities, including the satellites of Eastern Europe. These resentments and frustrations when compounded by economic difficulties could result in pressure for political change. Now haunted by the rapid progress in Soviet nuclear testing and in military production, *Hermitage* could no longer postpone action. We began implementing phase one of the conspiratorial plan: economic sabotage. Neither intending to nor having the power to seriously damage the huge Soviet economy, we could still do much to slow it down, to create a degree of chaos, and with it, fan the already spreading distrust of Soviet leadership that, we expected, would lead to a power struggle in the Kremlin and the elimination of the Georgian Joseph Vissarionovich Dzhugashvili Stalin, and his secret police chief Lavrenti Beria.

The "Anti-planning Committees", our veiled name for teams formed from natives of Murmansk, Kiev, Sverdlovsk, Baku and Makhachakala, had been trained to obstruct production. Their immediate prime targets were Leningrad's shipyards, its mechanical, electrical and chemical plants, textile and food producers. The motor vehicle, textile, iron and copper output of Gorki. Kuibishev's oil refineries and specialized engineering. In the Ukraine, coal mines as well as agriculture, Azerbaijan's huge oilfields. In Kazakhstan, copper, zinc, lead and heavy engineering. Georgia's iron, steel, manganese and motor vehicle plants..

Engineers, technicians, mechanics, clerks, administrators, chit supervisors, the Party men we bought, all participated in causing production failures throughout the Union. Oil refineries suddenly lacked spare parts. Incorrect fertilizer formulas burned crops, poisoned the soil. Badly calibrated tools ruined machinery. Railway ties separated, causing train wrecks and delivery delays. False production reports to ministries resulted in the removal of the more dangerous Ishaikas Party sniffer dogs.

Burst water mains, blown gas pipes, mildewed grain in silos, missing drilling equipment, fires, explosions, delays in money transfers to pay workers was only a part of the industrial nightmares. Republics grumbled. Apparatchiks accused of delinquency by the secret police were being arrested. The eight Communist countries in the Comecon economic association protested the shoddy goods, the poor packing, the incorrect instructions, the disappearance of entire shipments. This and much more disrupted their internal and external economic performances.

The territories were vast and the undertakings extremely dangerous. We had some failures but no desertions. Where patriotic fervor wore thin, the passions of hatred, jealousy, revenge and, above all, the loathing of the nomenklatura which controlled every aspect of our lives took over. There were also further passions, those of greed and possession which we were able to gratify thanks to the huge infusions of money from abroad.

Military garrisons were left untouched. None of us wanted to make life more difficult for the men of the armed forces. The traumas of war had eaten through their bodies and their souls, and there was little left of their pride.

We moved with great caution infiltrating political sinews. Uncle Alexander and Doctor Dobrovolsky made frequent trips to Moscow to attend medical conferences. They got to know the Minister of Public Health, Tretyakov, and became friends of Dr. Vasilenko, personal physician to Georgi Maximilianovitch Malenkov, Secretary of the Central Committee of the Communist Party. Vasilenko told uncle Alex that Malenkov's greatest ambition was to become Chairman of the Council of Ministers after Stalin's death. In his way stood his deadly enemy, Lavrenti Beria, the Minister of Interior and boss of the secret police who had an identical ambition. He would have to be discredited.

Prodded by uncle Alex, Dr. Vasilenko suggested to Malenkov that I was the best qualified person in the Soviet Union to find evidence of Beria's blunders in his management of Security Forces. Malenkov was hesitant until our mutual friend, Nikolai Alexandrovich Bulganin, assured him my intelligence network was second to none and that my personal dislike of Beria matched his own. Bulganin, with whom I had a cordial relationship, insisted that it was my duty to assist Malenkov. "Your being privy to Malenkov's secret operation, for which he knows Beria would have him hang, might prove very advantageous to us all, he told me". I agreed. That Bulganin had some stratagems of his own in mind was quite clear to me but I trusted the man.

Another concurrent development added incentive to our efforts. Kuperin, head of the Kremlin's medical department, confided to Dr. Tretyakov that Stalin was suffering from an enlarged heart and hardening of the arteries. Georgians were famous for their longevity, so at 74 Stalin could not be considered really old, he said. But, in his state any physical exertion or even mental stress could cause a fatal stroke. Malenkov's hopes were rising. As our aims coincided, I advised him to dispatch letters by secret couriers to officials of the autonomous Republics demanding urgent reports on the performance of Security Forces and on economic conditions. Through my own channels, senior apparatchiks, with whom *Hermitage* had forged alliance, were assured they would be covered. I urged them to conceal nothing and tell the unvarnished truth.

The reports from the Chairman of the Council of Ministers of the Ukraine, Korotchenko, and from Mgeladze, Secretary of the Party's Central Committee of Georgia, described the disastrous economic conditions in their regions. Same was said in further accounts from the Baku oilfields in Azerbaijan and about the state of agriculture in Kazakhstan. The reports also stressed that the effectiveness of Security Forces had disintegrated.

Malenkov rushed the reports to Stalin's attention hoping their impact would kill him. Stalin suffered shock but survived under the care of doctors Glazunov, Konovalov and Strukov, two of whom were recommended by Minister Tertyakov and brought in by Stalin's watchdog, the ever faithful doctor Kuperin. Meantime Beria, informed by his spies of the existence of the negative reports on his Security Forces, counter-attacked. He did not dare touch officials in Georgia, Stalin's birthplace, and always close to his heart, but he purged senior Party officials in the Ukraine. When, in an outrageous action he arrested Dr. Vinogradov -the personal friend of Bulganin- and Dr. Vasilenko, Malenkov's personal physician, it became evident Beria was no longer thinking rationally. Bulganin and I knew why. Every one of the dozen or so medical men looking after Stalin including Lukomsky, Pegov, Tkachov, Migunov and others, hated Beria to the depths of their souls. Beria now rarely left the Kremlin as if fearing to find himself isolated from his sole protector, Stalin. It was a simple matter to mix some disabling drugs with the daily pill intake of this hypochondriac, whose only medical problem was glaucoma.

With winter fast approaching, Dr. Kuperin persuaded Stalin to leave Moscow for the warm climate of the Crimea. With my help, Malenkov continued procuring reports of ever increasing economic difficulties and collecting evidence of serious deficiencies in the administration of Soviet Security. Then Malenkov, assured of the support of Bulganin, Molotov, Krushchev, Kabanov and Suburov, suddenly announced that he was calling an urgent meeting of the Praesidium to discuss the economic crisis and the problems of State Security. Never had it happened before that a meeting of the Praesidium was announced without Stalin's prior approval. Malenkov counted on Stalin being jolted into returning to Moscow and its dangerous 40 below zero temperatures. When he did return, the ferocious infighting inside the Kremlin, combined with further news of economic reversals, was too much for Stalin to handle. At the end of February he had his final and fatal stroke.

With Malenkov in charge, major decisions were quickly made concerning Party control. The Ministry of State Security was taken over by the Ministry of Internal Affairs. And, most important, Malenkov paid his debt to me by placing all overseas espionage in the hands of army intelligence, the GRU. At Bulganin's instigation and to his personal satisfaction, Beria was arrested by colonel Ivan Serov and later put to death.

I had to gain access to the files of the Ministry of State Security before the Internal Affairs Ministry took them over. It nearly cost me my life. As I turned the key of one of the many inner gates one evening, in the dim lights of the underground archives, I felt the cold steel of a gun pressed against my cheek. "Move and I'll blow your head off". I was not to be gainsaid a goal so nearly reached.

I reacted in anger: "Idyota. Take that gun out of my face or I'll skewer you like a pig". He recognized my voice. "Comrade General, this is lieutenant Kharadze at your orders. You know me. I am sorry. You took a terrible risk. I could have shot you". "Lieutenant, don't blubber. Just stand in back of me as you did before. Watch and learn". There was a sound of ripped cloth and ten centimeters of steel shaft affixed to my lower arm now extended beyond my bent elbow. "In one single motion taking less than a second, Lieutenant, I could have shoved this hidden weapon right through your gut". "Bohze Muy", he cried out. "A minute ago you were ready to kill me, now you invoke God to have mercy on you. Cheer up, Lieutenant, this is just a little life-saving trick I picked up in Spain during the civil war. But remember, it is unwise to move too close to your suspect. I won't mention any of this to your superiors". I had made a friend of the keen comrade Kharadze.

In Moscow, the main files were transferred, over period of time, to the new Soviet authority. But selected contents of these frightening means that could influence the future of Russia and her Allied Republics, now meticulously collated, became also part of the Vatican's *Walrus-Tricheco* secret records.".

"Grigori, are you saying that the very instruments of terror that for so many years deprived Russians of freedom were now to be used to restore democracy?"

"Evgenii. Caveat instantaneous democracy. In a country that for so many years relied on death and treachery to change leaders, it would take a near miracle to assure a smooth transition from the swollen-with-medals old guard to a new democratic government. *Hermitage* knew that the virgin gold of respect of human rights would be too soft without some alloy of fear.

The 20th Congress of the Communist Party brought us the first sign of a break with the past when it denounced the personal cult of Stalin and admitted the principle of peaceful co-existence between countries of different social systems. Unfortunately, this new socio-political consciousness went up in smoke when the Party Central Committee fired Krushchev and installed Kosygin, then later Brezhnev.

When Krushchev said we will bury America, he had hoped to fool you only into believing we had an economic edge over your country. He did not have in mind any military action. To neutral observers this was perfectly clear. However, virtually everyone on your side, including your paranoid Pentagon analysts, convinced of our overall strike superiority, immediately assumed exactly the contrary.

Well, let me assure you, Evgenii, that during these critical years the Soviet Union did not want armed conflict with the United States. I know because I was part of the policy-making body in Moscow and privy to all State secrets.

Through our own and foreign diplomats, in off-the-record meetings, and even with the intermediation of Vatican personages, we preached negotiated solutions, addressing your intellectuals, your scientists, your congressmen and your senators. With innate caution, the Soviets avoided the initiating of any policies that could even remotely be construed as aggressive toward your country. In every way we could think of, we emphasized that once both sides had nuclear weapons and the ability to accurately launch them, war could only mean mutual annihilation. Rather than accept our proposals for reciprocal nuclear disarmament, your leaders, while professing concurrence, kept us on permanent alert by continuing to build up America's arsenals."

Grigori's face was white. He seemed to be struggling to collect his thoughts. I did not dare disturb him, but when I tried to leave he motioned me back. "I become very distressed, he finally continued, over the incessant propaganda portraying us Russians as evil monsters, only looking to annihilate you. Had it never occurred to you that apart from the fear of world destruction there were also important psychological reasons for which the Soviets wished to avoid conflict with you? In many ways we were still living the war with Germany which cost us 20 million men. We could not easily forget that without American equipment arriving at our northern ports, without the second front in Europe which you spearheaded, our bloodied nation would have had to sacrifice many more of her sons, perhaps even collapsing in defeat.

So far the Soviets and the Americans have failed to exorcise the spectre of global holocaust but nil desperandum. We of the *Hermitage Coefficient*, having long primed the dynamics and set the calendar for political and social change in the Soviet Union, will not desist but soon cause the emergence in Russia of a statesman-reformer whose persuasive rationale to fundamentally revise the Communist Party's orthodoxy will inspire other enlightened men and have profound effect not only on Russia but the entire world. When this happens, I fervently hope America is ready to welcome them. And, Evgenii, don't have such a blank look. When the time comes, you will understand. It will all fit together. I promise you.

The *Hermitage Coefficient* was groping for an antidote to the Soviet nuclear paranoia. We had to have not just another dissenter but one who was open, quotable and celebrated. Our "Anti-Planning Committee" decided to enter into secret dialogue with Russia's most illustrious physicist, Andrei Sakharov, whose moral torment over the race in atomic weaponry was increasingly evident to his friends. Sakharov's superior intellect would not brook mediocrity. He had to be reached and persuaded to declare himself by someone capable of learnedly discussing theoretical physics as well as philosophy.

My choice fell on a talented scientist born in Smolensk, on the Upper Dnieper, graduate of Leningrad's Zhdanov University in physics and philosophy, who later in his career was appointed to the Soviet Academy of Sciences as editor of the Zhurnal Eksperimentalnoi i Teoreticheskoi Fiziki (Journal of Experimental and Theoretical Physics). Told what was expected of him, he at first refused the assignment fearing he could not begin to match Sakharov's brilliance. Was is not Sakharov who said that inside the atom is where things happen that don't? But, he yielded to my pressure, immersing himself in the fields of applied astrophysics, matter and antimatter and general relativity which were Sakharov's pre-eminent interests. He also prepared himself to argue in his own chosen specialty, Academic and Gestalt psychology, where he knew Sakharov had been probing. To play on Sakharov's known sensitivity to the opinions of his peers, *Hermitage* had readied letters addressed to him by three eminent physicists: the Dutchman Zernike, the German Botha and America's Segré. The Russian needed no convincing about the horrors of atomic weapons. After Hiroshima and the Soviet bombing of the Totsk area in the Southern Urals with an atomic weapon more powerful than the one Americans dropped on Japan, to see whether Russian soldiers could fight in conditions of nuclear war, Sakharov was never able to free himself from the ever tightening garotte of guilt. He knew that after the atomic blast Marshal Zhukov ordered some 40,000 troops into the area and that thousands later died from exposure to radioactivity.

But the question was whether Sakharov could reconcile his need to denounce Russia's frenetic buildup of her nuclear strike forces with the abiding loyalty he felt for his country, especially when Soviet leaders claimed to have a list of 100 cities the Americans were prepared to bomb.

I cannot tell you, Evgenii, just exactly what finally persuaded Sakharov, but it is more than likely my man from Smolensk brought him to perceive the essential configuration pattern of the situation as a whole and not as a mere sum of isolated parts. In any event *Hermitage* got its eminent Russian dissident and Rome inherited a brilliant immigrant scientist from a town on the Upper Dnieper".

The Augeias Adventure

"I am getting bored sitting here in Rome, I told Grigori. Our meetings are less and less frequent. I think I shall go to Greece. For a very long time now I have had the yearning to see a project of mine become reality. My dream will perhaps finally come true".

"Tell me about it, Evgenii. How did it all begin?" "The origin of my dream goes back some years. When vacationing in Greece I came upon the little church of the prophet Elia situated on the slopes of Mount Hymettus near Athens. These hills, the priest told me, was where the Turks had made their headquarters at the beginning of their occupation of Greece in the 15th century so as to dominate the city and the Saronic Gulf. I was so struck by the beauty, the magic of the place that I kept returning to admire it again and again. I knew that the day would come when I would be compelled to try and create something grandiose and meaningful there. Don't you think Grigori, I should pursue my *idée fixe*, my obsession?" "I suppose you must, but don't let it consume you."

I could see that Grigori was not too pleased with my leaving Rome. Nonetheless, this man's political mind never stopped churning. "You might do me a favor by keeping your eyes open in Greece. Let me tell you why. Moscow's Central Committee is confronted with serious problems created by the leadership of the Greek Communist Party. It is too fiercely independent, straying from directives, making no secret of its ambitions for political control of the country and becoming resistant to all discipline, even when Moscow threatens to cut off financial support. For once Moscow's official party line for Greece coincides, albeit accidentally, with the core aims of the *Hermitage Coefficient* which is equally discomfitted by the Greek nonconformists whose rash behavior could jeopardize our strategies in the entire Balkan region. Greek Communists stubbornly choose to ignore long range strategy, clinging instead to orthodoxy and simplistic devotion to dogmatism. This is counter-productive. With lack of foresight they continue to blindly tread in a mined field which might explode in the form of strong-armed intervention by the Greek military, followed by a disastrous political tidal wave for everyone, bushwacking the Americans in particular.

Should a military regime be installed, the Greek Communists would not miss the opportunity to accuse America's dirty imperialists of blatantly intervening in Greece's internal affairs. Whatever advantages the Americans may have gained in Greece through their official policy or the surreptitious manoeuvering of the CIA to wean the country's leftist elements away from Moscow would be instantly brought to naught. And then, considering the Greek legacy of loving to hate, spawned by four hundred years of Turkish occupation, the Communists would make sure the heavily propagandized Greek populace blamed the Americans for years to come for any evils that might beset it. So, potentially and ironically, the negative psychological impact on the Greek nation of a military coup would benefit Moscow. But Moscow is also aware the Western Powers would not tolerate a Communist bid for political control, remembering that after the end of the Second World War the Communist guerrilla army - E.L.A.S.- was prevented from seizing power by British and American intervention. In brief, Moscow at this time prefers the status quo, admonishing the Greek Communists to lie low. Your State Department, getting no cooperation from the laissez-faire self-serving Greek politicians, is jittery, not quite sure how to keep the lid on".

"Grigori, you never cease to amaze me. Don't you ever miss? Is there anything you don't know?" "Very little, as long as I have access to the *Trichèco* files", he replied smiling. "I'll do what I can and keep you informed through the usual channels", I said. It shouldn't be too difficult, I told myself, to gage the temperature in Athens. After all, I did have a good number of friends among the cultural and political elite from the days I kept them dazzled with the latest Hollywood fabrications and feminine pulchritude. I promised myself not to get even marginally involved in Greek politics but devote all my time to Mount Hymettos of the Prophet Elia. Little did I know.

Not sure where and how to begin, I asked my friend, the talented Italian architect Carlo Tevini, to accompany me to Greece for an inspection of Mount Hymettos. When it was completed, Tevini's enthusiasm and creative imagination could not be contained. "You must create a cultural and scientific center here in homage to the Golden Age of Pericles and give it the eponymous name *Europolis*, meaning City of Europe". Finding the idea inspiring, I asked Bill Sevenhuysen, a retired Shell Oil man living in Greece, if he could help. Typically, the big Dutchman wasted no time arranging for the renowned Netherlands Consulting Engineers, NEDECO, and for a second team of experts from Middle East Consultants, MECONI, of the Hague, to survey Mount Hymettos in order to select the most suitable area for a major development. The Dutch engineers devoted many weeks conducting an on-the-spot comprehensive study. Not only were they captivated by the beauty of the surroundings but, more importantly, they found unexpected treasures beneath a plateau situated at 1400 feet above sea level consisting of a rich formation of very rare red-veined white marble under the mountain's surface skin and then, as they drilled deeper, a huge and heretofore unknown source of fresh water forming an underground lake. They were ecstatic. Their finds offered a supply of exquisite marble and an abundance of water for the future fountains and the flower gardens.

Meconi-Nedeco already knew from my original, and well received memorandum to the Greek government that I envisaged a large complex comprising a cultural center - thus returning to Greece the Olympic competition in arts-, several scientific laboratories, an outdoor classic amphitheater, three conference halls, an international festival palace, television studios, a television ground station to permit global transmissions via satellite, a 400 room hotel linked to an ocean beach on the coast by its own téléphérique. Last, but not least, a series of one and two bedroom luxurious bungalows to be put at the disposal of the in-residence foreign scientists and scholars.

The Dutch experts undertook to complete a master plan and detailed hotel designs within five months. My Athens attorneys Michael Sideratos and the Lambadarios Brothers advised me not to ask the government for a long-term lease of the site until I could present the development studies. An outright purchase was not possible as Greek laws prohibited land sales to foreign nationals.

I filled the waiting time by presenting the *Europolis* concept to various international cultural and scientific organizations, soliciting their advice. I could not have been more pleased with the results. After only three months of correspondence, telephone conferences and travel, I had an impressive list of enthusiastic supporters, offering counselling and, predicated on the approval of my project by the Greek government, their ongoing collaboration. They were the Weizmann Institute of Science in Israel, The Israel Institute of Technology-Technion, The International Exchange Service of the Smithsonian Institution of Washington, The Ford Foundation, The Rockefeller Foundation, Walt Disney Studios. Later I would add ABC International Television.

The Meconi master plan was rejected by the government ostensibly because no Greek nationals had a part in its preparation. I was tired, stunned, disgusted, ready to go on a binge. God protects the inebriated. Half sloshed at a hotel bar, I poured out my woes in conversation with George Georgiadis, head of a group of young Greek architect- engineers. He offered me their professional assistance. Some thirteen weeks later, these talented enthusiasts made me a gift of a new set of architectural drawings, model- maquettes, including photo blow-ups of two hotels they had designed during incredibly long hours of labor, often at the expense of paying jobs. The work they delivered was not only good, it was brilliant. Together, we marched through the streets of Athens, carrying armfuls of designs to the ministry. Nobody would even look at them. This was a cruel insulting blow which deeply hurt and humiliated these young, wonderful, patriotic Greeks. That night, frustrated and deeply saddened, I cried for them. And for myself too.

My energetic attorney, Michael Sideratos, refused to give up. Day after day he bombarded ministers as well as members of parliament with notes, memoranda and telephone calls. After several weeks we were told that approval was denied because the project would result in the destruction of precious trees. I had tremendously good fortune counteracting this new obstructionist argument. The Governor of the State of Oregon, having seen my report and the analysis of Hymettus soil made by the Dutch, offered us a gift of 4,000 suitable saplings. They would be packed and shipped to Greece at his treasury's expense. I so informed the minister responsible for agriculture and forests, inviting him to inspect the proposed area of development with me so that he could personally ascertain there would be no damage to his imaginary trees as none existed on the proposed construction site. The minister, who spoke excellent English, did not address a single word to me while we tredded up the mountain. On reaching the plateau we were embraced by a fabulous panorama. I caressed the horizon with outstretched arms. "Well, minister", I asked, "what do you think?" I could tell he was furious. "I piss on it", he said, and proceeded to do exactly that, without the benefit of a tree.

Next I was advised that a lease on the land could not be granted until I furnished proof of foreign financing. The bureaucrats knew that without prior approval of the project by the government it would be next to impossible to get a financing commitment estimated by Meconi at 55 million dollars.

With scant hope of success, I hurried to find my friends at the *Neue Heimat* organization in Hamburg. Due to the virtues of the combined Dutch-Greek studies and fascinated by the concept of Europolis, the president of this giant German construction and finance group, Dr. Weiskampf, agreed that if an inquiry were to be made by the Greek government or any of its banks or agencies he would formally confirm Neue Heimat's readiness to provide total financing for my project.

I had now fulfilled all prerequisites imposed by the government. And still that was not enough. The officials continued to invent new obstacles. For the second time in my life I began to feel like a modern day Sisyphus, rolling a huge block of stone to the brow of the hill, over and over again, only to be forced back by its weight to the bottom just before reaching the summit. Strained financially, played out physically and emotionally, after nearly two years of ceaseless but useless effort, I lost courage. It was time to acknowledge that City Hall had succeeded in turning my dream into a nightmare.

I told the whole miserable story to Evangelos Averof, a wise friend, political sophisticate, author historian, and member of one of Greece's most distinguished philanthropic families. We emptied a bottle of wine while he listened to the sequence of events. "I am deeply distressed, he said, that there is nothing I can do to save your wonderful project. You see, I myself am prisoner to this execrable political mess Greece is in. Anyway, it is now too late. Two very influential persons, a banker and a minister who returned to Greece from your country with a deep resentment of anything American, have done a Uranus job on you". I shuddered, recalling from mythology that Uranus was castrated by the merciless Cronus.

"You must accept the nature of things in Athens, Evangelos continued. The more it changes, the more it remains the same. The Roman emperor Hadrian, who in the second century of the Christian era travelled widely throughout his empire, visiting Athens when it formed part of the Roman province of Achaea,was an admirer of Hellenistic civilization and of the Greek philosopher Zeno, founder of Stoicism. Nonetheless, in his memoirs he could not resist observing: "From the Ionian tyrants to the Athenian demagogues, from the austere integrity of Agesilaos to the excesses of a Dionysius or a Dimitrios, from the treason of Demaratos to the fidelity of Philopimen, everything that any of us could do to help or hinder his fellow man has been done at least once by a Greek."

I was not the only one to get his butt kicked in Athens. Greece had no television. I thought it a brilliant idea to introduce it. The president of ABC International Television, Donald Coyle, submitted a proposal to the Greek government under which ABC offered to build, entirely at its own expense, a complete TV network consisting of prime transmitters and booster stations covering all of the mainland and the islands, provide fully equipped studios, a ground station for the transmitting of Greek programs abroad via satellite, train Greek technicians, directors and producers at its American facilities, supply free of charge any filmed programming selected by Greece, regardless of its source. All installations to belong exclusively to the Greek State which would have full control of programming and censorship. In addition, ABC undertook responsibility for the procuring of international avertising clients, with a portion of the revenues accruing to the American network only until it recouped its investment.

To illustrate the miracles of television in the modern age, Coyle brought to Athens a staff of expert technicians with sophisticated electronic sound and light equipment. We rented the Hilton Hotel conference hall for the demonstration and hired a prominent Greek journalist with a good voice to act as anchor-man commentator.

Several days before our big TV show, I arranged, through the American ambassador, for Donald Coyle and me to be received by King Constantine. When we arrived, John Broudos, His Majesty's High Chamberlain, asked us not to invite the King to our television demonstration. "But that is what we came for" we protested. "Better not, he said, because it will only embarrass him. You see, he will not be able to attend." I had had several rather costly previous meetings with Mr. Broudos, putting trust in his assurances that His Majesty would intervene with the government on my behalf in connection with the Europolis project. Now his comment, which sounded more like warning, set off loud, disquieting alarms in my brain, especially after he whispered to me behind Donald's back: "I will listen, so not a word about the mountain either."

Alone, but for the 'bugs' Broudos implied, Donald and I spent an hour with the tall, handsome and charming King of the Hellenes who spoke of his devotion to Greece and his hopes for the future of her citizens. Still, there was something ominous in the atmosphere and I had the strong feeling that Constantine was a political prisoner in his own palace. I also realized that he had never heard my name before. The Greek government rejected the ABC proposal, describing it as an attempt to impinge on Greek sovereignty.

I reported to Grigori regularly every Friday night by phone, always to repeat that I saw nothing in the Greek political cauldron to be seriously worried about. "Evgenii, he scolded me on one particular occasion, your powers of observation, your instincts have gotten blunted. Stay alert before the Ides of May". I took this to mean that the Reds were contemplating some drastic moves round the middle of May to overthrow the government. But how and where I could not imagine. My neighbor, Alan Charak, a retired American colonel, was always remarkably well informed. "Bullshit, he said. Nothing is going to happen". Only a few days later, during an April night while most citizens were still fast asleep, the Greek military seized power in a lightning, perfectly executed and bloodless coup d'état. Grigori was right about the scapegoats. "Only they, the Americans and their CIA, it was whispered, could have masterminded such a smooth operation". True to form, the State Department could muster no credible response.

Four months later, largely thanks to the able mediation of a Greek American from Chicago ,Spyros Karavitis, I had an agreement in hand, signed by the Prime Minister, the Minister of Finance, the Minister of

Coordination and the Secretary General for Tourism, leasing to me 180 acres of land for the construction of Europolis and granting me facilities and privileges I had not even asked for. There was only one thing wrong with my contract. It bore the signatures of men that many foreign governments declared members of a military junta to which diplomatic recognition could not be extended.

Never mind that under the new regime acts of political delinquency against the nation were being punished and eradicated. It was not what the ejected politicians and the priviligentsia wanted to hear or admit. For years in postwar Greece, these clever mandarins managed to substitute oligarchy for democracy, professing devotion to the latter while assiduously practicing the former, without the psyche of the common citizen ever recognizing the difference. Now, when their influence and their cookie jar were taken away, they vociferously protested to the international community against the curtailment of their hegemony. In the name of democracy, of course.

"Herr Van Dee, Dr. Weiskampf told me in Hamburg, you must realize that *Neue Heimat* is an emanation of German Socialist trade unions and would never allow me to invest our money in a dictatorship". The story was repeated nearly everywhere I turned.

After being threatened, blackmailed and beaten up by very democratic thugs one night as I was returning to my apartment in the coastal town of Kalamaki, I told myself enough is enough. I packed my suitcase and flew to Rome to see Grigori before going on to beautiful Oregon.

Some people say that the happiest days in one's life are those you can't remember because nothing happened to invade your peace of mind. For me, life in beautiful Oregon was like that. But only in the very beginning. Soon I found it to be an excuse for laziness, for sitting on my derrière while I let the world pass me by. I felt sure my old friend, maestro Paul Baron would have some exhilarating ideas so I flew to Rome. "You're just the man I was looking for, he said. Let's do something wild, like stealing oil from the Arabs". Paul was mocking the many self-styled promoters, "these Ph. D.'s in scatology", he called them, who on the promise of securing an allocation of Arab oil from the Ministry of Petroleum and Minerals, known as Petromin, with the help of their nonexistent prince-sponsors, often succeeded in collecting substantial expense monies or even advance commissions from gullible buyers of crude.

Members of the Royal family, however numerous, never got involved with these interlopers. The founder of the Kingdom, Abdul Aziz, alone spawned forty-three sons and twenty daughters. After his extraordinary performance, there came the numerous progenies of King Faisal, of King Khalid, of Abdullah ibn Abdul Aziz, and then more sons of sons, eventually nearly countless in number, each sharing in the oil wealth. They needed no help in accumulating or spending it.

Facetious or not, Paul needed action, something to take his mind off his heart condition that now forbade the strains of conducting symphony. I noticed that arthritis was beginning to curl his virtuoso fingers. I wanted to cry. He would still sit down to his grand piano and play for me late into the night, but it was Chopin, not Liszt any more.

Learning that the Saudis were granting contracts for prefabricated housing ordinary citizens would be able to purchase at low cost, Paul promptly convinced the giant Italian construction firm of the Caltagirone Brothers to give us representation rights for Kuwait and Saudi Arabia. Though I had visited their country a score of times in the past, invariably finding everyone exquisitely courteous, I really did not know how the Saudis felt about Americans. Even those who wore rings from American colleges avoided comment, leaving me with the impression that they were worried anything they said could cause mutual embarrassment. Hoping to get a better reading in this matter before leaving Rome for Riyadh, I asked Grigori's advice. He introduced me to one of his associates, a Middle East specialist from *Trichèco*.

"It is a very long and convoluted story spanning several decades, he told me, but as you have little time I can only give you a simplified version and tell you that Americans are highly unpopular with members of the Royal House. In practical terms this means also with anyone who has a part in the country's administration. I suppose you already know that any Saudi can have you arrested and imprisoned by merely picking up the phone, if he feels in any way slighted, so be very careful what you say and how you say it. They are resentful not only of America's support of Israel but convinced the evil Americans began to manipulate their history virtually from the day oil was discovered in the Kingdom, bringing phenomenal profits to the American companies of Aramco, thanks to the monopolistic control they maintained over production, shipping and world-wide marketing of the Saudi crude.

King Saud tried to break the American transport monopoly by secretly sponsoring a private Saudi tanker fleet with the participation of the Greek ship owner Aristotle Onassis. When the disgruntled Onassis middleman,

Spyros Catapodis, talked, the Aramco companies sprang into action resorting to a series of what could only be called 'dirty tricks'.

First they agreed with Onassis' brother-in-law and main rival, Stavros Niarchos that he should despatch a special agent to Jeddah for the purpose of stirring up trouble over the proposed shipping deal. They followed up by persuading the State Department and the American President's office to place CIA's network and codes in Jeddah at the disposal of Niarchos' agent, hoping that by setting Greek against Greek, the negative publicity in the international press would embarrass King Saud, forcing him to drop the idea of a Saudi tanker fleet. They succeeded and Aramco was able to continue its exclusive shipping privileges.

In the long run, the State Department's and the CIA's blunderhead lack of finesse would have dire consequences. Their sabotaging of Saudi Arabia's king would never be forgotten or forgiven. There were infinite sequels to this kind of American crapulence with astonishing effect on Saudi-American relations. Come back when you have more time and I shall show you some interesting documents on how Aramco got hoisted by its own petard". "How will I find you?" "Just ask for me. My name is Rybak."

I was not at all encouraged by what the *Tricheco* man told me, but we had already airfreighted the component parts of sample houses to Riyadh. Two weeks later we had them erected and ready for inspection by the Ministry of Housing expecting my personal friends there to give their approval. Unfortunately, the Saudi King himself decided to inspect the compact Italian-designed bungalows.. "No, No, No, he said. I do not want to see my people living in horse stalls... Could you design some high-rise apartment buildings instead?" Paul knew that the costly designs would have to be made at our own expense because the Saudis never advanced money to anyone for anything, bankrupting many an eager but naive company that way. The road to the imagined Mecca was strewn with their corpses. To the obvious mortification of the ministry officials present, Paul did not hesitate to ask: "If Your Majesty likes the designs, will we get the building contract?" The king smiled. "Insh'allah", he said. I groaned inside. Greeks answering "No", even before they heard the question is annoying enough but at least you knew where you stood. "Insh'allah" -God willing-, though a respectful invocation, leaves one absolutely nowhere for it is a combined "Yes", "No" and "Maybe". We could not afford to play bluff with super rich Saudis so that was the end of our housing venture. We had no reason to stay on and anyway our limited visas were about to expire. Off we went to our favorite Arab country, Kuwait. For several weeks we trespassed on the exquisite hospitality of my dear friend Hamad Al Alban. One memorable evening we were invited to dine with Kuwait's ruler, the Emir. It was not exactly an intimate affair, since there were at least thirty other guests there, tearing pieces of lamb apart with greasy fingers. Paul and I quickly lost our appetite when the Emir's guards placed themselves round the room with sleek, hooded and murderous falcons on their padded shoulders. My neighbor explained: "all they have to do is pull the leather hood from the falcon's head, loosen the jesses that secure its yellow scaled gaiters, point at you, and you're dead".

Back in Rome I was unable to get through to Grigori and feared he might be seriously ill. I called Monsignor Grotto. It was only the second time that he agreed to speak with me alone. When he assured me that Grigori's inability to see me was only due to the unexpected arrival of important foreign dignitaries, it occured to me this might be a good opportunity to ask Grotto to clarify some points that had kept me puzzled since the last time he spoke with me. "Monsignore, you once told me of the remarkable initiative General Grigori took in the Sakharov matter. How is it you knew so many details?" "Good question, and I don't mind giving you an answer. You see, my name is Leopold Grotovsky and I am from Smolensk, on the Upper Dnieper."

"Well, well, well, I mumbled. Do you have any other astounding revelations for me? Matters I have not been told about? Like what made the general decide to leave Russia?" "As a matter of fact, Monsignore Grigori authorized me to tell you a thing or two, so if you will bear with me, I will let you in on some old secrets.

My communications from Rome to the General were frequent, either by letter or cable, sometimes even by phone. I would always use the identification codes of the Soviet intelligence unit in Rome so as to clear through Moscow's controls. I used phrases that only the General could understand. My messages repeatedly made it clear we were anxious to have him in Rome, to personally formulate directives for *Hermitage* activities in Russia, Poland, Czechoslovakia and Hungary.

Though I could never specifically mention it in our communications, I was quite sure he also knew that Rome wished to interrogate him about the report he had written extolling the political skills and intellectual attainments of Karol Wojtyla, the 44-year old Archbishop of Krakow, that so profoundly impressed the Curia Romana. What the Curia did not know was that there were certain phases of this matter the General kept very quiet about to avoid upsetting certain powerful individuals in the Vatican hierarchy. I was privy to it all and knew that after submitting his report on Wojtyla, the General had several secret meetings in Madrid with the founder of *Opus Dei*, José Maria Escriva de Balaguer and with his spiritual confrère, Alvaro de Portillo, who brought him into *Opus Dei* during the Spanish Civil War.

It was, therefore, no random coincidence that the General's encomium was soon followed by equally laudatory letters sent to the Curia concerning Wojtyla by the two Spaniards, describing Krakow's archbishop as a "persevering opponent of Marxism and Leninism with an unquenchable appetite for learning, who preaches the usefulness of anything fine and noble and speaks so compellingly of the dignity of man".

In contrast, the mission of Grigori's emissaries to America was a rigor mortis. They reported back that the bishops there were more concerned with the enriching of their treasuries than with the struggle against Communism in distant Poland.

Meantime, the indefatigable and farsighted Wojtyla established a much talked about institute in Poland devoted to sexual morality. Always diligently reporting to his superiors, he also sent Pope Paul VI confidential material that was later incorporated in the *Humanae Vitae* encyclical. When he received the Cardinal's Hat, Poland and *Hermitage* felt jubilant. Alvaro del Portillo made sure that the predominantly lay group of more than 70 thousand intellectuals and professionals, members of *Opus Dei* across the world, remained Wojtyla's most effective advocates. Grigori's men in Warsaw, with some arm twisting, had the Polish secret police send a report to Moscow that the new cardinal was a friend of the working class, a ponderous man, unlikely to create many political headaches.

In Moscow, our General was never in any imminent danger.. His few intimate friends in Military Intelligence had a pretty good idea that he would eventually be going somewhere abroad, never to return. Admitting to themselves that given the opportunity they would do the same, they envied him and kept their silence.

From Rome we continued applying tactful psychological pressure which our friend Grigori pretended not to notice, but eventually, he agreed to join us, realizing his continued presence in Russia was no longer essential to the smooth functioning of the *Hermitage Coefficient*.

This is how it happened. However, try to avoid harping on it when you see him. You know how he prizes his dignity, and the method we chose for him to arrive in our midst, while well thought out, might seem patterned on a typical CIA scenario. Off the record I can tell you that the old fox enjoyed every minute of it.

Comrade General took a regular diplomatic duty flight from Moscow to Paris, booked into the Château Frontenac Hotel. Pleading fatigue, he then sent his two sidekicks on the town, told them he would retire early but to meet him for late breakfast the next morning. He boarded the night train for the Riviera, got off at the town of Grasse, where a flashy Ferrari car, an American baseball cap, dark glasses, an Italian passport and a ravishing blonde were awaiting him. They drove at break-neck speed to Rome, parked in front of the Trinitá Dei Monti church, overlooking the Piazza di Spagna. He handed the car keys to the sacristan, said "grazie" to the blonde, put on a drooping black hat, walked out of the church, got into a van with SCV (Santa Cittá Vaticana) license plates and was never seen again."

"Monsignore Grotto, this can't be true. You are kidding me", I said. "No. It is exactly how we did it, If asked, the French and Italian border controls would vividly remember the sexy blonde in a red Ferrari but, merde, who paid attention to a blasé, rude, middle-aged Italian playboy returning home from a weekend of dissipation in Monte Carlo".

Looking out the window of my study where I have labored over these memoirs, years after the events took place, I see the television antenna of the little church on the slopes of Mount Hymettus sticking out over the trees, just a stone's throw away. I can nearly hear Prophet Elia telling me it is not the victory or the defeat but the worthiness of the battles one waged that counts. It sells poorly with me. I have little faith in prophets except the worldly ones like Grigori and he is now dead. Gone too soon to know that his own words would be echoed when Mikhail Gorbachev, the very kind of man he predicted would emerge in Russia, asked President Reagan: "why don't you believe us when we say we will not use missiles against you?" Gone too soon to see the Berlin wall crumble, this symbol of Communist suppression, of the xenophobic regime that had to lock its people in just as the Soviet regime did, lest they be tempted by a freer life. Gone too soon to know that "his" Cardinal of Krakow, whom he had seen elevated to the papal throne as Pope John Paul II, met with Gorbachev and described him as a "statesman-reformer, a man of principle who is ready to accept the consequences, however unpleasant, of his acts". Or, that the Pope had beatified José Maria Escriva de Balaguer, founder of *Opus Dei*.

Grigori was not just all analyst-philosopher. Among the many papers he bequeathed to me there is a Russian manuscript. He entitled it: "My gift from Agnieszka". I am reading it now. It is the story of his love, her passion and the palpitating joy of having a son.

He reposes in the small cemetery of a convent in Assisi, birthplace of Saint Francis. Just as he bid me, I waited a long time to speak of him and after this, I may say no more.

J'ai eu le courage de	(I have had had the courage
regarder en arrière	To look back
Les cadavres de mes jours	The cadavres of my past
Marquent ma route	Mark my course
Et je les pleure	And I grieve for them
Les uns pourrissent	Some putrefy in Italian
dans les églises Italiennes	churches
Ou bien dans les petits bois	Or in small groves
de citronniers qui fleurissent	of lemon trees
et fructifient	That blossom and fructify)

From collection of poems, *ALCOOLS*, *by Guillaume Apollinaire*, (1880-1918)

Index

A
A Branch (support or liaison departments of MI5) - p 163
Aardvark (Vatican most secret intelligence files) - p 169
ABC International Television (American television organization) - p 190, 192, 193
Abdul Aziz, 'ibn Sa'ud' 1876-1953 (founder of the Kingdom of Saudi Arabia) - p 194, 195
Abdullah, ibn Abdul Aziz 1923-   (Commander of Natinal Guard)
Abwehr (German Secret Service) - p 195
Achard, Marcel 1899-1974 (French playwright) - p 67, 77
Acheson, Dean Gooderham 1893-1971 (U.S.Secretary of State) - p 82
Across the River and into the Trees (Hemingway novel) - p 125
Addams, Charles 1912-1988 (American cartoonist) - 92
AFTS (Advanced Flying Training School.Royal Air Force) - p 23
Agesilaos 444-3611 B.C. (King of Sparta) - 192
Aïda (Giuseppe Verdi opera) - p 128, 129
Ajeel, Sultan (Kuwaiti businessman) - p 139
Al-Alban, Hamad Rashid (Kuwaiti businessman) - p 197
Alfredo's (fettucine restaurant in Rome) - p 104
Algonquin (New York hotel) - p 98
Allen, Larry 1908-1975 (American journalist) - p 43
Allen, Rupert (American film and PR executive) - p 65
Allied Artists (American film company) - p 70
Allport, Fayette (American film executive) - p 90
Amazons (female warriors in Greek legend) - p 126
Amon, Michelle (American film actress) - p 121

Amon, Robert (French film producer) - p 97, 121, 122
Amor y Padagogia (novel by Miguel de Unamuno) - p 77
Anderson, Hans Christian 1805-75 (Danish fairy tale writer) - p 99
Andreotti, Giulio 1919- (Italian statesman) - p 86
Anti Planning Committees (code name for Russian sabotage teams) - p 181, 186
Aphrodite (goddess in Greek mythology) - 120
Apollinaire, Guillaume 1880-1918 (French lyric poet) - p 200
Apparatchik (permanent government employee) - p 52, 59, 181, 183
Aramco (Arabian American Oil Company) - p 195, 196
Ascarelli, Giulio (20th Century Fox publicity manager) - 106, 107
Assisi (birthplace of St. Francis, Italy) - p 200
Atatürk, Kemal 1880-1938 (Turkish statesman) - p 129
Atomic Energy Commission, (AEC) (U.S.government agency) - p 167
Auschwitz (Nazi extermination camp, Poland) - p 42
Averof - Tositsas, Evangelos 1909-1990 (Greek statesman and philanthropist) - p 191
Azarian, Paula (executive film secretary) - p 84

B
Balaban, Barney 1888-1971 (president Paramount Pictures) - p 112
Balinska, Irena (US Government employee) - p 30
Balzac, Honoré de 1799-1850 (French novelist) - p 145
Banca Commerciale Italiana (Italian bank) - p 134
Banco di Santo Spirito (Italian bank) - p 134
Bank of Italy & America (bank in Italy) - p 113
Bardot, Brigitte 1934- (French film actress) - p 121, 122
Baroja, Pio 1872-1956 (Spanish novelist) - p 147
Baron, Paul (composer and conductor) - p 91, 98, 100, 126, 139, 194
Basov, Nikolai G. 1922- (Russian physicist) - p 180
BBC (British Broadcasting Corporation) - p 26, 27, 37, 40
Beane, A. Joynes 'Jack' (American business executive) - p 123, 129, 130, 138, 139
Beatrix Infanta of Spain (daughter of King Alfonso XIII) - 93, 94
Beck, Józef 1894-1944 (Polish political leader) - p 2
Beethoven, Ludwig van 1770-1827 (German composer) - p 99
Beix, Maxime de (French journalist) - p 71, 72
Ben Bella, Ahmed 1916 -   (Algerian statesman) - p 68

Bennet, Joan 1910-1990 (American acttess) - p 74
Bentinck, William Cavendich (British diplomat) - p 43, 59
Benvenides, Antonio (Spanish bullfighter) - p 127
Berger, Jean-Paul (French film producer) - p 79
Berger, Jean-Pierre (French film producer) - p 79
Beria, Lavrenti 1899-1953 (Soviet minister of the interior) - p 169, 170, 174, 181-184
Berlin, Irving 1888-1989 (American composer) - p 28
Bessy, Maurice (French journalist) - p 72
Bestegui, Charles de (European socialite) - p 101
Betts, Thomas colonel (American military attaché) - p 62, 64
Beurton, Ursula (Soviet spy) - p 164
Bezpieka (common name for Polish security police) - p 39, 45
Bigart, Homer 1907-1991 (American journalist) - p 43
Blackboard Jungle (American motion picture) - p 116, 117, 123
Blasco Ibañez, Vicente 1867-1928 (Spanish novelist) - p 142
Bocek, Ottomar 1926- (Czech general) - p 172
Bogdan, Norbert (financial executive) - p 131, 135
Bohlen, Charles E. 1904-1974 (American diplomat) - p 178
Bor-Komorowski, Tadeus 1895-1966 (Polish general) - p 36, 176, 177
Borah, William E. 1865-1940 (U.S. Republican senator) - p 19
Borges, Jorge Luis 1899-1986 (Argentine poet and novelist) - p 118
Borgia Apartments (inner chambers of the Vatican) - p 140
Borgia, Cesare 1475-1507 (Italian politician) - p 97
Boris Godunov (Opera by Mussorgsky) - p 155
Borodin, Alexander Porfyrievich 1834-87 (Russian composer) - p 155
Bosquet, 1810-1861 (French Army Marshal) -p 24
Bowmaker (British finance company) - p 131
Brady, Jack (American company executive) - p 139
Brezhnev, Leonid Ilyich 1906-1982 (Russian statesman) - p 185
Brooks, Richard 1912-92 (American film director) - p 116
Broudos, John (High Chamberlain to the King of Greece) - p 193
Browder, Earl (Russell) 1891-   (U.S.Communist Party leader) - p 24
Brummel, George Bryan "Beau" 1778-1840 (British dandy) - p 92
Bryan, William Jennings, 1860-1925 (U.S.political leader and orator) - p 61
Buchwald, Art 1925- (American journalist, humorist) - p 74, 75
Bujak, Tadeusz (Polish fighter ace, RAF) - p 51

Bulgakov, Sergei Nikolayevich, 1871-1944 (Russian philosopher and theologian) - p 9
Bulganin, Nikolai Alexandrovich 1895-1975 (Russian leader) - p 182, 183, 184
Bunker, Ellsworth 1894-1984 (American diplomat) - p 107
Burgess, Guy 1911-1968 (Soviet agent in British intelligence) - p 162
Bush House (BBC'S London studios for overseas broadcasting) - p 26
"Bustarella" (Italian slang for "pay-off") - p 113, 115
Buydens, Ann (representative of French Film Office) - p 78
Byrnes, James F. 1879-1972 (American statesman) - p 178

C

Cadogan, Alexander Sir 1884-1968 (British government official) - p 179
Café de la Rotonde (coffee house in Paris) - p 142
Cahiers de la Quinzaine (writings by Péguy) - p 156
Calder, (RAF Squadron Leader) - p 23, 24
Caltagirone Brothers (Italian construction firm) - p 195
Calvet, Corinne 1925- (French actress) - p 107
Canon Law (ecclesiastical law) - p 141
Capitol (Congressional building in Washington, D.C.) - p 168
Carabinieri (Italian gendarmes) - p 16, 90
Carol, Martine 1922-1967 (French film actress) - p 121
Cartier (French jeweler) - p 101
Casablanca Conference (1943 meeting between Roosevelt and Churchill) - p 68
Castel Gandolfo (the pope's summer residence near Rome) - p 153, 173
Catapodis, Spyros (Onassis middleman) - p 196
Catilina, Lucius Sergius 109-62 B.C. (Roman politician) - p 103
Chaliapin, Fyodor Ivanovich 1873-1938 (Russian bass singer) - p 155
Chaplin, Charles Spencer 1889-1977 (film, actor, director) - p 75, 102, 103
Charak, Alan (American army officer) - p 193
Charles, Nicholas (British Foreign Office employee) - p 49
Charlotte Grand Duchesse 1886-1985 (reigning head of Luxembourg) - p 101
Château Frontenac (hotel in Paris) - p 199
Chesterton, Gilbert Keith 1874-1936 (English poet and novelist) - p 156
Chevalier, Maurice 1888-1972 (French songster,actor) - p 71, 72, 73

Index 205

Chicago Council on Foreign Relations - p 19
Chopin, Frédéric François 1810-49 (Polish composer) - p 4, 99, 195
Christian-Jacque 1904- (French film director) - p 121
Churchill, Sir Winston Leonard Spencer, 1874-1965 (British statesman) -
 p 27, 31, 33, 43, 44, 68, 103, 165, 175, 178, 179
Cicero, Marcus Tulius 106-43 B.C. (Roman orator) - p 103
Cidonio (Italian construction company) - p 139
Cinèmonde (French film magazine) - p 72
Clausewitz, Karl von 1780-1831 (Prussian general) - p 130
Clemenceau, Georges 1841-1929 (French statesman) - p 68
Club of Rome (exclusive playboy club in Rome) - p 129
Cocteau, Jean 1889-1963 (French poet and novelist) - P 73
Cohn, Harry 1891-1958 (president Columbia Pictures) - p 112
Cohn, Roy (investigative assistant of senator McCarthy) - p 166
Colbert, Claudette 1905- (American film actress) - p 108, 109
Colette, Sidonie Gabrielle 1873-1954 (French writer) - p 73
Comecon (economic association of Communist block countries) - p 181
Comédie humaine (novel by Honor, de Balzac) - p 145
Confucius, 551 B.C. -479 B.C. (Chinese philosopher) - p 40
Constantine 1940-   (Constantine XIII, King of Greece) - p 193
Cooper, Diana (English socialite) - p 85
Cornfield, Albert (American film executive) - p 115
"Cosi fan tutti" (Italian for "they all do it") - p 114
Cossack (national group in S.Russia and famous horsemen) - p 155
Coudert, Fréres (French-American law firm) - p 75
Coyle, Donald (American television executive) - p 192, 193
Crawford, Joan 1906-1977 (American actress) - p 69
Crazy Horse Saloon (Paris striptease) - p 71
Credito Italiano (Italian bank) - p 134
Cripps, Sir Stafford 1889-1952 (British statesman) - p 164
Croix de Guerre (French decoration) - p 73
Cronus (one of the Titans in Greek mythology) - p 192
Crosby, Bing 1904-1977 (American songster and actor) - p 108
Crowther, Bosley 1905-1981 (NY film critic) - p 116
Cruna, Oliver (Swedish brain surgeon) - p 136, 137
Cugat, Xavier 1900-1990 (Spanish musician) - p 149
Czartoryski (Polish princely family) - p 62
Czetwertinski, Janusz (Polish nobleman) - p 39, 41

D

D Branch (MI5's counterespionage) - p 164
Daily Worker (American Communist Party newspaper) - p 24
Davis, Bette 1908-1989 (American movie actress) - p 55
Dayton, Leon (American diplomat) - p 44, 128, 129, 149
De Beauvoir, Simone 1908-1986 (French writer and philosopher) - p 76, 77
De Gasperi, Alcide 1881-1954 (Italian statesman) - p 86
De Pirro, Nicola (Italian government official) - p 86
Deep Purple (Popular melody during WW2) - p 31
Demaratos end 6th.cent.B.C. (King of Sparta) - p 192
Denaro (Italian for money) - p 114
Department "S" (KGB department controlling deep cover agents) - p 162
Descartes, René, 1596-1650 (French philosopher, physicist and mathematician.) - p 122
Deuxième Bureau (French Security) - p 167
Diaghilev, Sergei Pavlovich 1872-1929 (Russian ballet impresario) - p 146
Dionysius c.430-367 B.C. (tyrant of Syracuse) - p 192
Disney, Walt 1901-66 (American film cartoonist and director) - p 104, 190
Dobrovolsky, (St.Petersburg physician) - p 159, 174, 182
Doge (chief magistrate in the republics of Venice and Genoa) - p 15, 92
Domino (play by Marcel Achard) - p 77
Double Cross Committee (MI5's recruitment of double agents) - p 163
Douglas, Kirk 1916- (film actor) - p 78, 79
Dulles, Allen 1893-1969 (wartime head of the OSS) - p 65, 75
Dunne, Irene 1898-1990 (American actress) - p 101
Dupplin Castle (a Castle in Perth, Scotland & WW2 Military hospital) - p 24, 25

E

Eagle Club (club for American servicemen in the U.K.) - p 31
Ecole Nationale d'Administration (provides training for higher ranks of French the Civil Service) - p 71
Eden, Robert Anthony 1897-1977 (British statesman) - p 178
EFTS (Elementary Flying Training School, Royal Air Force) - p 23

Eisenhower, Dwight, David, 1890-1969 (U.S.general and statesman) - p 33, 101, 175-178
El Otro (Play by Unamuno) - p 142
ELAS (Greek pro-communist guerilla army) - p 188
Elephant Blanc (Paris nightclub) - p 71
Eliot, Thomas Stearns 1888-1965 (American poet and critic) - p 100
Elizabeth "Lizzy", (British secret agent) - p 171, 172
Ellington, Edward Kennedy "Duke" 1899-1979 (American pianist and composer) - p 99
Enver, Ali (Turkish, military officer) - p 128
Enver, Pasha 1881-1922 (Turkish general and statesman) - p 129
Epp, John major (member of.U.S.army intelligence) - p 64
Escriva, de Balaguer José 1902-1975 (Spanish founder of Opus Dei) - p 148, 198, 200
Europolis ("City of Europe") - p 189-191, 193, 194
Existentialists (followers of the Kierkegaard philosophical doctrine) - p 71
Expressionists (artists belonging to expressionist mode of artistic expression) - p 71

F

Fairbanks, Douglas 1883-1939 (American film actor) - p 103, 104
Faisal, ibn Abdul-Aziz 1904-75 (King of Sauii Arabia) - p 195
Falkland, Lucius Cary,Viscount 1610-1643 (British parliamentarian) - p 71
Fath, Jacques 1912-1959 (French couturier) - p 83
Favarger, Yvonne (executive film secretary) - p 84
FBI, Federal Bureau of Investigation (U.S.) - p v, 21, 22, 163, 167
Felcours, Amanda de (French socialite) - p 88
Fellini, Federico 1920-1993 (Italian film director) - p 108
Ferrara, Massimo de Santamaria (Italian film attorney) - p 120
Ficodoro, Franco (Italian finance manager) - p 135
Fields, W.C. 1879-1946 (American comedian, actor) - p 123
Film Français, Le (French movie magazine) - p 72
Film Polski (Polish film monopoly) - p 50, 60
Finauto (finance company) - p 135
Finmeccanica (Italian government Holding Company) - p 113-115, 130, 134

First Chief Directorate (division of KGB) - p 161, 162
Fitelberg, Grzegorz 1879-1953 (Polish composer and conductor) - p 177
Flaubert, Gustave 1821-80 (French novelist) - p 145
Fluency Committee (MI5 and MI6 joint committee to investigate Soviet penetration of British intelligence) - p 164
Fontaine, Joan 1917- (American actress) - p 105-108
Fontane, Lynn 1887-1983 (American theater actress) - p 28
Ford, Glenn 1916- (American actor) - p 116
Fouquet's (Paris resturant) - p 138
Fourth Republic (French consitutional Republic 1946) - p 68
Fox (Twentieth Century Fox film company) - p 70, 71, 75, 106, 115
Franco, Francisco 1892-1975 (Spanish general and head of state) - p 148

G
Gabin, Jean 1904-1976 (French actor) - p 69
Garcia Lorca, Federico 1898-1936 (Spanish poet and playwright) - p 147
Garde Republicaine (French parade regiment) - p 74
Gardner, Ava 1922-1990 (American actress) - p 127
Gaulle, Charles de, 1890-1970 (French statesman and general) - p 67, 81, 82
GCHQ (British Government Communications Headquarters) - p 162, 163
Gemini, Italo (Italian film exhibitor) - p 88, 90
Georgiadis, George (Greek architect-engineer) - p 190
German American Bund (Association of German Americans) - p 20-22
Germinal (novel by Émile Zola) - p 145
Gide, Pierre (French attorney) - p 78
Giraud, Henri Honoré (French general) - p 68
Girondist (member of political party during French Revolution) - p 68
GKNIIR (joint KGB & GRU intelligence group) - p 161
Gladstone, William Eward, 1809-98 (British statesman & PM) - p 29
Glazunov, Aleksandr Konstantinovich 1865-1936 (Russian composer) - p 156, 157, 183
Gluchowski, Mathew (Polish American escapee from war) - p 18
Gobbi, Tito (Italian baritone) - p 98
Goethe, Johann Wolfgang von, 1749-1832 (German poet and novelist) - p 27
Goldwyn, Samuel 1882-1974 (American film producer) - p 81
Gorbachev, Mikhail Sergeievich 1931- (Russian statesman) - p vii, 199

Index 209

Gorky, Maxim (Aleksei Maksimovich Peshkov)1868-1936 (Russian author) - p 145
Goya y Lucientes, Francisco 1746-1828 (spanish painter) - p 94
Grable, Betty 1916-1978 (American actress) - p 69
Grabowski, Zbigniew (Polish journalist) - p 30
Grampians (Grampian mountain system in Scotland) - p 24
Grant, Cary 1904-1986 (English-American film actor) - p 121
Green Lake (Czech spa) - p 55, 56, 170
Griffis, Stanton (American financier and diplomat) - p 49, 57, 58, 149
Gronchi, Giovanni 1887-1978 (President of Italy) - p 139
Grotovsky, Leopold (Russian scientist) - p 197
Grotto, Clemente (scientist Monsignore Grotovsky) - p 143, 144, 197, 199
GRU (Soviet military intelligence) - p 161, 163, 168, 172, 175, 179, 184
Gruson, Sidney 1916- (American journalist) - p 43
Gutzwiller (Swiss finance company) - p 131
Guys and Dolls (American musical by Frank Loesser) - p 98, 99

H

Hapsburg, Otto von 1912- (of Austrian royal dynasty) - p 20
Harper, Kenneth (English film producer) - p 119-122
Harriman, Averell 1891-1986 (American financier and diplomat) - p 35
Harrison, Rex 1908-1990 (English actor) - p 109-111
Harvard (oldest university in the U.S.A.) - p 75, 84, 167
Hearst, William Randolph 1863-1951 (American publisher) - p 18
Hegel, Georg Wilhelm Friedrich 1770-1831 (German philosopher) - p 26
Heidegger, Martin, 1889-1976 (German philosopher) - p 26, 76
Heidelberg University - p 26, 34
Heliogas Brazil (Vatican company) - p 134
Hemingway, Ernest 1898-1961 (American novelist) - p 124, 125
Hepburn, Audrey 1929-1993 (film actress) - p ix, 121
Hermitage Coefficient (secret anti-communist Society) - p vi, vii, 174, 180, 186, 188, 198
Hermitage Museum (State Museum in St. Petersburg) - p 174
Hitler, Adolf 1889-1945 (German Nazi dictator) - p 2, 8, 20, 34, 160, 173
Holden, William 1918-1981 (American film actor) - p 97, 100, 125, 126
Hollis, Roger Sir 1905-1973 (Director General of MI5) - p 164

210   *Sleeping Dogs and Popsicles*

Hollywood Reporter (American show-business journal) - p 85
Holmes, Oliver Wendell 1841-1935 (American jurist) - p 61
Hugo, Victor Marie 1802-85 (French poet and novelist) - p 145
Huis Clos (Play by J-P Sartre) - p 76
Hussman, Max (Swiss educator and economist) - p 111, 112

I
Ibert, Jacques François Antoine 1890-1962 (French composer) - p 98
Il Duce (Italian for "The Leader") - p 15, 112
Impressionists (artists belonging to impressionist school of art) - p 71
Inspectorat Génerale de Finance (French Inspectorate for Finance) - p 71
Institut Catholique de Paris (institute of higher learning) - p 144
IRI Institute for Industrial Reconstruction (Italian government Industrial
    Holding Company) - p 134
Ishaikas (Communist Party spies) - p 181
Ivanhoe (novel by Sir Walter Scott) - p 105, 106
Ivanov, Evgenii (KGB agent) - p 165

J
Jacobin (member of political club during French Revolution) - p 69
Jimenez Arnau, José Antonio (Spanish government official) - p 149
Joan of Arc 1412-41 (French national heroine) - p 39, 68, 74, 75
Jockey Club (Madrid restaurant) - p 127
Johnson, Van 1916- (American film actor) - p 122
Johnston, Eric 1896-1963 (American film executive) - p vi, 80-83, 94, 96,
    114-118, 123, 138
Johnston, Griff (American film executive) - p 80, 117
Joint Distribution Committee (Jewish relief organization) - p 55, 60

K
Kabanov, (Communist Party official) - p 183
Kalugin (Russian military intelligence officer) - p 176
Kandinsky, Wassily 1855-1944 (Russian painter) - p 9
Karavitis, Spyros (Greek-American businessman) - p 193
Katyn (town near Smolensk, USSR) - p v, 28, 29, 47, 166
Katzander, Howard (American journalist) - p 122

Katzander, Shirley (American journalist) - p 122, 123
Keeler, Christine (mistress of Britain's War Minister) - p 165
Keith, Gerald (American career diplomat) - p 64
Kennedy, Joseph Patrick 1888-1969 (U.S.financier) - p 19
Kerensky, Alexandr Feodorovich 1881-1970 (Russian revolutionary leader) - p 158
Kerr, Archibald John Clark 1882-1951 (British diplomat) - p 178
KGB (Committee of State Security, USSR) - p 133, 161-163, 165, 166, 169, 172, 175
Khalid, ibn Abdul Aziz 1912- (King of Saudi Arabia) - p 195
Kharadze, (lieutenant of Russian State Security) - p 184
Kielce (Polish town, scene of Jewish pogrom) - p 41, 42
Kiepuna, Jan 1902-1966 (Polish opera tenor) - p 35
Kierkegaard, Sören Aaby 1813-55 (Danish philosopher) - p 76
King's Regulations (regulations of the British Armed Forces) - p 24
Kitezh (Opera by Rimsky-Korsakov) - p 148
Koestler, Arthur 1925-1983 (writer) - p 109
Kornilov, Lavr Georgievich 1870-1918 (Russian general) - p 158
Korotchenko, (Party official in the Ukraine) - p 183
Kosciuszko, Tadeusz 1746-1817 (Polish General Served in American Revolutionary War) - p 4
Kosygin, Alexei 1904-1980 (Russian statesman) - p 185
Kovtun, (NKVD officer) - p 177
Krasnaya Zvezda (Soviet newspaper) - p 179
Krause Wichman, Joseph (German Consul General) - p 21-22
Kriminalka (Czech criminal police) - p 56, 170, 171
Kropotkin, Prince Piotr Alexeyevich 1842-1921 (Russian social philosopher and anarchist) - p 156
Krupskaya Institute of Culture (Institute in St. Petersburg) - p 8, 147
Krushchev, Nikita 1894-1971 (Russian statesman) - p 183, 185
Kuczynski, Réne (Soviet spy at Oxford University) - p 164
Kuibishev project (radio operation of KGB Disinformation) - p 174, 175, 181
Kuomintang (Chinese political party) - p 40
Kuperin, (Kremlin's chief physician) - p 182, 183

L
L'Éducation sentimentale (novel by Gustave Flaubert) - p 145

L'Être et le Néant (J-P Sartre's philosophical work) - p 76
La Agonía del Cristianismo (philosophical essay by Unamuno) - p 147
La Bohème (An opera by Puccini) - p 15
La Nausée (J-P Sartre's novel) - p 76
La Romana (Alberto Moravia novel) - p 95
La Scala (Italian Opera House in Milano) - p 71, 98
Lake Ladoga (Lake near St.Petersburg) - p 144, 159
Lambadarios Brothers (Greek firm of attorneys) - p 190
Landau, Lev Davidovich 1908-1968 (Russian physicist) - p 180
Lane, Arthur Bliss 1894-1956 (American diplomat) - p 35, 42, 47, 49
Lapin Agile (Paris bistro) - p 71
Laroche, Daniel (nom de guerre of British secret agent) - p 54, 170
Lawrence, David 1888-1978 (American journalist) - p 43
Le Roi d' Yvetot (opera by Jacques Ibert) - p 98
Lebret, Favre (director of Paris Opera) - p 75
Leduc, Jean (French government official) - p 81, 82
Legendre, Maurice (French author) - p 148
Légion d' Honneur (French order of distinction) - p 68, 82
Lehar, Franz 1870-1948 (Hungarian composer of operettas) - p 168
Lenin, (Vladimir Ilyich Ulyanov) 1870-1924 (Russian revolutionary) - p 47, 144, 148, 160
Les Ambassadeurs (dinner club in London) - p 119
Les Mains Sales (Play by J-P Sartre) - p 76
Lesueur, René (French tennis coach) - p 17
Lewis, David (film company executive) - p 117
Lewis, Flora 1923- (American journalist) - p 43
Lewitanski, Julius (1939 refugee from Warsaw) - p 16, 17
Library of Congress (the national library of the U.S.A.) - p 167
Liszt, Franz 1811-86 (Hungarian composer and pianist) - p 99, 195
Loesser, Frank 1910-1969 (American songwriter,composer) - p 98, 100, 126
Loew, Arthur M 1897-1977 (president MGM International) - p 112, 117
Lomas Verdes (Vatican interest company in Mexico) - p 134
Longchamps (Paris race track) - p 71
Loren, Sophia 1934- (Italian film actress) - p 119, 121
Louis XIV "the Great", "le Roi-Soleil" 1638-1715 (king of France) - p 154
Louvre (National museum of France) - p 66, 71

Index 213

Luce, Clare Boothe 1903-1987 (U.S.playwright and ambassador) - p vi, 85, 94-96, 115-119, 123
Luger (German military pistol) - p 63
Lukomsky, (Kremlin physician) - p 183
Lunacharsky Library (State Library, St. Petersburg) - p 156
Lunt, Alfred 1893-1977 (American stage actor) - p 28
Lynn, Vera 1917- (English songstress) - p 27

M
Maas, Irving (American film executive) - p 65
Machiavelli, Nicoló, 1469-1527 (Florentine statesman and writer) - p 27, 86
Maclean, Donald 1913-1983 (Soviet spy in British intelligence) - p 162
Madras Aluminium (Vatican company in India) - p 134
Mafia (Sicilian criminal organization) - p 169
Maginot Line (France's eastern frontier fortifications) - p 67
Malenkov, Georgi Maximilianovich 1902-1988 (Russian statesman) - p 182-184
Malevich, Kasimir 1878-1935 (Russian painter and sculptor) - p 9
Mallarmé, Stéphane 1844-1898 (French Symbolist poet) - p 77
Mannikin Pis (fountain statue in Bruselles) - p 25
Mao Tse-tung 1893-1976 (Chinese statesman) - p 40
Maquis (French military underground) - p 55
Marañon Moya, Gregorio (Spanish attorney, justice minister) - p 93
Marañon, Gregorio 1887-1960 (Spanish physician, writer and statesman) - p 93, 94
Marco Polo, 1254-1324 (Venetian traveler) - p 15
Marks, John (English naval officer) - p 31
Marks, Julian (English financier) - p 31
Marks, Nancy (American wife of Julian Marks) - p 31
Marks, Nancy Joan (daughter of Julian Marks) - p 31
Marks, Susan (daughter of Julian Marks) - p 31
Marlow, Christopher 1564-1593 (English drammatist and poet) - p 100
Marshall, George Catlett 1880-1959 (U.S.general and statesman) - p 33
Martin, Theodore Sir 1881-1924 (British statesman) - p 78
Marzotto, Paolo (Italian industrialist) - p 96
Matterhorn (Peak in Swiss Alps) - p 139
Matisse, Henri 1869-1954 (French painter and sculptor) - p 9

Mattheis, Belisario baron de (Italian government official) - p 85, 87, 90, 91, 124, 128
Maxim's (Paris restaurant) - p 70
Maxwell, Elsa 1883-1963 (public relations hostess) - p 87
Mayakovsky, Vladimir Vladimirovich 1893-1930 (Russian poet and playwright) - p 9
Mayer, Gerald M (American film executive) - p 65, 82, 84
McCarthy, Frank (American film executive and producer) - p 65
McCarthy, John Gilman (American business executive and diplomat) - p 65, 83-87, 101, 102, 114, 118
McCarthy, Joseph Raymond 1909-57 (American Republican senator) - p 166
McClure, Robert A. 1897-1957 (American general) - p 31
McCormick, Robert Rutheford 1880-1955 (American publisher) - p 18
McMillin, John (American company executive) - p 138, 139
MECONI (Firm of Dutch consulting engineers) - p 189-191
Merry Widow (KGB code name for the director of CIA) - p 166, 168
Mesta, Perle 1890-1975 (American socialite and diplomat) - p 101, 102
Metro Goldwyn Mayer (American motion picture company) - p 70, 105, 106, 116, 121
Mgeladze (Party official in Georgia) - p 183
MI5 (British Internal Security) - p 162, 163, 164, 171
MI6 (British Secret Intelligence) - p 162, 163, 164, 167, 172
Migunov (Russian physician) - p 183
Mikolajczyk, Stanislaw 1901-1966 (Polish statesman) - p 47, 62
Millay, Edna St Vincent 1892-1950 (American poet) - p ix, 100
Milton, John 1608-74 (English poet) - p 100
MIT (Massachusetts Institute of Technology) - p 167
Mitterrand, François 1916- (French statesman) - p 78
Molotov-Ribbentrop pact (1939 Russo-German nonaggression pact) - p 173, 183
Monroe Doctrine (declaration of U.S. hegemony in Latin America) - p 138
Monsignore (title of Catholic Church dignitary) - p 140, 141, 143, 197, 199
Montana (boys' school in Switzerland) - p 112
Montmartre (art district of Paris) - p 71
Moravia, Alberto (Alberto Pincherle) 1907-1990 (Italian writer) - p 95, 96

Index 215

Morgan, Michelle 1920- (French actress) - p 69
Morin, Philippe (French professor of medicine) - p 160
Morrow, Vic 1932-1982 (American actor) - p 116
Morse, Wayne 1900-1974 (American senator) - p 95
Motion Picture Association of America (film trade association) - p 50, 52, 60, 65, 70, 90, 94, 118, 149
Moujik (Russian peasant) - p 93, 155
Mount Hymettos (part of Greek mountain chain in Attica) - p 189
Mozart, Wolfgang Amadeus 1756-91 (Austrian composer) - p 99
Murphy (British air attaché) - p 91
Musset, Alfred de 1810-57 (French Romantic writer) - p 145
Mussolini, Benito 1883-1945 (Italian Fascist dictator) - p 15, 16, 18, 86, 103, 112, 160
Mussorgsky, Modest 1839-81 (Russian composer) - p 155

N

Napoléon, Bonaparte 1769-1821 (emperor of the French) - p 66
Nassr, Hassan Bey (Egyptian diplomat) - p 40, 41
National Security Agency (NSA) (U.S government agency) - p 167
NATO (North Atlantic Treaty Organization) - p 82, 129
NEDECO (firm of Dutch consulting engineers) - p 189
Neue Heimat (German financial and construction Group) - p 191, 194
Nevsky Prospect (avenue in St. Petersburg) - p 157
New Yorker (New York magazine) - p 18, 100, 122, 150
Newcastle (British merchant ship) - p 23
Niarchos, Stavros 1909- (Greek fleetowner) - p 196
Nibelung (German epic used by Wagner in his cycle of musical dramas) - p 27
Nicolai (member Soviet Secret Police) - p 38, 41
NKVD (Forerunner of KGB) - p 32, 177, 178
Notre Dame (American Catholic university) - p 153, 154
Nouvelle Eve (Paris nightclub) - p 71
Novamont Corporation (Vatican controlled company in Virginia) - p 134

O

Oak Park (town in Illinois, U.S.A.) - p 19
Office of Strategic Services -OSS- (forerunner of CIA) - p 65

OGPU (a forerunner of the KGB) - p 160
Olomouc (industrial town in Czechoslovakia) - p 55, 56, 141, 170-172
Onassis, Aristotle 1906-1975 (Greek ship and tanker owner) - p 195, 196
Operation Overlord (code name for Allied invasion of Europe) - p 175
Opus Dei (Catholic Order) - p 71, 133, 140, 141, 148, 149, 153, 198, 200
Orlov, Yuri Sergeievich (assumed name of Russian exile) - p 7, 9, 10, 123, 140, 142, 160, 177
Ornstein, George 'Bud' (American film executive) - p 87, 92, 104
Ornstein, Gwenn (socialite niece of Mary Pickford) - p 92, 102
Orsini, Philipo (Italian nobleman) - p 97
Ortega y Gasset, José 1883-1955 (Spanish esayist and philosopher) - p 147
OWI, Office of War Information, (US WW2 propaganda agency) - p 27, 28, 30, 31, 34

P

Palmer, Lilli 1914-1986 (actress) - p 109-111
Palmieri, Dino (Italian tennis star) - p 17
Pao-Yii (Chinese ambassador to Poland) - p 40
Paramount (American film company) - p 70, 106
Pate, Hedy (Polish patriot) - p 38, 39, 63
Pate, Maurice (American diplomat) - p 39
Patton, George Smith 1885-1945 (American general) - p 178
Pavlov, Ivan Petrovich 1849-1936 (Russian phisiologist) - p 122
Pavlova, Anna 1885-1931 (Russian ballerina) - p 155
Pavlow, Muriel, 1922 (English actress) - p 28
Pegov, (Stalin's doctor) - p 183
Péguy, Charles 1873-1914 (French poet and essayist) - p 156
Penhollow (Penny) (American military) - p 61, 62
Perdicari, John (American-Italian journalist) - p 85, 87, 102
Pericles c.495-429 B.C. (Athenian statesman) - p 189
Pétain, Henri Philippe, 1856-1951 (French soldier and statesman) - p 67, 68
Peter I "the Great" 1672-1725 (czar of Russia) - p 154
Petromin (Saudi Ministry of Petroleum and Minerals) - p 194
Petronius, c.66 A.D. (Arbiter Elegantiae at Nero's court) - p 98
Petrucci, Antonio (director of Venice Film Festival) - p 105
Philby, Kim 1912 (Soviet "mole" in British intelligence) - p 162

Philopimen 252-184 B.C. (King of Sparta) - p 192
Phlaum, Irving, (Chicago newspaper columnist) - p 20, 21
Pickford, Mary 1893-1979 (American actress) - p 102, 104
Pienkowski, Karol (director of Polish Radio) - p 2, 3, 26
Pignatelli, Maria (Italian noblewoman) - p 62, 64
Pilate, Pontius c.26-c.36 A.D.(Roman procurator) - p 144
Plato, c.428- c.348 B.C. (Greek philosopher) - p 99
Plaza de Toros (bullring in Madrid) - p 127
Poitier, Sidney 1924- (American actor) - p 116, 144
Polignac Memorandum (French declaration of 1823, supporting the Monroe Doctrine) - p 138
Polignac, Guy prince de (French businessman) - p 138
Polignac, Jules Armand prince de 1780-1847 (French statesman) - p 138
Pombo, Ovsaldo (Argentine diplomat) - p 40
Ponti, Carlo 1913- (Italian film producer) - p 120
Ponti-de Laurentis (film studios in Rome) - p 120
Pontifical Academy of Science (Vatican Academy) - p 143, 180
Pontifical Institute for Oriental Studies (Vatican institute) - p 133
Pontilov industry (heavy industry in St.Petersburg) - p 157
Poor No More (novel by Robert Ruark) - p 124
Portillo, Alvaro de (leading member of Opus Dei) - p 148, 198
Potash, Shirley (American PR executive) - p 123
Prado (Museum in Madrid) - p 94
Prince Igor (Opera by Borodin) - p 155
Princess Elizabeth (British Royal Family) - p 26
Princess Margaret (Britsh Royal Family) - p 26
Princeton (private university in New Jersey) - p 91, 167
Profumo, John D. 1915- (Britain's War Minister) - p 165
Prokofiev, Sergei Sergeievich 1891-1953 (Russian composer) - p 146
Proust, Marcel 1871-1922 (French novelist) - p 81, 145
Puccini, Giacomo 1858-1924 (Italian operatic composer) - p 15
Pushkin, Alexander Sergeievich, 1799-1837 (Russian writer) - 9, 10, 61, 171

Q
Quinn, Anthony 1915- (American film actor) - p 79, 97

R

Rachmaninoff, Sergei Vassilievich 1873-1943 (Russian composer) - p 146
Racconti Romani (Alberto Moravia novel) - p 95
Radkiewicz (Mrs) (wife of Polish Security Minister) - p 50, 60, 64
RAF, Royal Air Force - p 23, 26, 31, 52, 91
Ravera, (Italian physician) - p 136, 137
Ray, Nita (Chevalier's companion) - p 73
Reagan, Ronald 1911- (American statesman) - p 199
Redbrook Estates (Canadian company with Vatican interests) - p 134
Revolt of the Masses (a social critique by Ortega y Gasset) - p 147
Richelieu, Armand-Jean du Plessis de 1585-1642 (French cardinal and statesman) - p 102
Rigoletto (Giuseppe Verdi opera) - p 128
Rimbaud, Arthur 1854-91 (French poet) - p 77
Rimsky-Korsakov, Nikolay Andreyevich 1844-1908 (Russian composer) - p 155
Rizzoli, Angelo 1889-1970 (Italian publisher) - p 108
Robespierre, Maximilien François Marie-Isidore de 1758-94 (French revolutionist) - p 69
Roche, France (French journalist) - p ix, 72
Rockefeller American Overseas Finance corporation - p 131
Rockefeller Foundation (a philantropic organization) - p 190
Rogers, "Buddy" (musician-actor.husband of Pickford) - p 102
Rokossovsky, Konstantin Konstantinovich 1896-1968 (Russian army commander) - p 176
Roland Petit Ballet (French ballet company) - p 71
Romancero Gitano (book of verse by Garcia Lorca) - p 147
Romodanov, Alexander (St.Petersburg physician) - p 159
Roosevelt, Franklin Delano 1882-1945 (president of the U.S.A.) - p 12, 18, 19, 24, 28, 33, 43, 68, 178
Rosenbaum, (American music conductor) - p 34, 64
Round the World in Eighty Days (title of motion picture) - p 126
Ruark, Robert 1915-1965 (American novelist) - p 124, 127
Rubinstein, Arthur 1887-1982 (concert pianist and composer) - p 98
Rudzin, Theo (Swiss businessman) - p 139
Rundstedt, Karl Rudolf Gerd von 1875-1953 (German field marshal) - p 33
Russell, Aliki, née Diplarakos, (wife of John Russell) - p 43, 85

Russell, John Sir (British diplomat) - p 43
Russell, Thomas Pasha, Sir 1879-1954 (British diplomat) - p 43
Rybak (Vatican researcher) - p 196

S

Sa'ud, ibn Abdul Aziz 1902-69 (King of Saudi Arabia) - p 194, 195
Saint Peter's (the basilica of Vatican City) - p 100
Sakellaropoulo, Michael (American economist) - p ix, 84
Sakharov, Andrei 1921-1989 (Russian physicist) - p 181, 186, 187, 197
Sampsonievsky Prospect (Avenue in St. Petersburg) - p 157
San Marino (a republic in the E.Appenines) - p 87, 89, 90, 93
Sartre, Jean-Paul 1905 -1980 (French philosopher and writer) - p 76, 77
Schiller, Johann Christoph Friedrich von 1759-1805 (German poet, historian and critic) - p 12, 26
Schine, G.David (investigator for senator McCarthy) - p 166
Schroder (banking corporation) - p 131
Schwinn, Walter (American Foreign Service officier) - p 49
Scotland Yard (Criminal Investigation Dept.of the British Metropolitan Police) - p 163
Sedan (town N.E.France, scene of French army surrender to Prussia in 1870) - p 67
Segrè, Emilio Gino 1905- (U.S.physicist) - p 187
Selfridges (London department store) - p 29
Serov, Ivan (colonel of Russian State Security) - p 184
Sevenhuysen, William J.C. (Dutch Shell Oil executive) - p 189
SHAEF (Supreme Headquarters Allied Expeditionary Forces) - p 31, 32
Shakespeare, William 1564-1616 (English poet and playwright) - p 100
Sherwood, Robert Emmet 1896-1855 (American playwright) - p 19, 28
Shipley, Ruth (Head US Passport Division) - p 30
Shirer, William (American journalist broadcaster) - p 3
Sideratos, Michael (Greek attorney) - p 190
Siegel, Chuck (Polish American athletic coach) - p 12
Sienkiewicz, Henryk 1846-1916 (Polish novelist) - p 51
Signoret, Simone 1921-1985 (French actress) - p 69, 76
Sinatra, Frank 1915- (American singer) - p 127
Sinfonia Concertante for Oboe (concerto by Jacques Ibert) - p 98
Sir Galahad (knight in Arthurian legend) - p 102
Sisyphus, king of Corinth, (Greek mythology) - p 19, 191

Skorzeny, Otto (Nazi paratrooper who liberated Mussolini) - p 160
Skouras, Spyros 1893-1971 (president 20th Century Fox) - p 75, 115
Slowik, Jerzy (Polish agent for KGB) - p 53, 54, 58, 170
Smetana, Bedrich 1824-84 (Czech composer) - p 99
Smith, Mary (Executive secretary) - p 123
Smithsonian Institution (educational institution the U.S.A.) - p 190
Snoxhall (a home in Surrey) - p 31
Something of Value (novel by Robert Ruark) - p 124, 125
Sousa, John Philip 1901-1966 (American composer) - p 49
Special Branch (Secret Service of Scotland Yard) - p 163
Spellman, Francis, Cardinal 1889-1967 (Cardinal of New York) - p 112
Spiegel, Mark (American film executive) - p 70
St. Andrews (university town in Scotland) - p 25
St. Mark's Square (location of San Marco Basilica in Venice) - p 110
Stalin, Joseph Vissarionovich Dzhugashvili 1879-1953 (Russian statesman) - p 9, 32, 33, 143, 146, 160, 166, 169, 176-178, 180-185
Stark, Ray 1909- (American film producer) - p 121
Starzynski, Stefan 1893-1943 (Mayor of Warsaw in 1939) - p 3
Steinbeck, John Ernst 1902-68 (American novelist) - p 14
Stettinius, Edward Reilly Jr. 1900-49 (U.S. statesman) - p 33
Stewart, James 1908- (American actor) - p 90, 91
Stokowski, Leopold 1882-1977 (American conductor) - p 95, 96
Stravinsky, Igor 1882-1971 (Russian composer) - p 146, 157
Studebaker (U.S.car manufacturer) - p 130, 137
Suburov, (Communist Party official) - p 183
Sunset Boulevard (American motion picture) - p 100
Svoboda, Ludvik 1895-1979 (Czech minister of defense) - p 172
Swanson, Gloria 1897-1983 (American actress) - p 100
Swensen, John (Swedish American in British army) - p 25

T
Tannenberg, Battle of (German army defeats Russians, 1914) - p 155
Taylor, Elizabeth 1932- (film actress) - p 126
Taylor, Robert 1911-1969 (American actor) - p 105
Tcherenkov, P.A. 1904- (Russian physicist) - p 180
Tcherepnin, Nikolai 1873-1945 (Russian composer) - p 156
TECHNION- Israel Institute of Technology - p 190

Tennyson, Alfred, Lord 1809-92 (English poet) - p 100
Tevini, Carlo (Italian architect) - p 189
The Broken Axis (Book by Max Hussman) - p 112
The Four-poster (title of motion picture) - p 109
The Honey Badger (novel by Robert Ruark) - p 124
The Lucy Ring (Soviet spy organization in Switzerland) - p 164
The Man from Prague (Czech clergyman) - p 55-57, 64
There shall be no Night (Play by Robert Sherwood) - p 28
Third Reich (Nazi regime in Germany, 1933-45) - p 12, 20, 67
Tkachov, (Kremlin physician) - p 183
Todd, Michael 'Mike' 1907-1955 (American film producer) - p 126
Tolstoy, Alexy Nikolayevich 1882-1945 (Russian novelist) - p 9, 33
Torem, Charles (American attorney) - p 75
Torlogna, Alessandro (Italian nobleman) - p 93
Traviata (Giuseppe Verdi opera) - p 128
Tretyakov, (Soviet government official) - p 182
Trichèco file (Vatican secret file) - p 180, 189
Trinder, Tommy 1909-1989 (English comedian) - p 27
Trinitá Dei Monti (Church in Rome) - p 199
Trotsky, Leon (Lev Davidovich Bronstein) 1879-1940 (Russian revoluionist) - p 160
Truman, Harry S 1884-1972 (33rd president of the U.S.) - p 82, 118
Turgenev, Ivan Sergeyevich 1818-83 (Russian writer) - p 9

U
Uhuru (novel by Robert Ruark) - p 124
Ullastres, Alberto (Spanish government minister) - p 149
Unamuno, Miguel de 1864-1936 (Spanish philosopher and essayist)- p 76, 77, 94, 142, 143, 147, 148
Uranus (god of the heavens in Roman mythology) - p 192
Use Enough Gun (novel by Robert Ruark) - p 124

V
Vagnozzi, Egidio Cardinal 1906-1980 (Vatican's head of economic affairs) - p vi, 133
Variety (American show business magazine) - p 71, 74
Vasilenko, (Malenkov's physician) - p 182, 183

Vatican Bank for Religious Works (prime Vatican bank) - p 112
Vatican City (Papal State) - p 100, 139, 140
Veil, Simone 1927- (French attorney and politician) - p 78
Velazquez, Diego Rodriguez de Silva y 1599-1660 (Spanish painter) - p 94
Ventura, Ray (French film producer) - p 121
Verlaine, Paul 1844-96 (French lyric and Symbolist poet) - p 77
Versaille Palace (royal palace built for Louis XIV) - p 154
Vestnik Pravitelstva (Russian government newspaper) - p 155
Viberti, Angelo (Italian industrialist) - p 130, 131, 134, 135, 137-139
Vichy (French town, seat of Pétain's government) - p 74, 81
Victoria 1818-1901 (queen of Great Britain) - p 78
Vila, Claudio (Italian singer) - p 108
Vilar, Antonio (Portuguese actor) - p 149
Villa Taverna (U.S.ambassador's residence in Rome) - p 94-96
Vinogradov, (Communist Party official) - p 183
Voice of America (US Government radio network) - p 30, 33
Vyborg (industrial quarter of St.Petersburg) - p 157

W

Wagner, Wilhelm Richard, 1813-63 (German operatic composer) - p 16, 27
Walrus Profile (Vatican secret file) - 169
Walt Disney Studios (motion picture studios) - p 104, 190
Wanger, Walter 1894-1968 (American film producer) - p 75
Warner Brothers (American film company) - p 70, 106
Washington, George 1732-99 (first American president) - p 40
Watergate Improvement Corporation (American company with Vatican) - p 134
Waugh, Evelyn 1903-66 (British novelist) - p 85
Weiskampf, (president of Neue Heimat) - p 191, 194
Weizmann Institute of Science (research institute in Isael) - p 190
White's (an exclusive Club in London) - p 26
Whitehead, Tommy (English naval officer) - p 1, 8, 31
Wilde, Oscar 1856-1900 (Irish playwright) - p 92, 119
Wilkens, Barbara (American heiress and socialite) - p 101
Wilson, James Harold 1916- (British Labour statesman) - p 165
Windsor duke of 1894-1972 (Edward VIII of Great Britain) - p 88

Wise, Rinaldo (Polish-Egyptian-English pressman) - p 13
Witkowski, Lech (Polish colonel, Katyn murder witness) - p 29
Wojtyla, Karol Josef 1920- (Pope John Paul II) - p vi, 197, 198

Y

Yale (private American university) - p 167
Yalta (Conference) (1945 conference in the Crimea between Roosevelt, Churchill and Stalin) - p 47, 178, 179
Young Poland (a group of young Polish composers) - p 177
Young, Terence 1915-1994 (English film director) - p 120, 122

Z

Zeno, 'Zeno of Citium' c.334-c.262 B.C. (Greek philosopher) - p 192
Zernike, Fritz 1888-1966 (Dutch physicist) - p 187
Zhukov, Georgi Konstantinovich 1896-1974 (Russian marshal) - p 180, 187
Ziv, John Marshall (American PR writer) - p 19
Zloty, Polish currency worth 20 US cents in 1939 - p 14, 39, 55, 64
Zola, Émile 1849-1902 (French novelist) - p 145